The Early Date of Revelation and the End Times:
An Amillennial Partial Preterist Perspective

ROBERT HILLEGONDS, MST (Mathematics)

Fountain Inn, South Carolina

"Proclaiming the kingdom of God and teaching those things which concern the Lord Jesus Christ, with all confidence."

The Early Date of Revelation and the End Times:
An Amillennial Partial Preterist Perspective
Copyright © 2016 by Robert Hillegonds

All rights reserved. No part of this book may be reproduced in any form or by any means, except for brief quotations for the purpose of review, comment, or scholarship, without written permission from the publisher.

Unless otherwise noted all Scripture quotations are from the ESV® Bible (The Holy Bible, English Standard Version®), copyright © 2001 by Crossway, a publishing ministry of Good News Publishers. Used by permission. All rights reserved.

Some Scripture quotations are marked NASB. These Scripture quotations are taken from the New American Standard Bible®, Copyright © 1960, 1962, 1963, 1968, 1971, 1972, 1973, 1975, 1977, 1995 by The Lockman Foundation. Used by permission.

Published by Victorious Hope Publishing
P.O. Box 1874
Fountain Inn, South Carolina 29644

Website: www.VictoriousHope.com
Printed in the United States of America

ISBN 978-0-9964525-2-6

Victorious Hope Publishing is committed to producing Christian educational materials for promoting the whole Bible for the whole of life. We are conservative, evangelical, and Reformed and are committed to the doctrinal formulation found in the Westminster Standards.

Dedicated to

Alice Dorothy Cooper (Kuiper) Hillegonds

mother who kept me on course

when we were young

by each day reading to our family

the Word of God

The earth did not tremble the night your

light faded. But it should have.

Endorsement

Are there many amillennial partial preterists? There may be more after reading this book. Robert Hillegonds leaves no stone unturned in his quest for the date of Revelation. His early date conclusion framed within a partial preterist and amillennial perspective is very well presented. His meticulous research, sane interpretations, irenic spirit, and love for God and His truth lead the reader on an exciting journey to discover the date of the book of Revelation, with all of its interpretive implications.

Was Revelation written before AD 70? Did Nero or Domitian banish John? Is Revelation John's Olivet Discourse? These and several other questions are explored by Hillegonds in this enlightening work. I felt like a spiritual Sherlock Holmes trying to follow the clues and resolve the questions of a whodunit mystery. Mostly, however, one senses the pressing need to figure this out. So much seems to ride on how we understand this great final book of the Bible.

Hillegonds provides a very intriguing and helpful guide to understanding why more of us in modern evangelicalism are leaning to an early date of John's Revelation. In reading this you may not agree with his conclusions, but you will be forced to answer them. Whatever your eschatological bent, I hope this book will ravish your heart for the day when God will make all things new.

A robust combination of exacting scholarship and spiritual feast. I commend it for professional theologians, pastors, and interested laity.

I have occasionally wondered why scholars lean toward a late date for John's Revelation. Now I have a thoroughly researched book to help me vie for an early date.

Rev. Michael Pitsenberger
MDiv Western Theological Seminary
Pastor, Carmel Reformed Church

Front Cover & Neronian Coin

There are two key pieces of physical evidence that are referred to in this book. The first is architectural: the temple at Jerusalem. The second is an inscription found on many Neronian coins.

The front cover of this book addresses the first line of evidence, which relates to the destruction of the Temple in AD 70. How is it possible for John to write "they will trample" the holy city for forty-two months if John is writing the book of Revelation more than twenty-five years after the fall of Jerusalem?

The two photos shown below address the second line of evidence, which pertains to an inscription on a number of Nerorian coins. The photos are of a Roman provincial coin with an image of Nero on the obverse. The coin was minted under Agrippa II in the early to mid AD sixties. The photos were taken from a coin in my personal collection.[1]

Neronian coin minted under Agrippa II

---

[1] Photos of the Neronian coin were taken by Richard Lanenga Photography, Inc. http://www.richardlanenga.com.

Although the inscription on the obverse is worn, the reverse side of the coin is in better condition, making the coin identifiable from the information provided by the Roman Provincial Coinage Project.

The bronze quarter denomination shown in the above image is from the Soefar Collection and was identified as Roman Provincial Coinage (Vol 1 - 4990) which gives the inscription on the obverse as ΝΕΡΩΝ ΚΑΙΣΑΡ ΣΕΒΣΤΟΣ. This inscription is key to the 666/616 puzzle of Revelation 13:18.

The Roman Provincial Coinage Project at the University of Oxford is an international initiative that began in 1992 with the publication of *Roman Provincial Coinage* Vol 1 (44 BC - AD 69).

The purpose of the Roman Provincial Coinage Project was to complement the Roman Imperial Coinage series and provide a standard treatment of all Roman coinage. As opposed to imperial coinage, provincial coinage was minted in lower quantity and was of a lower quality. However, provincial coinage, in the words of the project authors, has "great importance for the study of cultural, religious, political, economic, and administrative history . . . "[2]

Agrippa II had the coin minted "in the Name of Nero." No Jewish ruler prior to Agrippa had a coin minted in the image of Caesar and his name.

His sister became the mistress of Titus, Vespasian's son, not long after committing troops to Vespasian. Meanwhile, Agrippa led his Judean forces under Vespasian and Titus against Jerusalem. For more information on Agrippa, see Appendix F.

---

[2] Roman Provincial Coinage Online, University of Oxford, rpc.ashmus.ox.ac.uk/intro/project/.

Contents

Dedication ... iii
Front Cover & Neronian Coin ... v
Acknowledgments ... 1
Introduction ... 3

Part I: The Early Date of Revelation
1. My Interest, Presuppositionalism, Bertrand Russell, and Eschatology ... 11
2. The Eyewitnesses and Form Criticism ... 19
3. Eusebius, Papias, the Author of Revelation and the Muratorian Canon ... 23
4. The Sixth King, the Banishment of John to the Island of Patmos, and the dating of Revelation ... 41
5. Nerva and the Release of John – AD 71 or after the Death of Domitian ... 59
6. Centralized Persecution of Christians and the Imperial Cult ... 75
7. The Syriac Tradition, Epiphanius, and Jerome ... 83

PART II: Topics in Preterism Explained and Defended
8. The Olivet Discourse and Double Fulfillment ... 93
9. Revelation is John's Version of the Olivet Discourse ... 111
10. Recapitulation and the Gog/Magog Battle ... 117
11. Nero is the Beast ... 129
12. Nero Redivivus ... 143
13. The Ten Kings and Local Persecution ... 153
14. The Temple Was Clearly Standing ... 159
15. Objection from the Point of that View that the Temple is Symbolic ... 163
16. Mathison on Why Preterism is Essentially Correct ... 169

Part III: Eschatological positions
17. Definitions ... 175
18. Thumbnail Sketch of Eschatological Positions ... 177

19. The Dispensational Hermeneutic versus the Historic
    Protestant Hermeneutic   181
20. Amillennial and Postmillennial Reformed Eschatology   185
21. Reformed View of the Old Testament Land Covenant   189

Part IV: Israel and the End Times
22. Israel and Prophecy   195
23. R.C. Sproul, James Stuart Russell and
    Duncan McKenzie   199
24. Romans 11 and the Fullness of the Gentiles   203
25. Satan's Little Season and the Gog/Magog Invasion   213
26. The Amillennial Solution   217
27. Final Conclusions   219

Appendix A: Peter Steen   223
Appendix B: Dutch Reformed Theological History
starting with Kuyper   225
Appendix C: Bertrand Russell   231
Appendix D: Objection to a Literal Interpretation of
the Number of Kings   233
Appendix E: First Century History, Halley's Comet,
and Miracles   239
Appendix F: Agrippa II and the Expansion of his Territories   249

Bibliography
Bibliography I: Modern Writings   253
Bibliography II: Ancient Writings   260
Notes   263

Acknowledgments

A word of thanks goes to Dr. Francis Gumerlock for reviewing the portions of this book which pertain to his work and for his helpful comments and advice. Thank you, Dr. Kenneth Gentry, for reviewing and publishing this book, and thanks for the fine editor that you assigned to me, Mischelle Sandowich. Thank you Mischelle for the thorough work you did on the line editing and also for your helpful suggestions. Thanks also to Rev. Michael Pitsenberger for his advice on the work of Kim Riddlebarger. I am also grateful for the work of Marie Eenigenburg Min, Kenneth Decker, and Harry Hillegonds who read every word of the manuscript numerous times including the initial draft and then again after each revision. Thank you Richard Lanenga for photographing the Neronian coin from my collection. A special word of appreciation goes to the youngest of my two daughters, Marjorie DeVries, who took time from her writing schedule to read through the manuscript a final time. Thank you, Jacqueline, my oldest daughter, for your encouragement and a word of thanks to your husband, Dr. Tae'Ni Chang-Stroman, for his advice on the manuscript. Finally, a special note of gratitude to my wife Dolores, who read the initial manuscript, encouraged me, and faithfully provided moral support along the way.

Introduction

A few months ago, I went to my accountant to have my taxes done, and as I spent some time in the waiting area outside of his office, I read a portion of Kenneth Gentry's *Before Jerusalem Fell*. When I was called into his office, I was carrying a folder with the paperwork for my taxes along with Gentry's book. I will refer to my accountant as "Joe." We exchanged greetings and I handed him the folder with my paperwork for my taxes. Joe, who noticed the hefty book in my hands, asked, "What are your reading?"

Now, Joe is not an ordinary accountant. I noticed more than one diploma displayed in picture frames mounted on his office wall. Before he became an accountant, he taught at a local college in Chicago. Joe has an interest in history. I mentioned a few words to him about the dating of the book of Revelation and it immediately perked his interest. He mentioned a date pertinent to the rule of Nebuchadnezzar in the Old Testament. He clearly knew his Old Testament history. He asked me, "Are you a Christian?" I replied in the affirmative and he said,

> So am I. I'll tell you though, there are two things that I believe no one can do. No one was ever raised from the dead, and no one can foretell the future.

We had a brief conversation on these two topics, and then we had to turn our attention to the task at hand. However, if you are like Joe, and have an interest in history and prophecy, we will together, continue the discussion through this book.

Jesus was the greatest prophet. He did know specifically what the future held. In the Olivet Discourse, Jesus prophesied about the coming fall of Jerusalem in amazing detail. When people normally think of prophecy, they think of predictions made with a certain amount of ambiguity. The prophecy of Jesus was of a different nature.

The detail of the prophecy of the destruction of the Herodian temple was astounding.

> Some of his disciples were remarking about how the temple was adorned with beautiful stones and with gifts dedicated to God. But Jesus said, "As for what you see here, the time will come when not one stone will be left on another; every one of them will be thrown down." (Luke 21:5-6).

> When you see Jerusalem being surrounded by armies, you will know that its desolation is near. Then let those who are in Judea flee to the mountains, let those in the city get out, and let those in the country not enter the city… (Luke 21:20-21).

Typically, when people at the time of Jesus saw an army approaching, they would go to the city for safety. Jesus told them to do exactly the opposite. He told them to leave the city. Jewish believers fled the city when they saw the unexpected retreat of the Roman legions under Cestius Gallus. This was a temporary retreat that allowed Jewish believers time to leave Jerusalem. Cestius Gallus was replaced by Vespasian, the best general of Rome.[3]

We also see in Luke 21:32 a timing restriction for the prophecy that was remarkable in its accuracy.

> Truly I tell you, this generation will certainly not pass away until all these things have happened. Heaven and earth will pass away, but my words will never pass away.

---

[3]According to Josephus, "It then happened that Cestius was not conscious either how the besieged despaired of success, nor how courageous the people were for him; and so he recalled his soldiers from the place, and by despairing of any expectation of taking it, without having received any disgrace, he retired from the city, without any reason in the world." See Flavius Josephus, *The Complete Works of Flavius Josephus, Jewish Wars*, trans. William Whiston (London: T. Nelson and Sons,1860), Bk. 2, Ch. 19, Section 7, 642.

Introduction 5

The possible destruction of the Temple within a generation was an event that was totally foreign to the mind of any Jew living at the time of Jesus. The temple was one of the wonders of the world at the time Jesus made his prophecy. Millions had worshiped at the temple. Jesus did not just prophesy that one of the greatest structures on earth would be taken by an enemy. Jesus made the amazing prophecy that not one stone would be left upon another.

The words of Jesus had a stunning, lasting effect on the apostles. Their world would be shaken. His words inspired Matthew, Mark, and Luke to each write a version of what we know as the Olivet Discourse. His words are known as the Olivet Discourse since the major part of the discourse was given by Jesus on the Mount of Olives. There is a version in the book of Matthew, in the book of Mark, and in the book of Luke.[4]

I believe that the book of Revelation is John's version of the Olivet Discourse or at least contains John's version of the Discourse. Sometime after the prophecy of Jesus of the destruction of the Temple, John had a series of visions. In response to the prophecies of Jesus on the Mount of Olives and after receiving the visions, John wrote the book of Revelation. The book of Revelation starts with the words, "The revelation of Jesus Christ." However, now the "time is short" before the fulfillment that not one stone would be left upon another. Through the inspired words of John, we are given another

---

[4] F.F. Bruce dates the gospel Mark to around AD 64 or 65. He dates Luke shortly before and Matthew shortly after AD 70. Says Bruce, "One criterion which has special weight with me is the relation which these writing appear to bear to the destruction of the city and temple of Jerusalem by the Romans in AD 70. My view of the matter is that Mark and Luke were written before the event, and Matthew not long afterwards."

Bruce, commenting on the work of John A.T. Robinson, tells us that outside of one or two New Testament documents which do imply that the fall of Jerusalem had already taken place that Robinson's case is so well researched that no one should deal with the question of dating without paying attention to his arguments. See F.F. Bruce, *The New Testament Documents: Are They Reliable?* 6th ed., (Grand Rapids, MI: Wm. B. Eerdmans Publishing Co.; Downers Grove, IL: InterVarsity Press, 1943, 1946, 1950, 1953, 1960,1981), 6-15.

version of the Discourse with prophecies that were shortly to be fulfilled in the first century as well as prophecies that are still to be fulfilled after the millennium.

The first three chapters of Revelation contain specific details concerning the seven churches. The most common way to interpret the book of Revelation today is that the visions and prophecies beginning in Chapter 4 of Revelation are future to us. However, the book of Revelation was not written "to us;" it was written "for us." It was written to the Christians of the first century. If Revelation is John's version of the Olivet Discourse, then at least some of the prophecies in the book of Revelation were fulfilled with the destruction of the temple in AD 70.

Let us compare Luke 21:24 from the Olivet Discourse to Revelation 11:2.

Luke 21:24

> They will fall by the sword and will be taken as prisoners to all the nations. Jerusalem will be trampled on by the Gentiles until the times of the Gentiles are fulfilled.

Revelation 11:2

> ... do not measure the court outside the temple; leave that out, for it is given over to the nations, and they will trample the holy city for forty-two months.

The Romans besieged the city of Jerusalem from the Spring of AD 67 to September of AD 70 – about forty-two months. Both judgment on those who "say they are Jews but are not" and the public affirmation of the already established new covenant were made visible to the whole Roman world in AD 70. There was an earlier time when God made a covenant with his people at Sinai.

At Mount Sinai, God spoke and an *entire nation* heard him make a covenant with Moses and the children of Israel.

> And you came near and stood at the foot of the mountain, while the mountain burned with fire to the heart of heaven, wrapped in darkness,

cloud, and gloom. Then the Lord spoke to you out of the midst of the fire. You heard the sound of words, but saw no form; there was only a voice. And he declared to you his covenant. (Deut. 4:11-12).

As opposed to other religions of the world, where "god" gives revelation *only* to an individual person; the God of Jacob, the God of Abraham reveals himself so that a *whole nation of people* could simultaneously hear his voice. The *whole world saw*, in AD 70, the expansion of the old covenant to include all the nations of the earth. This was the public verification of the new covenant and the passing of the Jewish Age.

Just a few years before the fall of Jerusalem the Apostle Paul warned listeners to remember Moses words at Mt. Sinai when the Old covenant was established.

> See that you do not refuse him who is speaking. For if they did not escape when they refused him who warned them on earth, much less will we escape if we reject him who warns from heaven. At that time his voice shook the earth, but now he has promised, "Yet once more I will shake not only the earth but also the heavens." This phrase, "Yet once more," indicates the removal of things that are shaken—that is, things that have been made — in order that the things that cannot be shaken may remain (Hebrews 12:25-27).

The earth and heavens were shaken when the temple system was removed. We are now, through Christ, a part of the everlasting kingdom that cannot be shaken.

Part I
The Early Date of Revelation

Chapter 1
MY INTEREST, PRESUPPOSITIONALISM, BERTRAND RUSSELL, AND ESCHATOLOGY

You may have noticed that the MST listed after my name is not a master's degree in theology. It is a Master's Degree in the Teaching of Mathematics from the University of Illinois at Chicago. I spent the majority of my teaching career teaching mathematics and computer science at the secondary level. In addition, however, to my interest in mathematics, I have a strong interest in philosophy, theology, and in studying the Word of God.

Early in my academic career, I accumulated a number of hours in philosophy and theology at Trinity Christian College and Calvin College. I was, for a year, a preseminary student at Calvin College. However, in my senior year, I changed majors to secondary education and transferred to the University of Illinois at Chicago. My original teaching certificate in the State of Illinois showed that one of the areas where I was certified to teach was philosophy. Since that time I have continued my lifelong study of philosophy, theology, and the Scriptures.

While attending Trinity Christian College, I had the privilege of studying under Calvin Seerveld and Peter Steen. Under these professors, I was introduced to a philosophy known as presuppositionalism. In this philosophy the basic suppositions or assumptions of thought are examined.

That any logical system of thought *must* have a postulate outside of that system of thought that *must be accepted without proof* was proved by the German mathematician Gödel in 1931. His theorem, known as the incompleteness theorem(s), shook the philosophical world of the day that was led by the great mathematician, Bertrand Russell, and his followers. The importance of Gödel's theorems and the importance of presuppositonalism are still underestimated today.

See Appendix C for more detail and an introduction on an early important book by Bertrand Russell.

Gödel proved that *any closed system depends on something outside of that system that you have to assume to be true but cannot prove.*

All of science rests on the *assumption* that the universe is orderly and subject to logical investigation.

It cannot be proved that the universe is orderly and subject to logical investigation. That the universe is orderly and can be understood is because God created the universe to be orderly and knowable. This is a basic presupposition. Law is the boundary between God and the cosmos. Scientific advancement in the Western World was due to a *belief* that the laws of the universe could be discovered. Copernicus, Galileo, Kepler, Descartes, Boyle, Newton, Leibniz, Ohm, Pasteur, Maxwell, and Planck were all Christians. They believed we live in a world that can be measured and in the discovery of laws that can be described mathematically.

According to presuppositionalists, every person accepts suppositions that are the most basic convictions that a person has regarding reality and what can be known. These suppositions cannot be proved. They are fundamental and unproven, but necessary. Now by unproven, we do not mean unreasonable. The assumptions or postulates made in Geometry, for instance, cannot be proved; however, they are not unreasonable.

The basic presuppositions that one has are the most fundamental beliefs one adheres to and, at times, a scholar will appeal to these basic assumptions in a proof or if pushed far enough in a particular argument. I, for instance, believe that God created the world. I believe that there was a fall that corrupted all of creation. I believe that Jesus paid the price to redeem creation and that he physically rose from the dead. I believe that Jesus changed water into wine. I believe that miracles occurred in the first century. I believe that there were inspired prophets who foretold the birth of Christ. These fulfilled prophecies and miracles are "signs" that Jesus, who was born of the Virgin Mary, was the Word who became flesh. The text of Scriptures containing the fulfillment of prophecies foretelling the birth of Christ and his miracles have been subject to redating in modern times. It is argued that they were added at a later time by editors. A new category for analysis emerged in the late 1800s. That miracles may have occurred in the past has become myth.

However, just because we no longer see the followers of Christ perform miracles or prophesy, *like Jesus did*, does not mean that Jesus did not walk on water. It does not mean that the dead were not raised. These miracles were recorded by the eyewitnesses. We, in turn today, read the words attributed to those eyewitnesses to understand that Jesus is God. The miracles of Jesus were not added in by a community of followers after a long period of oral development. The miracles were observed by eyewitnesses. That brings us to the "what-if" that is the basis of this book.

What if the basic "facts" accepted by theologians can be shown to fit together better with a pre-AD 70 authorship for the book of Revelation rather that a post-AD 70 approach. This does require the belief that it is possible that John saw visions directly from God and made prophecies in the book of Revelation prior to AD 70 that were shortly to be fulfilled.

The approach I will defend is essentially the position of R.C. Sproul and Kenneth Gentry, specifically, that the book of Revelation was written in approximately AD 65 or 66 and that the "time was short" when it was written. Much of prophecy in the book of Revelation was fulfilled in AD 70 with the destruction of the Temple just three or four years after it was written. I will defend the viewpoint that the book of Revelation is essentially John's version of the Olivet Discourse. Just as there is near-term prophecy and far-term prophecy in the Olivet Discourse, there is near-term prophecy and far-term prophecy in the foretelling of the same events in the book of Revelation.

The particular beliefs of a person about the possibility of miracles and beliefs about direct revelation from God to man through the prophets are a part of his basic set of presuppositions that cannot be proved or disproved. Every scholar has a set of presuppositions, a particular pair of colored glasses that is worn that filters the data processed. In some cases, the color of the glasses can actually cause one to view the data is such a way that new data is constructed. Eusebius was a scholar whose presuppositions are well documented. We will take a look at some of the well-known presuppositions of Eusebius and discuss how they colored his interpretation of the data he had at his disposal and influenced his choices in writing history. We will, in addition, take a look at prophecy and eschatology.

My interest in eschatology began at the age of thirteen when I read William Hendriksen's, *More than Conquerors*.[5] My thoughts on eschatology took the next step when I read *The Coming of the Kingdom*[6] by Herman Ridderbos. Although I never had the opportunity to take a course with Anthony Hoekema while at Calvin, his book *The Bible and the Future*[7] had a great influence on my thinking concerning eschatology. Kim Riddlebarger's *The Man of Sin*[8] and *The Case for Amillennialism*[9] are the two works which, in my opinion, are among the best in current amillennial thought.

---

[5] William Hendriksen, *More Than Conquerors* (Grand Rapids, MI: Baker Books: 1940, 1967).

[6] Herman Ridderbos, *The Coming of the Kingdom*, trans. by H. de Jongste, (Philadelphia: P & R Pub Co., 1962).

[7] Anthony A. Hoekema, *The Bible and the Future* (Grand Rapids, MI: Wm. B. Eerdmans Pub. Co., [1979], 1994).

[8] Kim Riddlebarger, *The Man of Sin Uncovering the Truth about the Antichrist* (Grand Rapids, MI: Baker Books, 2006).

[9] Kim Riddlebarger, *A Case for Amillennialism: Understanding the End Times* (Grand Rapids, MI: Baker Books, 2003).

Two years ago, I read R.C. Sproul's, *The Last Days According to Jesus*.[10] On the second page of the introduction to his book he discusses a small book by Bertrand Russell that is entitled *Why I am not a Christian*.[11] Sproul's discussion immediately caught my attention. Russell had a tremendous influence on the world we live in today. After debunking the logical proofs for the existence of God, Russell believes he goes on to show that Jesus was a *failed prophet*. Jesus correctly foresaw the destruction of Jerusalem but totally failed as a prophet, according to Russell, when Jesus prophesied that the world would end within a generation. The prophecy of Jesus is turned around by Russell from being one of the most remarkable in history into ultimately a failed one. However, to understand the prophecy, Sproul says that we must ask what the time-frame of "this-generation" is and what is meant by "all these things"?[12]

Could it be that the perception of Jesus as a failed prophet is the result of a faulty *understanding of what "all these things" are that Jesus prophesied would be fulfilled within a generation*? What is the meaning of the phrase "end of the age" in the Olivet Discourse? What is the meaning of the words the "latter days" that are prophesied in Scripture?

It was at that point that I noticed the references of Sproul to Kenneth Gentry.[13] What does the time-frame reference "shortly to take place" mean in the book of Revelation? Would not events that are "shortly to take place" be more meaningful to members of the seven churches within a time-frame of one to five years, as claimed by Gentry, rather than two or three hundred years or even two thousand years? Gentry, I noticed, was a student of Greg Bahnsen. I did know

---

[10] R. C. Sproul, *The Last Days According to Jesus*, 8th ed., (Grand Rapids, MI: Baker Books, 2009).

[11] Bertrand Russell, *Why I am not a Christian* (New York: Touchstone, 1967).

[12] R.C. Sproul's foreword to James Stuart Russell's book, *The Parousia*, (Grand Rapids, MI: Baker Books: New Ed., 1999), xi. Emphasis mine.

[13] Sproul, op. cit., 137.

that Bahnsen was a student of VanTil and that VanTil represented the best in Reformed scholarship. I realized that Gentry came through a strong tradition of reputable scholarship. For more detail on Reformed scholarship see Appendix B.

I followed up my reading of Sproul's book with Kenneth Gentry's *Before Jerusalem Fell: Dating the Book of Revelation*.[14] From the early date perspective, the symbols of the book of Revelation reflect real coming historical realities that would be to a great degree fulfilled in just a few short years in the fall of Jerusalem in AD 70. It was like a shot of adrenaline to my eschatological thinking which was based on an idealist interpretation of Revelation. The possibility of real events and real historical armies as prophecy that was shortly to be fulfilled awoke me from my own "dogmatic slumbers" of interpreting Revelation through symbols that are timeless.

Behind any symbol there must be a *real historic event* that was *meaningful to the first century Christians* to whom the book was written. I could visualize the hailstones that weighed a hundred pounds each falling from the sky in the symbolism of Revelation and literally see their fulfillment in the hundred pound boulders launched from the catapults of the Roman legions as described by Josephus.[15] Could it be possible that John was prophesying just three or four years before the Romans launched their boulders? If the book of Revelation was written just several years prior to the fall of Jerusalem, then its prophecies have amazing "shortly to take place" fulfillment in AD 70.

I felt like amillennialist Sam Storms, who after reading Gentry's work, said that he felt drawn to Gentry's position but was not yet fully persuaded.[16]

After an entire year of doing my own research since first reading *Before Jerusalem Fell: Dating the Book of Revelation*, I have changed my

---

[14] Kenneth L. Gentry, Jr., *Before Jerusalem Fell: Dating the Book of Revelation*, 3rd ed., (Fountain Inn, SC: Victorious Hope Publishing, 1998, 2010).

[15] Ibid., 245-46.

[16] Sam Storms, *Kingdom Come* (Fearn, Scotland: Mentor Imprint of Christian Focus Pub., 2013), 413.

almost life long held position on the dating of the book. I believe that a *strong* argument can be made that the book of Revelation was written before AD 70. This book is a result of a year of research on the dating of the book of Revelation.

I am still amillennial in my thinking, but favor the early date for the authorship of Revelation. To my knowledge, there are no recently published books, other than one written by Jay Adams, on the end-times from the amillennial perspective from authors favoring the early date. Jay Adams wrote *The Time is at Hand*[17] back in the sixties.

I will include in this book some of the arguments made by Gentry, John A.T. Robinson, George Edmundson, and others along with one or two of my own thoughts that persuaded me to change my view on the dating of the book of Revelation. Although specific arguments by themselves seem convincing on either side, we need to see how they fit together as a whole. I will revisit the arguments made by George Edmundson that the late dating of the authorship of Revelation became prominent due to questionable suppositions made by Eusebius.

---

[17] Jay Adams, *The Time is at Hand* (Woodruff, SC: Timeless Texts. 1966, 2004).

Chapter 2
THE EYEWITNESSES AND FORM CRITICISM

The perspective of many textual scholars today is based on the view of Rudolph Bultmann developed in the 1920s. With the advent of "form criticism," the miracles of Jesus became part of a special type of history labeled "sacred history." The miracles of Jesus are simply myths which were added later over time by his followers years after his death in order to show that he is God.

The bible, contends Bultmann, is not "historical" in the objective sense that we know history today. The actual history is of no consequence since it is the eternal truths in the end that matter. R.C. Sproul comments:

> They [the higher critics] assigned later and later dates to the writing or compilation of New Testament books . . .The Gospel account of Christ's life and work was ripped from the arena of history . . . It was left to scholars like Oscar Cullmann and Herman Ridderbos to argue that, though the Bible's theme is redemption and though biblical history is redemptive, the Bible is nonetheless redemptive *history*.[18]

Recently, Richard Bauckham emphasized the importance of the testimony of the eyewitnesses as it relates to form criticism in his book *Jesus and the Eyewitnesses: The Gospels as Eyewitness Testimony*.[19] In 2007, the writers of *Christianity Today* gave this work its book award in the area of Biblical studies.

According to Bauckham, form criticism still has a dubious hold over the way New Testament critics think about how the original

---

[18] R.C. Sproul's foreword to James Stuart Russell's book, *The Parousia*, (Grand Rapids, MI: Baker Books: New Ed., 1999), vii-viii.
[19] Richard Bauckham, *Jesus and the Eyewitnesses: The Gospels as Eyewitness Testimony* (Grand Rapids, MI: William B. Eerdmans Publishing Company, 2006).

stories circulated and changed over time. Form critics tell us that the eyewitness *started* the stories about Jesus, after which the stories then went through a lengthy oral transmission phase and were developed communally rather than being attributed to a single author such as Peter or John. It is these communally developed stories that were picked up by the evangelists and are what we read today. Some form critics view the process of the communal circulating of the stories as being done faithfully. However, many critics believe the stories changed considerably over time. Stories were lengthened and detail was added.

Critics would take a "miracle story" and then ask how it functioned in the teaching within the community. Critics would ask how the "miracle stories" were told (or invented) in teaching and preaching. This process, Bauckham says, has been overdone because the eyewitnesses were still around during this process, which occurred between the death of Jesus and the writing of the earlier gospels.

Bauckham argues that the period between the life of Jesus and the writing of the Gospels was spanned by the continued presence of the eyewitnesses who continued to be the authorities for their traditions until their death. Bauckham explains that because of this, the usual ways of thinking about oral tradition are not appropriate.[20]

Paul, tells us who some of these eyewitnesses were. In his account of the resurrection appearances in 1 Cor. 15:3-8, which is one of the earliest records of these appearances, Paul said that Jesus appeared to over five hundred believers most of whom were still alive when he was writing about these events about twenty years after the crucifixion. The comment about the five hundred also tells us something about the type of witnesses which were available to contemporaneous writers. Some of the witnesses, like those in the five hundred, witnessed a specific event and possibly a few other events from the life of Jesus. Other witnesses, like Peter, were with

---

[20] Ibid., 8.

Jesus continually. Some of these witnesses would come into contact with writers that were contemporaneous to them such as Papias.

Bauckham tells us that there is no reason to have a prejudiced attitude towards Papias just because Eusebius called Papias a stupid man, a man of very little intelligence. Eusebius does this because Papias believed that, at the second coming of Christ, there would be a millennium which would be a paradise on earth. In addition, Eusebius did not agree with some of the writing of Papias on the origins of the New Testament writings.[21]

Close to two hundred years after Papias wrote, Eusebius used Irenaeus to justify using Papias as a source. Papias is a key source because, according to Irenaeus, Papias was a hearer of John. Eusebius later discredits Papias for his views on the millennium.

The earliest writer contemporary to the time of these eyewitnesses was Papias. The writers following Papias were not contemporaneous to the eyewitnesses, *so it is critical to analyze how they interpret him.*

The following table contains information on three contemporaries of Papias followed by important works or authors of important works in the early church.

Name	Birth	Death	Residence
Clement		c. 101	Rome
Papias	c. 60[22]	c. 155	Phrygia
	collected data c. 80 - c. 100		(per Bauckham)
Polycarp	c. 69	c. 155[23]	Smyrna
Muratorian Canon	written about c. 150		
dating - a contemporary of Pius is mentioned in the Canon (Pius died in the c. 150s)			
Irenaeus	c. 130	c. 202	Gaul
Hegesippus (wrote about c. 175)			Palestine?

---

[21] Ibid., 12-13.

[22] Ibid., 18. Bauckham cites Bartlet who tells us that Papias could easily have been born as early as 50 C.E. but no later than AD 60.

[23] Although disputed, the early date of c. 155/156 is now given preference. See Everett Ferguson, *Church History* (Grand Rapids, MI: Zondervan 2005), 80.

Name	Birth	Death	Residence
Clement	c. 150	c. 215	Alexandria
Tertullian	c. 160	c. 230	Carthage
Origen	c. 185	c. 254	Alexandria
Victorinus		c. 304	
Eusebius	c. 260	c. 339	Caesaria
Epiphanius	c. 315	c. 403	Palestine, Cyprus

Commentary (Tyconius of Carthage), was written about c.380, Nero is listed as the Sixth King of Rev. Used by Jerome as a source

Jerome	c. 357	c. 420	Bethlehem

Syriac (Philoxenian) translation of Bible c. 508 (Syriac tradition dated earlier)

Chapter 3
EUSEBIUS, PAPIAS, THE AUTHOR OF REVELATION, AND THE MURATORIAN CANON

Eusebius, the Bishop of Caesarea, was also called Eusebius Pamphili. He was born in the year AD 260, a hundred years after Tertullian was born. Eusebius was an historian and scholar of the Biblical canon. As the first historian of the early Church, he needed to chronologically order a mass of letters, sermons, and documents.[24]

British educated classicist, Timothy Barnes, comments that no survey or summary can cover the wealth of detail this *Ecclesiastical History* contains.[25] His writings have had an influence in the development of Christian thought that few other writers have had.

Eusebius was the first to argue that John the Elder was the author of the book of Revelation rather than the apostle John.

Many consider the arguments of Eusebius to be convincing. Although Eusebius strongly believed that the apostle John wrote the Fourth Gospel, many scholars today have extended the work of Eusebius to also attribute the Fourth Gospel to John the Elder. Among them is the great New Testament scholar, Richard Bauckham. Bauckham defends the position of Eusebius and appeals to the prologue of Papias to show that there was a second John who wrote the book of Revelation. However, there may or may not have been a separate person known as the "Elder John" who is distinct from the apostle John. There are two contrasting points of view. It could be that "the Elder" is simply used as another name for the apostle John.

---

[24] Timothy D Barnes, *Constantine and Eusebius* (Harvard Univ. Press. 1981), 141.
[25] Ibid., 140.

A defense of the traditional point of view that the apostle John was the author of the book of Revelation is given by Robert H. Gundry. Gundry is certainly no conservative New Testament scholar. Because of his liberal approach to source criticism he has the dubious distinction of being ejected from the Evangelical Theological Society. He is, however, noted for his insights and pulls no punches. He received his PhD from Oxford University and studied under F. F. Bruce. Gundry's textbook, *A Survey of the New Testament*, is a classic that was first published in 1973 and has gone through five editions.[26] His defense of the Johannine authorship of the book of Revelation, in which he interacts with Bauckham's position, is worth walking through in some detail.[27]

Before considering the arguments given by Gundry and Bauckham, however, we will first consider some historical background that influenced the basic beliefs of Eusebius — his presuppositions.

There is a well-accepted reason that Eusebius questioned the credentials of Revelation. The heretical sect of Montanism based some of their millennial beliefs and prophecies on the book of Revelation. The sect was spreading rapidly throughout Asia and made its way all the way to Gaul (modern day France). In the year AD 230, shortly before Eusebius was born, the Synod of Iconium declared all baptisms performed by the sect following the teachings of Montanus to be invalid. The early Church considered the sect to be heretical, as did Eusebius.

Montanus believed that a new age was coming to pass in the second century, the age of the Spirit. He believed that he was a special recipient of the Holy Spirit.

In the words of Eusebius:

---

[26] Robert H. Gundry, *A Survey of the New Testament*, 5th ed. (Grand Rapids, MI: Zondervan, 2012).

[27] Robert H. Gundry, "The Apostolically Johannine Pre-Papian Tradition concerning the Gospels of Mark and Matthew," *The Old is Better: New Testament Essays in Support of Traditional Interpretations* (Tübingen: *Mohr Siebeck*, 2005. Reprinted, Eugene, OH: Wipf and Stock Publishers, 2010), 49-73.

The enemy of God's Church, who is emphatically a hater of good and a lover of evil, and leaves untried no manner of craft against men, was again active in causing strange heresies to spring up against the Church. For some persons, like venomous reptiles, crawled over Asia and Phrygia, boasting that Montanus was the Paraclete, and that the women that followed him, Priscilla and Maximilla, were prophetesses of Montanus. [28]

In the book of Revelation, John was taken by an angel to the top of a mountain where he sees the New Jerusalem come down to earth. Priscilla and Maximilla made a prophecy that the New Jerusalem would come down from heaven after a series of wars, not at Jerusalem, but in a town called Phrygia. Eusebius identified this sect with the book of Revelation. Eusebius had an extreme distaste for this particular sect which was spreading rapidly throughout Asia Minor.

According to Timothy Barnes, Eusebius questioned the credentials of Revelation even though no early writer had. Barnes notes that Eusebius conceded that Justin and Origen both attributed the book of Revelation to the apostle John and twice cited Irenaeus, who believed the book of Revelation was written by the apostle John. However, Eusebius appeals to Papias that there were two Johns, and the younger less authoritative John wrote the Revelation.[29]

In other words, Eusebius had a motive for denying the apostolic authorship of Revelation and looking for another John of a lesser authority. Eusebius wished to counter the spread of Montanism.

In addition to the comments of Barnes, that no previous early writer denied Johannine authorship, it was not helpful for the position

---

[28] Philip Schaff and Henry Wace, ed., *A Select library of Nicene and post-Nicene fathers of the Christian Church*, Second Series, *Vol. 1, Eusebius: Church History, Life of Constantine the Great, and Oration in Praise of Constantine* (New York: The Christian Literature company, New York. 1890), 229.

[29] Timothy D Barnes, *Constantine and Eusebius* (Cambridge: Harvard University Press. 1981), 140.

of Eusebius that the Muratorian Canon contained the book of Revelation in its list of acceptable books for worship.

The Muratorian Canon, also known at the Muratorian Fragment, is the oldest known manuscript that contains a list of New Testament books. It is called a fragment because the first part of the manuscript is missing. The book of Revelation was accepted by many, although not universally. Bauckham, however, noticed a distinction made in the canon which had parallels to the work of Papias.

Bauckham argues that the tradition found in the Muratorian Canon regarding John is dependent upon Papias. There are several interesting similarities in language between existing Papian fragments and the Canon. Bauckham notes that the Canon distinguished the author of the Gospel of John as a "John" who was only one of the "disciples" from Andrew who was referred to as one of the "apostles." The words translated from the Canon are:

> The fourth of the gospels is of John, one of the disciples. To his fellow-disciples and bishops, who were encouraging him he said: "Fast with me today for three days, and whatever will be revealed to each of us, let us tell to one another." The same night it was revealed to Andrew, one of the apostles, that all should certify what John wrote in his own name.[30]

Bauckham tells us that a similar distinction is made by Papias in his prologue. Bauckham contends that there are indications that the Muratorian Canon was written by an individual, although he does not claim that Papias wrote the Canon. Traditionally scholars have dated the authorship of the Canon to AD 170. There is in the fragment several statements about the *Shepherd of Hermas,* which self-dates the fragment to about AD 150. The Fragment rejects the *Shepherd of Hermas* as Scripture with the claim that it is written by the brother of Pius who was bishop of Rome. It states that the book could be read but could not be read publicly in worship. Pius died about AD 152.

---

[30] Richard Bauckham, *Jesus and the Eyewitnesses: The Gospels as Eyewitness Testimony*, (William B. Eerdmans Publishing Company, 2006), 426.

Based on this reference, some scholars endorse an earlier date prior to AD 150. Per Gentry:

> The portion of this important manuscript dealing with the canon of Scripture claims to have been written by someone who was a contemporary of Pius, Bishop of Rome, sometime between A.D. 127 and 150.[31]

Given the amount of attention scholars have paid to this portion of the canon, it is worth quoting in full.

> The Pastor, moreover, did Hermas write very recently in our times in the city of Rome, while his brother bishop Pius sat in the chair of the Church of Rome. And therefore it also ought to be read; but it cannot be made public in the Church to the people, nor placed among the prophets, as their number is complete, nor among the apostles to the end of [their] time.[32]

Some scholars have argued that the Muratorian Canon should be dated to the fourth century. Sundberg wrote an article in the early 1970's arguing that the phrase "very recently, in our times" in the fragment does not refer to the author's time as understood in its ordinary meaning. Sundberg distinguishes between the time of the apostles and a post-apostolic time. He argues that the phrase, "in our times" refers to "post-apostolic times."

Hahneman revives Sundry's argument and notes that Irenaeus uses similar wording in his *Against Heresies*, where the vision was seen "not a very long time ago, but almost in our own generation towards

---

[31] Kenneth L. Gentry, Jr., *Before Jerusalem Fell: Dating the Book of Revelation*, 3rd ed. (Fountain Inn, SC: Victorious Hope Publishing, 1998, 2010), 93.

[32] Cleveland Coxe, *Ante-Nicene Fathers, Vol. 5: Hippolytus, Cyprian, Caius, Novatian, Appendix*, ed. Alexander Roberts and James Donaldson. Revised and Chronologically arranged with brief prefaces and occasional notes by A. Cleveland Coxe (New York: Christian Literature Publishing Co., 1886), 604.

the end of the reign of Domitian." Most scholars look at this argument as being weak, however, because Irenaeus is not trying to separate his time from the apostle's time.

Hahneman listed a number of reasons in his book why the Muratorian Canon should be dated in the fourth century rather than at an earlier date. His main arguments center around a thesis of an Eastern origin of the Fragment rather than the commonly accepted view that the Fragment was written in the vicinity of Rome. This prompted a heated debate that the overall aim of Hahneman, according to Charles Hill, is to advance the work of Sundberg who claimed the Old Testament canon was not closed and the process of a fixed Old Testament canon did not begin until third century.[33]

Bauckham lists a number of discussions, which in his words "may be judged to have vindicated the earlier date."[34] Michael Kruger, author of the *Canon Revisited,* agrees. Kruger tells us that Joseph Verheyden rightly sums up the modern debate. "None of the arguments put forward in favour of a fourth-century, eastern origin of the Fragment are convincing."[35]

The date of AD 170 is the traditional date given scholars mainly because line 65 in the Canon refers to the "heresy of Marcion." However, Tertullian, in his *Adversus Marcionem,* dates the origins of this heresy to the early AD 140s, which is well before the death of Pius in AD 152. Given that it took a few years for the heresy of Marcion to spread would make a date of about AD 150 a more logical time for dating the authorship of the Fragment.

The canon itself claims that the *Shepherd of Hermas* was written "very recently, in our times," where "our times" is described as the

---

[33] C.E. Hill, "The Debate Over the Muratorian Fragment and the Development of the Canon," *Westminster Theological Journal* 57:2 (Fall 1995): 438.

[34] Richard Bauckham, op. cit., 425, 426.

[35] Michael J. Kruger, 'Ten Basic Facts about the NT Canon that Every Christian Should Memorize: #6: "At the End of the Second Century, the Muratorian Fragment lists 22 of our 27 NT books."' Canon Fodder. http://www.michaeljkruger.com/ten-basic-facts-about-the-nt-canon-that-every-christian-should-memorize-6-at-the-end-of-the-second-century-the-muratorian-fragment-lists-22-of-our-27-nt-books-2/ (accessed April 11, 2016).

time "while bishop Pius ... was occupying the [e]piscopall chair." In other words, the Shepherd was written by the brother of Pius before his death while he was officially performing the duties of his office as Bishop within the Church.

That the *Shepherd of Hermas* was written by the brother of Pius, however, is considered to be an error in the Fragment — but an error that is important to its date of authorship. Hermas, a foster-child sold into slavery in Rome, lists his family members (Vision 1:1:1). The brother of Pius is never mentioned as a family member. Gentry quotes details as to the origin of the error as described by Arthur S. Barnes:

> Pius I, about 150, "changed the house of Pudens into a church, and gave it precedence over all the other parishes of Rome as the dwelling of the Bishop, and dedicated it with the title of the *Pastor*, that is, the Good Shepherd." This seems to be the original and true story and is told in the Roman Breviary for his feast on July 11th. The "Acts of Pastor and Timotheus", which are not authentic but contain some true traditions, make "Pastor" the brother of Pius, whom he put in charge of this church. This is the first confusion. The author of the Muratorian Fragment takes it a bit farther. He says: "the 'Pastor' of Hermas is not really ancient, for it was written by the brother of Pius I quite lately." Thus we have a double confusion. The dedication of the church has been confused with the name of its priest, and he again with the name of the book which Hermas wrote.[36]

There is internal evidence that the *Shepherd* was written even earlier. The *Shepherd* makes contemporary reference to the apostles of Christ. Gentry quotes Hermas:

> the apostles and bishops and teachers and deacons, who walked after the holiness of God, and exercised their office of bishop and teacher and deacons in the purity and sanctity for the elect of God, some of them already fallen on sleep, and others still living.[37]

---

[36] Kenneth L. Gentry Jr., *Before Jerusalem Fell: Dating the Book of Revelation*, 3rd ed. (Fountain Inn, SC.: Victorious Hope Publishing 1998, 2010), 87.

[37] Ibid., 90. Quote is from Vision 3:5:1 from Hermas.

Both Gentry and Robinson date the Shepherd to the mid AD 80s based on the above quote.[38]

Philip Schaff dates the Shepherd even earlier to the Hermas mentioned in the book of Romans. Romans 16:14 gives a greeting, "Greet Asyncritus, Phlegon, Hermes, Patrobas, Hermas, and the brothers who are with them."[39]

The confusion on the part of the author of the Fragment as to the author of *the Shepherd of Hermas* is an additional reason why the Fragment should be dated to AD 150, as this is when, according to Barnes, the error occurred that caused the confusion. I see no reason to date the Muratorian Cannon to any date other than its self-attested date.

Bauckham makes a convincing case that the Canon is dependent on Papias. The parallels between Papias' work and the Canon would also indicate an early date for its authorship.

Bauckham goes on to argue, concerning the story about the origins of John's gospel recorded in the Fragment, that there is good reason for supposing that this story bears some relation to Papias and treats not John the son of Zebedee, but Papias's John the Elder, as author of the Gospel.[40]

Although it does seem to be the case that the language used in the Muratorian Canon is dependent on Papias, this does not mean the language itself indicates that there is an individual named John the Elder who is a distinct person from John the son of Zebedee. Let's take a look at the actual language from the prologue.

The lines interpreted by Eusebius from Papias that have been in dispute are as follows:

> And by way of guaranteeing their truth for you [sg.] I will not hesitate to concatenate for the Expositions [of the Lord's Oracles] both as many things as I once learned well from the elders and [as many things as] I remembered [or "noted down"] well. For I was

---

[38] Ibid., 87.
[39] Ibid., 87.
[40] Bauckham, op. cit., 428.

not delighting in those who were saying many things, as the majority [of people were delighting in them]. Rather, [I was delighting in] those [who were remembering] the commandments given to the faith by the Lord and deriving from the truth itself.

(P1)

And if somewhere anyone who had followed the elders happened to come, I was examining the words of the elders, what Andrew or what Peter had said, or what Philip or what Thomas or James or what John or Matthew or any other one of the Lord's disciples [**had said**],

(P2)

and what things Aristion and the elder John, the Lord's disciples, **are saying** [with reference to the time when Papias was examining these reports].

For I was not assuming that the things from books would benefit me so much as the things from a living and surviving voice[41]

I broke the key statement of Papias quoted above into two parts, P1 and P2, for reference purposes.

Gundry, in his argument, first considers the date and the reliability of Eusebius's tradition.

Gundry tells us that modern handbooks used to date Papias's writings concerning John the Elder to AD 130 or later.

A reassessment, however, indicating an earlier time has been taking place.[42] Eusebius himself, according to Gundry, "leads us" to an earlier date between 100 - 110 by stating that Papias became known during the time of Polycarp and Ignatius, with whom he associates Clement of Rome who died in AD 100. This is consistent with the current reassessment. Gundry then cites Yarbrough.

---

[41] Gundry, op. cit., 50. From *Hist eccl* 3.36.1-2; 3.39.3-4.
[42] Robert W. Yarbrough, "The Date of Papias: A Reassessment," *JETS* 26 (1983): 181-191.

Yarbrough notes that Eusebius's *Chronicon* puts together in order the apostle John, Papias, Polycarp, and Ignatius and assigns the date A.D. 100 to this entry; and J.B. Orchard shows that Eusebius is following a chronological order according to which all the events recorded in *Hist. eccl.* 3.34-39 take place during the bishopric of Evarestus at Rome (A.D. 101 - 108).[43]

Gundry mentions that the failure of both Irenaeus and Eusebius to quote Papias against Gnosticism is best explained by the fact that Papias at this earlier date wrote before Gnosticism became a widespread threat.

What this means is that the earlier days of learning for Papias overlapped with the ministry of the apostle John. In other words, a reference to "learning from John" is understood to be a reference to "learning from John the apostle."

The "older view" before the "reassessment" is that Papias was twice removed from the disciples. In this case there would be no overlap with the ministry of the apostle John. If the "reassessment" is correct, then Papias is only once removed from the disciples when he wrote.

Gundry cites U.H. J. Körtner who adds that it is easier to think of the earlier date since it is hard to think of the Elder John and Aristion as still alive toward the middle of the second century. The present tense "they are saying" implies they are still alive when Papias writes.[44]

The only "hard" evidence favoring a late date comes in a statement by Philip of Side, who dates Papias remarks to the reign of Hadrian (AD 117 - 138). However, Gundry suggests that we have good reasons to distrust Philip's statement. He is notoriously unreliable and wrote approximately a century later than Eusebius.

According to Gundry:

Comparison of Philip's statement with Eusebius's favor that Philip depended on Eusebius but garbled the information he got [45]

---

[43] Gundry, op. cit., p. 50.
[44] Ibid., p. 51.
[45] Ibid., p. 51.

In summary, a large number of considerations unite to disfavor a date of A.D. 130 or later in accordance with Philip of Side and to favor a date of A.D. 101 - 108 for Papias's report.[46]

By his own testimony Papias is not surmising but passing on an earlier report by a certain elder. If Papias writes during A.D. 101 - 108, then the tradition does not go back to merely Papias, the tradition reaches back even more.

Richard Bauckham also believes the traditional time for Papias completing his book in about AD 130 is based on the "very unreliable evidence" of Philip of Side.[47] Papias personally was acquainted with the daughters of Philip the evangelist. Bauckham believes the date should be earlier, possibly as early as the turn of the century.[48] Papias collected his data during or close to the decade AD 80-90. Bauckham essentially contends that Papias wrote as an old man on what he did when he was a young man. Bauckham explains,

> For our purposes it is much more important that, whenever Papias actually wrote, in the passage we shall study he speaks about an earlier period in his life, the time during which he was collecting oral reports of the words and deeds of Jesus. As we shall see the period of time of which he is speaking must be AD 80.[49]

It should be noted that this dating by Bauckham, for the collection of information on the part of Papias, is a shift from the traditional belief held by those who contend that John the Elder wrote the book of Revelation.

It is often argued by those favoring John the Elder as the author of Revelation, that Papias collected his data after AD 100. In other words, the apostle John would have been too old to be a candidate for Papias to communicate with; the more likely choice would be the younger John the Elder. Thus, Bauckham cannot make an identical

---

[46] Ibid., 52.
[47] Richard Bauckham, op. cit., 13.
[48] Ibid., 13-14.
[49] Ibid., 14.

argument. He agrees with Gundry that the time period that Papias collected his data was prior to AD 100, and this time period would overlap with ministry of the apostle John. This earlier time period is foundational for Gundry's argument.

Gundry argues that Papias, instead of being twice removed from the apostles, whom he refers to as "the Lord's disciples," is only once removed. The text indicates that Papias claims to have listened often to those who had themselves heard some of the disciples speak.[50]

Summarizing this in a diagram with the above listed dates we have the following:

Lord's disciples and elders ministered about AD 50: Andrew, Peter, Philip, Thomas, James, Matthew, John	⟵⟶	Some of those who heard what **was said** by the disciples and elders would still be around in AD 90 about (40 years later)	⟵⟶	Papias would talk to those **once** removed
John, whose name is repeated as the elder, and Aristion	⟵⟶	John and Aristion are still alive "they are saying"	⟵⟶	Papias talked to John & Aristion directly

Papias was only once removed from the original disciples of Jesus. Papias equates "the words of the elders" with what Andrew or Peter or Philip or Thomas or James or John or Matthew or any other of the Lord's disciples had said. There is no apparent indication that Papias means to distinguish the elders from the disciples in "P1."

The listing of the apostolic names under the designation "the Lord's disciples" certainly does not imply such a distinction, according to Gundry, for Papias immediately identifies John "the elder" as one of "the Lord's disciples."

Since Papias does not directly distinguish between elders and disciples, a little detective work is necessary.

The key is to distinguish between the words "they had said" in "P1" and "they are saying" in "P2". John the Elder is just another

---

[50] Gundry, op. cit., 52.

name for the apostle John. The name "John" is repeated (in italics in the above diagram) with the words "are saying", because *John is the last surviving elder.* Thus, the apostle John is the one whose statements Papias has been hearing by firsthand report.[51]

Bauckham also believes, as does Gundry, that Papias was collecting his data early, likely between AD 80 and AD 100. However, he does not believe Papias is repeating the name of John, rather that he is distinguishing the apostle John from another John named John the elder.

My diagram of Bauckham's grouping:

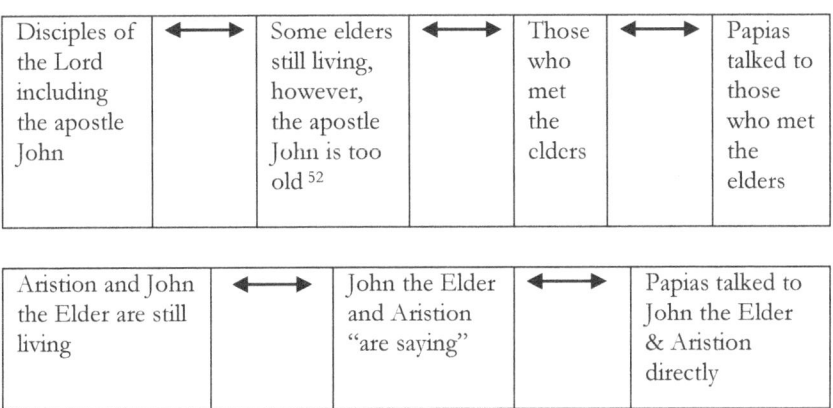

Papias, Bauckham concludes, seems to be using the terms "elders" to refer to the generation of teachers who knew the apostles but outlived them. This would be more consistent with the statement that Papias made earlier that he learned from them. Papias would not have spoken to the apostle John, but to John the Elder.

Gundry objects to this line of reasoning. The emphasis on the word "elders" makes better sense if it refers to the apostles as they deserve more emphasis than those who simply "handed on" their testimony. It is harder, says Gundry, to understand under Bauckham's

---

[51] Ibid., 55.
[52] Would the apostle John be too old or dead if Papias if gathered his data between AD 80 and AD 90? Most believe that the apostle John lived to AD 100.

view why Papias did not call Aristion an elder as well as a disciple.[53] This brings up an interesting question. Gundry asks,

> Does Bauckham slip in writing that as "prominent Christian teachers in the province of Asia," Aristion as well as the Elder John "deserved . . . both the epithet 'elder' and the epithet 'disciple of the Lord'"? Papias does not call Aristion an elder. Writing some eighty years later than Papias wrote makes it natural for Irenaeus to use "elders" for disciples of the apostles, for those disciples belong to a bygone age. But for Papias, "elders" more naturally referred to bygone apostles (with the exception of John).[54]

The elders emphasized truthfulness in repeating the commandments given by the Lord.

A supposedly earlier generation of disciples does not step in as "go-betweens to pass the commandments from Jesus to the elders."[55] We would have expected them to outright say that they received the Lord's commandments from the disciples. However, *Papias implies that he has not heard the elders.* He says, it is others who have heard them: "but if ever anyone came who had followed the elders, I inquired about the words of the elders."[56] Papias did not talk to any of the elders because they had all died by this time except for the apostle John. Papias repeated the name of John because he is the last surviving elder.

According to Gundry, Eusebius lets the truth slip out when he himself in *eccl.* 3.39.7 shows that Papias used both of the terms "elders" and "Lord's disciples" to mean "apostles." Eusebius writes that Papias "confesses that he had received the words of the apostles from those who had followed them." Says Gundry,

> To be sure, Eusebius distinguishes himself between the apostle John and the Elder John (*Hist. Eccl.* 3.39.6). But this distinction is John and

---

[53] Ibid., 53, footnote 9.
[54] Ibid., 53, footnote 9.
[55] Ibid., 54.
[56] Ibid., 54.

the Elder John (*Hist. Eccl.* 3.39.6). But this distinction is tendentious. Eusebius does not like the book of Revelation – the milleanarianism that Papias, Irenaeus, and others have drawn from it seem crassly materialistic to him ... so he wants to belittle the book by making it unapostolic.[57]

Gundry argues that Eusebius is manipulating the words of Papias. In addition to manipulating the words of Papias, Eusebius misuses the words of Dionysius when Dionysius mentions that there are two tombs with the name of John in Ephesus. In 7.25.16 of his *Ecclesiastical History* Eusebius almost exactly echoes the words of Dionysius when he says, "I think there was a certain other [John] of those who came to be in Asia, since they say that there also came to be two memorials in Ephesus and that each is called John's."[58] The "I think" of Dionysius is exceptionally weak and the "they say" is vague.

It might be there are rival burial sites similar to the ancient site rivalry for the claimed burial sites of Peter and Paul "between the *Memoria Apostolorum ad Cacacumbas* and the monuments on the Vatican Hill and the Ostian Way."[59] It is possible a second tomb belonged to a later Christian named John. Zahn notes the Greek word used by Eusebius for memorial could also mean monument. There could be a monument at a house where John lived, a monument at a Church where John met, and another where John was buried.[60]

Eusebius then buttresses his support by turning the words of Dionysius into a confident assertion. He not only says "there were two Johns," he replaces the vague "they say" of Dionysius with "the ones who have said" and adds the words "still now" to strengthen the argument from the two memorials.[61]

In the words of Gundry:

---

[57] Ibid., 54.
[58] Ibid., 58.
[59] Ibid., 57.
[60] Ibid., 57.
[61] Ibid., 58.

But Dionysius himself would not have recognized this use of his statement; for in his own context he has just identified the elder who wrote 2 - 3 John with the Apostle John, and he has made no mention of the tradition passed on by Papias. In all likelihood, then, *Eusebius gains the dubious honor of being first to make a false distinction between the Apostle John and the Elder John.* Since the distinction is not only false but also rests on an unnecessary inference from two memorials, the argument is doubly weak. Papias means to ascribe his information concerning Matthew and Mark to one and the same John, i.e. who was a disciple and elder, i.e., the famous apostle.[62]

There are reputable scholars who believe the book of Revelation was written by the apostle John. Although Richard Bauckham is a highly respected scholar whose work represents the view of many today, the defense of the traditional position given by Robert Gundry is strong.

What is important for our upcoming analysis is that there is an interesting use of sources and questionable choices made by Eusebius. According to Gundry, Eusebius is likely the first to make a false distinction between the apostle John and the Elder John. At the very least we can say that Eusebius makes a choice as to the identity of John as author of Revelation that none of the Church fathers previous to him made.

Most damaging to the argumentation of Eusebius and of importance for our upcoming analysis, however, is his misuse of the comments made by Dionysius of Alexandria. Eusebius misused the word of Dionysius even though he knew exactly what the original words of Dionysius were.[63]

We must ask, in a future chapter, if Eusebius made other questionable choices and misused statements to add strength to an argument.

---

[62] Ibid., 58. Emphasis mine.
[63] Ibid., 58. Gundry gives a side by side comparison of the words of Dionysius versus those of Eusebius written in 7.25.16 of his *Ecclesiastical History*. The phraseology is almost identical.

We noted earlier that the Shepherd of Hermas may have been written as early as the mid AD 80s. Interestingly, the Shepherd of Hermas uses the same imagery as the book of Revelation. Gentry quotes R.H. Charles: "The fact that Hermas used the same imagery as [the Apocalypse] may be rightly used as evidence that he knew it."[64]

In the Shepherd of Hermas, the Church is represented by a woman (Rev 12), the enemy of the Church by a beast (Rev 13), out of the mouth of the beasts come fiery locusts (Rev. 9:3), and the foundation stones of the heavenly Jerusalem bear the names of the twelve Apostles (Rev. 21:14). Also, the faithful in both Revelation and the Shepherd of Hermas are both clothed in white and are given crowns to wear.

Since Hermas knew the book of Revelation, we can reasonably date the writing of the book of Revelation before the mid AD 80s.

More importantly, in the Muratorian Canon we read:

> the blessed Apostle Paul, following the rule of his predecessor John, writes to no more than seven Churches by name ... John too, indeed, in the Apocalypse, although he writes to seven churches, addresses all.[65]

It is interesting that on the Muratorian Fragment, which Bauckham argues is dependent on Papias and in Bauckham's view supports his claim that John the Elder wrote the book of Revelation, a time is indirectly specified before which the Book of Revelation must have been written.

Kenneth Gentry asserts,

> This ancient writer [of the Muratorian canon] clearly teaches that John preceded Paul in writing letters to seven churches. And it is universally agreed among historians and theologians that Paul died before A.D. 70, either in A.D. 67 or 68.[66]

The position argued by Eusebius is that the book of Revelation was written by John the Elder during the period of time that Domitian

---

[64] Gentry, op. cit., 90.
[65] Ibid., 94.
[66] Ibid., 94.

was Emperor of Rome in the AD nineties. The Canon, on the other hand, tells us that the Letters to the seven churches in Revelation were written before the death of Paul. The Canon gives us direct extra biblical evidence. Eusebius, we shall see, gives us an argument in attempting to justify a position. We will examine his argument and in the process take a look as some of the choices he made along the way.

Chapter 4
THE SIXTH KING, THE BANISHMENT OF JOHN TO THE ISLAND OF PATMOS, AND THE DATING OF REVELATION

The book of Revelation itself directly gives us very little information as to when it was written and by whom. In Revelation 1:1-2, 9 we read:

> The revelation of Jesus Christ, which God gave him to show to his servants the things that must soon take place. He made it known by sending his angel to his servant John, who bore witness to the word of God and to the testimony of Jesus Christ, even to all that he saw . . . I, John, your brother and partner in the tribulation and the kingdom and the patient endurance that are in Jesus, was on the island called Patmos on account of the word of God and the testimony of Jesus.

The book itself only tells that the author is named John and that he was on the island of Patmos "on account of the word of God and the testimony of Jesus." This could mean that John was banished to the island of Patmos as tradition holds, or it could be that John was simply visiting Patmos to preach the gospel.

We will take the position that the dominant traditions are correct in saying that John was banished to the island of Patmos.

Based on the text in the Muratorian Canon that concerns the letters of John and Paul, the date for the authorship of the book of Revelation is prior to AD 67. Gentry sets the date in the mid-sixties and defends the position that John was banished to an island by Nero. It is argued by Eusebius, however, that the book of Revelation was written by John the Elder during the period of time that Domitian was Emperor of Rome in the AD eighties or nineties.

We do have a very strong indicator in the book of Revelation itself as to when it was written. Revelation 17:10 gives us a way to determine which "king" was in power – by counting the first seven kings (emperors) of Rome. The Jews viewed the Roman Emperors as kings. "We have no king but Caesar" (John 19:15).

The first problem to be solved in counting the kings is to identify the first king. Since the Roman Empire was officially established as an empire under Augustus, some commentators suggest that the count should start with Augustus.

Gentry, however, reminds us that:

> Julius did claim the title *Imperator*. Suetonius clearly records his claim to the *"praenomen Imperatoris."* This puts him in line with Augustus and the following emperors who naturally claimed the same. Indeed, the following emperors even called themselves by his name, "Caesar."[67]

Suetonius lists Julius as the first of the line in his *Lives of the Twelve Caesars*. Dio Cassius, another Roman Historian, lists Julius as the first of the emperors. Most importantly, though, is the answer to the following question posed by Gentry. Who would a Jewish historian from Palestine, living in the same time period as the author of Revelation, consider to be the first emperor? What clinches Gentry's argument for me is that the historian Josephus, who wrote works for *both the Romans and the Jews*, considers Julius Caesar to be the first Caesar. That, says Gentry, is the most important consideration for our purposes.[68]

Gentry interprets Revelation 17:10 as follows:

> "They are seven kings, five have fallen, [i.e., Julius, Augustus, Tiberius, Caligula, and Claudius], one is [i.e., Nero], the other has *not yet come;* and when he comes, he must remain a little while [i.e, Galba reigned from June, 68 to January, 69]." It seems indisputably clear that the book of

---

[67] Kenneth L. Gentry, Jr., *Before Jerusalem Fell: Dating the Book of Revelation*, 3rd ed., (Fountain Inn, SC.: Victorious Hope Publishing, 1998, 2010), 154-155.
[68] Ibid., 155.

Revelation must be dated in the reign of Nero Caesar, and consequently *before* his death in June, A.D. 68. He is the sixth king.[69]

A second reason that there is a difference of opinion by theologians as to the identity of the sixth king of Rome, also related to counting, is due to the determination if it is allowable to skip certain kings. Mathematically, in the process of counting whole numbers by ones, it would not be allowable to skip the next number of a sequence. In any ordered list we should always proceed to the next item on the list. The list is a matter of recorded history.

Some believe we should be able to skip Galba, Ortho, and Vitellius because of the brevity of their reigns in the year of the four emperors. However, Suetonius includes them in his list of the twelve Caesars.

Commentaries from the early church interpreting Revelation 17:10 and listing Nero as the sixth king have been translated from Latin into English. In 2012, Francis X. Gumerlock published *Revelation and the First Century*, which gives translations of patristic and medieval commentaries on Revelation 17 in which Nero is listed as the sixth king.

Gumerlock tells us that:

At least four commentaries on the book of Revelation, written between the eighth and thirteenth centuries, saw Nero as the sixth king of Rev. 17:10, the one who "is" reigning. Concerning the source of these comments, they are thought to have stemmed from a commentary that dates before 750 but is now lost (although there is great promise for its reconstruction), or from the lost, but now reconstructed commentary of Tyconius of Carthage, who wrote about the year 380. These rather widespread written records of Nero reigning as the sixth king is significant, because in them is the implication that John wrote the

---

[69] Ibid., 158.

Apocalypse at an early date, during the reign of Nero from 54 - 68 A.D.[70]

Despite this strong internal indicator that Revelation was written when Nero was in power, the dominant Church tradition holds that it is under the reign of emperor Domitian in the AD eighties that John was banished to the island of Patmos where he wrote the book of Revelation.

Traditionally, most writers since the time of Eusebius have viewed his writings as works that were written with his holding a set of presuppositions that did not color the way he wrote. We saw in our previous chapter that Bauckham does not view the presuppositions of Eusebius on the book of Revelation in the same manner Gundry does when examining the works of Papias.

In contrast to Bauckham, Gundry sees Eusebius as "twisting the words of Papias" in order to arrive at a desired conclusion. Probably almost all scholars recognize that Eusebius misuses the "I think" of Dionysius by turning them into what Gundry terms "a confident assertion." In light of this, a more detailed analysis of Eusebius's writings on the banishment of John to Patmos is warranted. We will now give a brief introduction to our analysis of Eusebius's writings of the banishment of John given by George Edmundson.

In 1913 George Edmundson gave a series of eight lectures before the University of Oxford entitled: *The Church in Rome in the First Century, an Examination of Various Controverted Question Relating to its History, Chronology, Literature and Traditions.*

---

[70] Francis X Gumerlock, *Revelation and the First Century: Preterist Interpretations of the Apocalypse in Early Christianity* (Powder Springs, GA: American Vision Press, 2012), 157-58. Gumerlock has just completed his translation of the recently reconstructed commentary of Tyconius of Carthage. This commentary which dates back to the time of Jerome was published in the Corpus Christianorum Series Latina, which is published by Brepols publishers out of Turnhout, Belgium. Although Tyconius has an error in his succession of emperors, he does list Nero as the sixth king. Gumerlock's translation was accepted for publication in the Fathers of the Church series.

One of the topics discussed by Edmundson in lecture six of his series was on the banishment of John. Political prisoners were banished by Domitian when he was emperor. These political prisoners were then later released by Nerva. Political prisoners were also banished by Domitian when Domitian temporarily accepted the name of Caesar from Vespasian in mid AD 70 and was then released by Nerva in AD 71.

John A.T. Robinson devoted considerable space in his *Redating the New Testament* to arguments given by Edmundson which he is intrigued by, however, ultimately rejects, a primary reason being that Edmundson's count of the emperors beginning with Claudius is strained.[71] With Claudius as the first king, Domitian, during his temporary tenure as emperor, would be the sixth king, the one who "is." Robinson tells us that he quoted Edmundson at some length because his work, which has some impressive points, has been ignored. I will do the same.

I will defend a modification of Edmundson's argument with Nero as the sixth king rather than Claudius. John would then have been at Patmos during the brief reign of Domitian in AD 70 and then released by Nerva in AD 71.

We will revisit some of the analysis given by Edmundson in detail. Edmundson starts out with a walk through of Eusebius's position that John was banished in the AD nineties. Eusebius starts out by considering accounts of the early Church fathers on the banishment of John by "the tyrant."

There are a number of accounts by the early church fathers of John being banished by a Roman emperor to an island, the Island of Patmos. It is on the Island of Patmos that John saw his visions and wrote the book of Revelation.

One of the earliest writers of an account in Church history on the banishment of John is that of Tertullian. Tertullian, in his Apology 5,

---

[71] John A.T. Robinson, *Redating the New Testament* (Philadelphia: The Westminster Press, 1976), 252.

written in AD 197, makes an amazing statement where he asserts that John was plunged into burning oil and suffered nothing.

That John was "plunged into burning oil and suffered nothing" could be considered to be an embellishment. Others consider this to be a miracle. Gentry points out, regardless of what one thinks about John coming out the burning oil unharmed, to plunge someone into burning oil would be consistent with the torture administered by Nero.[72] The account that John is then exiled to an island appears in a number of accounts given by early fathers of the Church. Tertullian associates the exile with Rome:

> where Peter had a like passion with the Lord [i.e. crucifixion]; where Paul hath for his crown the same death with John[the Baptist] [i.e., execution], where the apostle John was plunged in boiling oil, and suffering nothing, and was afterwards banished to an island.[73]

Notice that in this early account there is no mention of the name of the island to which John was banished or who banished him. We also know that Nero executed Paul and Peter. It is likely that Tertullian is implying that Nero attempted to execute John at this particular time in Rome, since all three names are used in the same sentence. However, it is also possible that the attempted execution of John took place at a different time. The banishment of John could have taken place later under Domitian or possibly earlier, before the executions of Paul and Peter by Nero. Gentry believes that all three were executed, maybe not at exactly the same time, but in the reign of Nero.

Gentry refers to a comment by Hort:

> Hort found it noteworthy that when Tertullian speaks of Domitian's evil in the fifth chapter of his Apology, he does not mention anything about John's banishment or suffering under him. . . . . Yet Hort's observation becomes especially remarkable in light of the prior Tertullianic

---

[72] Gentry, op. cit., 96-97.
[73] Ibid., 95.

statement, which unites the three Apostles under the Neronic persecution all of this becomes more intriguing when even Eusebius follows suit in his *Evangelical Demonstration* (3:5). Hort noted that Eusebius "groups in a single sentence Peter's crucifixion at Rome, Paul's beheading, and John's banishment to an island."[74]

Modern day scholar Jean Hardot writes nearly the same, according to Gumerlock. Hardot writes that, in Tertullian's view, Rome was the "theater of the triple martyrdom of Peter, of Paul, and of John."[75]

Jerome, in his exposition of Matthew 3:20, refers to the "ecclesiastical histories," where we see the influence of Tertullian.[76] Jerome adds the information that John was banished to the isle of Patmos.

In the early accounts of Origen and Clement on the banishment of John to the Isle of Patmos, *there is never mention of the name Domitian.* Clement refers to "the tyrant" and Origen refers to the "King of the Romans." Clement says,

> When after the death of the tyrant he [John] removed from the island of Patmos to Ephesus, he used to journey by request to the neighboring districts of the Gentiles, in some places to appoint bishops, in others to regulate whole churches, in others to set among the clergy some one man, it may be, of those indicated by the Spirit.[77]

Clement, however, in *Miscellanies* 7:17 writes:

> For the teaching of our Lord at His advent, beginning with Augustus and Tiberius, was completed in the middle of the times of Tiberius. And that of the apostles, embracing the ministry of Paul, end with Nero.

---

[74] Gentry, op. cit., 95.
[75] Gumerlock, op. cit., 42.
[76] Ian Boxall, *Patmos in the Reception History of the Apocalypse* (Oxford: Oxford Univ. Press, 2013), 42.
[77] Robinson, op. cit., 222.

So although Clement does not mention specifically that it was under Nero that John was banished, it is implied when combined with the above quote from Miscellanies 7:17. The teaching of the apostles ends with Nero. This would include the apostle John's book of Revelation.

However, in the writings of the church historian Eusebius, the name Domitian appears. Writers after this early historian, for the most part, follow his lead.

After establishing that "the tyrant" banishes John, Eusebius appeals to Irenaeus. He appeals to Irenaeus to show that the Apocalyptic vision was recently seen. Edmundson tells us, it was at this point in his narrative that Eusebius created the misunderstanding of Irenaeus that has stood since his time.

What makes the upcoming quote from Irenaeus particularly important is that he knew Polycarp, who personally knew the apostle John. This is the closest we come to the writings of someone who actually knew the apostle John outside of Papias. This makes Irenaeus extremely important, even though he was very young when he heard Polycarp speak.

Eusebius, who was born about fifty years after the death of Irenaeus, attributes the following quote to Irenaeus in a letter to Florinus where Irenaeus is recalling a memory of his *boyhood when he heard Polycarp lecture*. Eusebius writes:

> For when I was a boy, I saw thee [Florinus] in lower Asia with Polycarp, moving in splendor in the royal court, and endeavoring to gain his approbation. I remember the events of that time more clearly than those of recent years. For what boys learn, growing with their mind, becomes joined with it; so that I am able to describe the very place in which the blessed Polycarp sat as he discoursed, and his goings out and his comings in, and the manner of his life, and his physical appearance, and his discourses to the people, and the accounts which he gave of his intercourse with John and with the others who had seen the Lord. And as he remembered their words, and what he heard from them

concerning the Lord, and concerning his miracles and his teaching, having received them from the eyewitnesses of the Word of life, Polycarp related all things in harmony with the Scriptures. These things being told me by the mercy of God, I listened to them attentively, noting them down, not on paper, but in my heart.[78]

We know from Irenaeus in his *Against Heresies* that someone saw the apostle John "almost in our time [John died about AD 100]" near the end of Domitian's reign [Domitian died in AD 96]. It could be that it was someone other than Polycarp who saw John in the Churches John was visiting and Irenaeus took note of the information from this "someone else." However, the above mentioned memory of Irenaeus would qualify as recalling a time in which Polycarp recalled hearing John "almost in our time [time of Irenaeus]." The question is, was it John who was recently seen or was it John's vision that was recently seen by him "almost in our time."

The following statement by Irenaeus has been debated by modern scholars for over a hundred years because of its ambiguity. The ambiguity centers around a problem in translation.

The only complete text that we have of *Against Heresies* is in Latin, while the work was originally written in Greek. According to Gentry, we cannot correctly understand the statement apart from the original Greek in which the statement was written. We do, fortunately, have the following quote in Greek thanks to Eusebius. The English translation reads as follows:

> We will not, however, incur the risk of pronouncing positively as to the name of Antichrist; for if it were necessary that his name should be distinctly revealed in this present time, it would have been announced by him who beheld the apocalyptic vision. For *that* was seen no very

---

[78] Philip Schaff and Henry Wace, ed., *A Select library of Nicene and post-Nicene fathers of the Christian Church*, Second Series, *Vol. 1, Eusebius: Church History, Life of Constantine the Great, and Oration in Praise of Constantine* (New York: The Christian Literature company, New York. 1890), 238-239.

long time since, but almost in our day, towards the end of Domitian's reign.[79]

The ambiguity is that the sentence could be translated, "For *he* was seen no very long time since, but almost in our day, towards the end of Domitian's reign."

According to Gentry, the "that was seen no very long time since" is grammatically ambiguous in the Greek where it could be either that John was seen or that the Revelation was seen no very long time since. *However, the context of the statement by Irenaeus was that John was alive and people could have asked him about the identity of the Antichrist.*

It could have been asked of John as to the identity of the Antichrist in order to resolve a dispute concerning the number 666 found in Revelation 13:18. Revelation 13:18 in the English Standard Version reads as follows:

> This calls for wisdom: let the one who has understanding calculate the number of the beast, for it is the number of a man, and his number is 666.

The footnote in the ESV reads: Some manuscripts *616*

The alternate translation would be:

> This calls for wisdom: let the one who has understanding calculate the number of the beast, for it is the number of a man, and his number is 616.

In order to emphasize the nature of the dispute and to make the context and the implications of this context clear, I have arranged the points of the narrative given by Irenaeus in the form of a conversation between Irenaeus and a fictitious scribe. I have provided

---

[79] Kenneth Gentry, op. cit., 47.

documentation mapping each point of the conversation to the narrative of Irenaeus.[80]

Scribe:
> Irenaeus, I want to bring it to your attention that we have in our possession another copy of Revelation which gives the number of the beast as 616.[i]

Irenaeus:
> Yes, I am aware that there is more than one copy. I do not know how some scribes have made an error and have changed the middle number of the name.[ii]

Scribe:
> Some who have read the number have come up with a name of a man.[iii]

Irenaeus:
> Those who seek out a name from the erroneous and spurious number, we should assume, will be pardoned by God if they did this without evil intent.[iv]

Scribe:
> Some have done this, though, to make a name for themselves.

Irenaeus:
> Those who calculate a name from the spurious number and affirm this name that they came upon by themselves have led into error both themselves and those who confide in them.[vi]

---

[80] See endnotes i through xiii for mapping to narrative of Irenaeus found in Book V, Chapter 30, Paragraphs 1,3 of his *Against Heresies*.

Scribe:
> It is less hazardous to await the fulfillment of the prophecy than to make surmises.[vii]

Irenaeus:
> There are names found which have the number and it will be asked which shall be the man.[viii] I say this on account of the fear of God[ix] that I make no allegation for the name Evanthas. The name Latenios is a very probable solution to the puzzle since it is the name of the last kingdom as seen by Daniel.[x] It is the Latin who at the present time rule. Teitan also is a name that of all names is rather worthy of credit. Even the sun is termed "Titan" by those who currently rule. This name "Titan" has so much to recommend it.[xi]

Scribe:
> Should we choose one of these names positively as the name of the Antichrist?[xii]

Irenaeus:
> We will not incur the risk. If it were necessary that his name should be distinctly revealed in this present time, it would have been announced by him who beheld the apocalyptic vision.[xiii]

> *NOTE: at this point there is not enough information for Irenaeus to resolve the dispute concerning the spurious number or the correct name.*

Someone could have resolved the dispute by directly asking John. However, it would be necessary for John to be alive and be willing to tell him the solution. With this in mind, we must ask the question: which concluding statement would give "that someone" the possibility of getting the desired information from John?

> For John was seen no very long time since, but almost in our day, towards the end of Domitian's reign.

OR

> For the vision was seen no very long time since, but almost in our day, towards the end of Domitian's reign.

For the NAME to be revealed, it would in no way help Irenaeus resolve the dispute by using the information that John recently saw the vision.[81] However, if John was still alive, he could be asked the question directly by someone to resolve the dispute. Irenaeus notes that John could have announced the information if he felt it was necessary to do so.

Irenaeus did know someone who recently saw John. Irenaeus knew Polycarp and Polycarp knew John. What Irenaeus is saying between the lines is something like this, "Look, I knew Polycarp, and Polycarp could have received the solution from John by directly asking him." What we do know is that Polycarp never gave the solution to Irenaeus, and Irenaeus seems to have known Polycarp well. In his search for the solution, Irenaeus seems to imply the name of the Antichrist was yet to be revealed. Ian Boxall relates the situation as follows:

> Irenaeus is concerned to discourage speculation about the identity of the Antichrist, and has a vested interest in dating John's non-announcement of Antichrist's name as late as possible, so that it may still apply to Irenaeus' own day. Indeed, Alan Garrow has suggested a further reason why this Domitianic dating supports Irenaeus' concerns: namely his dependence upon Polycarp ... Closing the gap between Polycarp and the Apocalypse would have strengthened Irenaeus' claim that the name of Antichrist had never been announced publicly.[82]

Irenaeus does not say who saw John. He did not need to. Those who knew Irenaeus were also well aware that John knew Polycarp. *The full context is that John, who was the author of the riddle, could have made known the solution of the riddle to Polycarp when he recently saw John toward the end of*

---

[81] Kenneth Gentry, op. cit., 51.
[82] Ian Boxall, *Revelation:Vision And Insight* (London: SPCK. 2002), 90-91.

the reign of Domitian. Even in the possible but unlikely event that Irenaeus had someone other than Polycarp in mind, the fact remains that it was John who could have resolved the dispute if he were alive.

A reason that most still favor the standard reading may be that the ambiguity is not apparent in either the Latin or the English translations. The "that" of the "that was seen," which is italicized in the English translation above appears to correspond to the nearest previous noun (vision) as only two words separate "that" and "vision." In the Greek, however, verbs contain the subject within their form without having to explicitly add the subject, as is necessary in English.

However, to assume the word "that" must connect to the pronoun (vision) in the Greek is, in Gentry's words an error that is grave enough to be termed a "serious blunder."[83] In the Greek there is no noun before the verb "was seen."

Although it might seem unusual for us today to refer to a person as "that was seen", it was not at all unusual for Irenaeus. According to Hort, Irenaeus tended to use "that was seen" of persons more commonly than things like visions. That Irenaeus would be referring to "that" as being seen in "almost our time" when referring to John would not be unusual.[84]

Edmundson tells us that the misunderstanding of Irenaeus as seen in the common rendering of the above passage began with Eusebius and his interpretation of a comment by Origen.

> The misunderstanding about the meaning of the passage is largely due to Eusebius, who after a reference to Domitian's persecution proceeds "in this [persecution] report [he] affirms that the Apostle and Evangelist John, who was still living, in consequence of his testimony to the divine word was condemned to dwell on the island of Patmos," and then he quotes Irenaeus in support of his statement. Now Eusebius was very

---

[83] Ibid., 346.
[84] Ibid., 50.

familiar with the works of Origen, and more particularly his commentaries, he had in mind the following comment by Origen upon St. Matthew xx:22†: "And the sons of Zebedee were baptized with the baptism, since Herod killed James the [brother] of John with the sword, while the King of the Romans, as tradition teaches, condemned John bearing testimony through the word of truth unto the Island of Patmos. And John speaks of the things concerning his testimony, not saying who condemned him . . . and he seems to have beheld the Apocalypse in the island." Origen does not give the name of the Roman king, since, as he says, John does not tell us who condemned him. He certainly does not say that the Roman King was Domitian, indeed he is but repeating what Irenaeus had said before.[85]

† "Are you able to drink the cup that I am to drink?" They said to him, "We are able."

Edmundson is telling us that Eusebius is reading too much into the commentary by Origen. Eusebius takes the words of Origen and ties the words "King of the Romans" to Domitian based on his misreading of what is now the common rendering of Irenaeus. In other words, Eusebius assumed Domitian to be the "King of the Romans."

Eusebius follows the same pattern concerning his statements about John during the reign of Trajan. Edmundson refers to the words of Eusebius and then comments as follows:

Eusebius, again, after speaking of Trajan succeeding Nerva in the Empire writes: 'About this time also, John, the beloved disciple of Jesus, at once Apostle and Evangelist, still surviving in Asia, supervised the Churches, there, having returned from his banishment to the island

---

[85] George Edmundson, *The Church in Rome in the First Century: An Examination of Various Controverted Questions Relating to Its History, Chronology, Literature and Traditions. Eight Lectures Preached Before the University of Oxford in the Year 1913* (London, New York, and Bombay and Calcutta: Longsman, Green and Co., 1913), 165.

after the death of Domitian.' He then refers to Clement of Alexandria and Irenaeus as his authorities.[86]

Eusebius combines the persecution of Domitian, the above quote by Origen, the previous quote by Clement, and the now common rendering of Irenaeus to make the claim that John was banished to the isle of Patmos under Domitian and then returned from banishment under Nerva. Of course, as just noted, neither quote by Clement or Origen name Domitian as the tyrant or Domitian as King of the Romans!

What Edmundson seems to be saying here is that Eusebius is referring to Origen, Clement, and Irenaeus in order to *justify* an argument. It is his *claim* of Eusebius that after severe persecution John is banished by Domitian and then released by Nerva when he was emperor. He is not just reporting history; he is providing a justification for the history he is writing.

The opposite point of view is expressed by Lawlor a year before Edmundson's lectures in his *Eusebiana*.[87] This is a repeat of the same position Lawlor expressed in 1907 in an article in *The Journal of Theological Studies*. Lawlor says,

> Eusebius acted, it would seem, exactly as we might expect that a historian would act whose design was to give a narrative of a series of events, which should practically consist of extracts from earlier writers. He took as his basis Hegesippus, who had the fullest account known to him of the history of the Church during the period with which was concerned. And here and there he added to his Hegesippean narrative illustrations from other authorities—Irenaeus, Tertullian, Brettois, and the rest.[88]

---

[86] Ibid., 166.

[87] Hugh Lawlor, *Eusebiana: Essays on the Ecclesiastical History of Eusebius Bishop of Caesarea* (Oxford: Clarendon Press, 1912), 53.

[88] Hugh Lawlor, "Hegesippus and the Apocalypse," *The Journal of Theological Studies*, 8 (April 1907): 443.

Lawlor believes that Hegesippus has the fullest account available. So what does Eusebius give us in 3.20 of his *Ecclesiastical History*? An argument seeking justification with reference to a questionable source, or a historian simply giving a narrative of a progression of historical events based on a reliable source? We need to consider both the progression of the narrative (argument) and the mysterious "ancient sources" of Hegesippus.

Eusebius starts his narrative with the persecution of the "King of the Romans." Eusebius knows that there was persecution under both Nero and Domitian. He refers to "Nero" as the first emperor to persecute the Christians. He then identifies Domitian as the unnamed persecuting "King of the Romans" by reading "his own interpretation of the words of Irenaeus into the passages from Origen and Clement."[89] His conclusion is that John was banished by Domitian and ultimately was released by Nerva after the reign of Domitian.

---

[89] Edmundson, op. cit., 165.

Chapter 5
NERVA AND THE RELEASE OF JOHN – AD 71 OR AFTER THE DEATH OF DOMITIAN?

Before we consider the "ancient source" of Hegesippus, we will first ask the question: what was the historical dilemma that would motivate Eusebius to feel the need to build a case? A. J. Robinson reminds us in his classic work, *Redating the New Testament*, that Nerva was directly involved with the release of banished prisoners **twice,** once when he was emperor but also once when he was working directly with Vespasian.[90] Robinson[91] quotes George Edmundson from his Bampton Lectures given at Oxford in 1913:

> In the month of June of that year Domitian and Mucianus left Rome to take part in a campaign in Gaul, and a little later Vespasian arrived in Rome and at once assumed the direction of affairs. Suetonius informs us that from the beginning he was anxious to conduct himself with the great moderation and clemency. One of his first cares was to take in hand the administration of justice, which had been sadly interrupted by the civil wars, and to examine into the accumulation of law-suits which had arisen, and to provide for the restitution of what had been seized by violence in the disorders of the time. Now Vespasian associated Titus with himself in the government in the course of the year 71 A.D. and was very jealous during the whole of his reign of allowing authority to be vested in any but members of his own family. But Vespasian took as his colleague in the consulship in 71 A.D. M. Cocceius Nerva. Now Nerva – the future emperor – was the representative of a family distinguished for three generations as jurists, and no doubt his appointment at this particular time was due to Vespasian's desire to have

---

[90] John A.T. Robinson, *Redating the New Testament* (Philadelphia: Westminster Press. 1976), 250.
[91] Ibid., 252.

a skilled lawyer at his side for dealing with the mass sentences of exile and of confiscation which with the legacy of the successive revolutions [starting with Nero's suicide]. Nerva held office during the first *nundinum* of 71 A.D., and it is permissible to believe that in accordance with tradition one of the sentences quashed by him was that which sent John to Patmos.[92]

Nerva had much to do in AD 71 in that he had to deal with mass sentences of exile of the successive revolutions beginning with the death of Nero. Nerva had to deal with the sentences of exile under Nero, Galba, Otho, and Vitellius. In addition, Nerva had to deal with what seems to be sentences of exile imposed by Domitian when he was temporarily emperor before the return of Vespasian to Rome.

Again Robinson refers to Edmundson:

Though but a boy of eighteen his head became filled with ambitious ideas, and he began, says Suetonius, to use his power in so arbitrary a manner as to give proof of what he was to become later. To such an extent was this the case that Dion Cassius tells us that Vespasian wrote to him from Alexandria "I am much obliged to you, my son, for letting me still be emperor and for not having yet deposed me." [93]

What Domitian was to become later as emperor was one who executed twelve former senators of Rome in order to confiscate their property.

In December of AD 69, Vespasian became emperor. For the first half of AD 70 Vespasian was securing his power in Alexandria while his oldest son Titus was completing the siege of Jerusalem.

His younger son, Domitian, accepted the name of Caesar "and was invested with full consular authority (consulare imperium), his

---

[92] George Edmundson, *The Church in Rome in the First Century: An Examination of Various Controverted Questions Relating to Its History, Chronology, Literature and Traditions. Eight Lectures Preached Before the University of Oxford in the Year 1913* (London, New York, and Bombay and Calcutta: Longsman, Green and Co., 1913), 171.

[93] Ibid., 170.

name being placed at the head of all dispatches and edicts." † [94]

In June, Domitian left Rome. Shortly afterward Vespasian arrived as noted above.

John may have been released by Nerva after the reign of Domitian as tradition holds. However, John may have not been released by Nerva in the AD nineties as Eusebius claims, but in AD 71.

It now makes sense why the early church fathers may not have specified who the tyrant was. Their source may not have specified who the tyrant was or when John was released by Nerva. The names of Domitian and Nerva are tied with the exile and release of prisoners in both AD 71 and in AD 96. If Domitian was the tyrant, the release of John by Nerva could have been either in AD 71 or in the AD nineties. Likewise, if Nero was the tyrant, John could have been released in either AD 71 or in the AD nineties. It was up to Eusebius to specify the name of the tyrant.

Eusebius claims to have a source. Here are the words of Eusebius as translated by Philip Schaff *beginning in paragraph 7 as numbered by Lawlor and Oulton* with the words "*These things are related by Hegesippus.*" This ends the portion directly attributed to Hegesippus as a source.

The section that just ended is the account of Hegesippus of how Domitian freed Christians that were of the "seed of David" because they did not have enough money to make their banishment worthwhile. They owned only "nine thousand denarii, half of which belonged to each of them; and this property did not consist of silver, but a piece of land which contained only thirty-nine acres." The paragraphs attributed to Hegesippus ends with the words "These things are related by Hegesippus." Eusebius then turns his attention to Tertullian.

> 7 *These things are related by Hegesippus.* Tertullian also has mentioned Domitian in the following words:
>
> "Domitian also, who possessed a share of Nero's cruelty, attempted once to do the thing as the latter did. But because he had, I suppose,

---

[94] John A. T. Robinson, op. cit., 249. † Tacitus, *Hist.* 4.2; Suetonius, *Dom.* I.

some intelligence, he very soon ceased, and even recalled those whom he had banished."

8 But after Domitian had reigned for fifteen years, and Nerva had succeeded to the empire, the Roman Senate, according to the writers that record the history of those days [Roman Historians],[XI][95] voted that Domitian's honors should be cancelled, and that those who had been unjustly banished should return to their homes, and have their property restored to them.

9 It was at this time [return of the exiled prisoners], that the apostle John returned from his banishment in the island and took up his abode at Ephesus, according to an ancient Christian tradition [ancient men].[96]

Lawlor argues that the words of Eusebius in paragraph 9 are based on Hegesippus as the source.[97] I believe that probably most theologians and textual scholars agree today that Hegesippus is the source of paragraph 9. I do as well.

Paragraphs 8 and 9 have two different sources. First is the source of paragraph 8 that is attributed to the Roman historians, the historians who recorded that those banished should receive their property back. Of course, Eusebius does not remind his readers that it also happened in AD 71 that Nerva oversaw the legal proceedings and restored property of banished political prisoners that were to be released. The Roman historians themselves tell us nothing about John.

---

[95] Philip Schaff and Henry Wace, ed., *A Select library of Nicene and post-Nicene fathers of the Christian Church*, Second Series, *Vol. 1, Eusebius: Church History, Life of Constantine the Great, and Oration in Praise of Constantine* (New York: The Christian Literature company, New York. 1890), 149. Footnote xi by Schaff reads: "See Dion Cassius, LXVIII. I sq., and Suetonius' *Domitian*, chap. 23." The numbering of the paragraphs is that of Lawlor. See Eusebius. *The Ecclesiastical History and the Martyrs of Palestine. Vol 1*. trans. by H. J Lawlor and J.E.I Oulton, (SPCK, [1927], 1954, Book III, Ch. 7:6, 81.

[96] Ibid., 149. According to Schaff, the ancient traditions are literally "the word of the ancients among us." Also, according to Lawlor this should be translated as the "ancient men." See Eusebius. *The Ecclesiastical History and the Martyrs of Palestine*. Vol 1. Translated by H. J Lawlor and J.E.I Oulton. SPCK, [1927], 1954, 81.

[97] Hugh Lawlor, "Hegesippus and the Apocalypse," *The Journal of Theological Studies*, 8 (April 1907), 442.

All we know about a possible Christian being released from exile is that Domitian's niece who was in exile on the island of Pandateria on the Campanian Coast was released and received her property back.[98]

The second source of information in paragraph 9 tells us that after Nerva released the banished prisoners, John took up residence in Ephesus after his exile on the island. *Notice that likely the only information given by "the record of our ancient men" is that John resided at Ephesus after being exiled from the island.*

"It was at that time" that John was released by Nerva. This could have been in AD 71 after being exiled from the island and having "taken up his abode" again in Ephesus. We do know that John resided in Ephesus in the AD 70s and as the leader of the Churches in Asia Minor frequently would visit them. If the "ancient men" refers to a written source, it may not have been specific as whether the release was in AD 71 or in AD 96.

> John seems to have made a home in Ephesus for the rest of his life [after AD 67]. There he supervised all the Christian churches in the provinces of Asia. These included Smyrna, which was a large commercial center; Pergamum, the center of the parchment-manufacturing industry; and Sardis, Philadelphia, and Laodicea, all cities once prosperous but then in decline after an immense earthquake that ravaged them in A.D. 17. These were the churches which John mentioned in Revelation. According to The Constitutions of the Holy Apostles, John ordained bishops as well as priests in each of those cities.[99]

We must also consider the possibility, as noted earlier, that "the record of our ancient men" was not a written record. Philip Schaff in the written notes to his translation of the *Ecclesiastical History* says that the "ancient men" literally means the "the word of the ancients among us."[100] So who were these ancient men?

---

[98] Dio Cassius, *History*. Lxviii, 14.2.
[99] Bernard C. Ruffin, *The Twelve. The Lives of the Apostles After Calvary* (Huntington, IN: Our Sunday Visitor [1977], 1984), 94.
[100] Philip Schaff and Henry Wace, ed., *A Select library of Nicene and post-Nicene*

With the words "ancient men" we immediately think of Papias and Polycarp. Polycarp was close to ninety when martyred in AD 155 before Hegesippus made his journey to Rome. Papias died about the same time Polycarp was martyred. The apostle John died in approximately AD 100. We do know, however, that possibly as early as AD 155 that Hegesippus traveled across the Roman Empire and gathered information for his five books of *Memoirs*. During his trip to Rome he interacted with several ecclesiastical leaders in Corinth when creating a succession list of bishops.

Eusebius tells us of this journey to Rome during the tenure of Anicetus who was bishop from about AD 155 - AD 167.[101]

> And the church of the Corinthians continued in the true doctrine until Primus was bishop at Corinth .... With them I associated on my voyage to Rome, and I abode with the Corinthians many days; during which we were refreshed together in the true doctrine. But when I came to Rome, I made for myself a succession-list as far as Anicetus; whose deacon was Eleutherus.[102]

If the "ancient men" interviewed by Hegesippus were young in AD 96 when John was presumed to have been released, those individuals would be in their mid-seventies to eighties by the time Hegesippus made his journey to Rome in AD 155. Polycarp, thought by many to have been the last surviving person to have known John, was already martyred, and Papias had died about the same time, although probably earlier.[103]

---

fathers of the Christian Church, Second Series, *Vol. 1, Eusebius: Church History, Life of Constantine the Great, and Oration in Praise of Constantine* (New York: The Christian Literature company, New York. 1890)., 149.

[101] A wide variety of dates are given for the beginning of Bishop Anicetus' tenure as Bishop from AD 154 to AD 157. The Catholic Encyclopedia gives the beginning of his tenure as AD 157.

[102] Eusebius, *The Ecclesiastical History and the Martyrs of Palestine*, Vol. 1, trans. by H. J Lawlor and J.E.I Oulton (SPCK, 1954 [1927]), 127.

[103] If Papias was born AD 60, as recent scholarship indicates, it is more likely that Papias died in the AD forties than the AD fifties.

The more likely explanation would be that the "ancient men" would simply be those who knew that John was alive rather than men who had actually known John. There is no indication from the passage in the *Ecclesiastical History* that Hegesippus received any information from the "ancient men" other than that John was living in Ephesus after AD 96 during the time period that Nerva allowed the banished prisoners to return home. That he "took up his abode once more" could have been after one of his extended visits to a church in Asia Minor. That John was living in Ephesus after AD 96 does not invalidate the argument given by Edmundson. We cannot rule out the possibility that John was released by Nerva in AD 71 and continued to have a residence in Ephesus into the late AD 90s.

The question is: would Eusebius take two different sources, the Roman historians and the "ancient men," and combine them together in such a way that it is implied that the "ancient men" knew John was released from Patmos in AD 96 while in fact all that Eusebius knew from his source was that John was alive at that time?

One's first impulse is to say "no." However, consider that he did almost exactly the same thing when he wrote about the two tombs with the name John. The words of Gundry are worth repeating:

> To debunk the book of Revelation, then, Eusebius apparently turns Dionysius's cautious inference, "I think there was another John," into a confident assertion "there were two Johns." He then adds ... "still now," to strengthen the argument ...[104]

A necessary requisite for the "ancient men" to talk to Hegesippus and relate that John returned from the island of Patmos would be that they saw John was alive. However, that John was alive does not mean that he was just released from Patmos. Eusebius could be using a similar tactic here to the one given above to support an argument.

---

[104] Robert H. Gundry, "The Apostolically Johannine Pre-Papian Tradition concerning the Gospels of Mark and Matthew," *The Old is Better* (Tübingen: Mohr Siebeck, 2005. Reprinted by Wipf and Stock Publishers, Eugene, OH, 2010), 58.

Eusebius, it seems, is not just giving an historical narrative, he is building a case for the banishment of John under Domitian and his release under Nerva with a source that seems to show nothing more than that John was alive after AD 96.

There is a different problem that comes up when checking for the source of Victorinus of Pettau regarding the Patmos tradition. He does not give a source. We do believe, however, that he had one.

Victorinus was a contemporary of Eusebius who died a martyr's death either under Diocletian in AD 304 or possibly under Numerius in about AD 283 - 284. Victorinus wrote a commentary on the book of Revelation before one of these persecutions.

Boxall observes that the comments made by Victorinus are brief and confined to one verse, Rev. 10:11.[105] Victorinus comments on what John was told in his vision,

> "And He says unto me, Thou must again prophesy to the peoples, and to the tongues, and to the nations, and to many kings." He says this, because when John said these things he was in the island of Patmos, condemned to the labour of the mines by Cæsar Domitian. There, therefore, he saw the Apocalypse; and when grown old, he thought that he should at length receive his quittance by suffering, Domitian being killed, all his judgments were discharged. And John being dismissed from the mines, thus subsequently delivered the same Apocalypse which he had received from God. This, therefore, is what He says: Thou must again prophesy to all nations, because thou seest the crowds of Antichrist rise up; and against them other crowds shall stand, and they shall fall by the sword on the one side and on the other. [106]

According to Edward Earle Ellis, author of *The Making of the New Testament Documents*, Victorinus:

---

[105] Ibid., 37.

[106] Philip Schaff, ed., *ANF07. Fathers of the Third and Fourth Centuries: Lactantius, Venantius, Asterius, Victorinus, Dionysius, Apostolic Teaching and Constitutions, Homily, and Liturgies* (Reprinted, Grand Rapids, MI: Christian Classics Ethereal Library [1885]), 805.

seems to presuppose, however, that John's exile involved many years of labor and thus to support the conjecture that John was exiled under Domitian's brief exercise of imperial powers at Rome in early AD 70 while his father, the emperor Vespasian, was still in the East. It is also difficult to suppose that John would be condemned to the mines in his 80s or 90s.[107]

Says John A.T. Robinson when referring the Patmos passage of Victorinus:

> Yet the identification is by no means solid. Clement's disciple Origen writes in his Commentary of Matthew that the emperor of the Romans, as tradition teaches, condemned John to the isle of Patmos adding that John does not say who condemned him.[108]

Robinson continues with a comment on the banishment of John with Tertullian's early version of the Patmos tradition.

> Jerome in quoting the passage interprets Tertullian to mean that John's suffering, like that of Peter and Paul, occurred under Nero – despite his own acceptance from Eusebius's Chronicle of the Domitianic date.[109]

It is significant that Origen's teacher was Clement of Alexandria. As we noted earlier, Clement implies in his *Miscellanies* that the book of Revelation was written before the death of Nero.

We are left to speculate about the source of Victorinus. Edmundson suggests the following possibility about the source of Victorinus and later Jerome:

> Victorinus certainly did not write under the influence of Eusebius, and the similarity of his version of the tradition to that of Jerome seems to point to their common derivation from some documentary source to

---

[107] Edward Earle Ellis, *The Making of the New Testament Documents* (Leiden: Brill, 1999, 2002), 211.
[108] John A.T. Robinson, *Redating the New Testament* (Philadelphia: Westminster Press, 1976), 223.
[109] Ibid., 223.

Patmos and the subsequent release with the names of Domitian and Nerva.[110]

Edmundson argues that this source may have been a reference to the release of banished prisoners by Nerva *without being specific as to under which reign* John was banished. It is more than possible that Victorinus believed that John was banished as a much younger man in AD 70 and then released as an old man in AD 96. Only the names of Domitian and Nerva may have been tied together.

From the evidence that Edmundson gives, as noted above, I believe that the names of Domitian and Nerva were tied together. It seems that Domitian was involved in the banishment of prisoners in AD 70. My hypothesis is, however, that John was already banished by Nero and was already at the Island of Patmos when Domitian was temporarily Caesar in AD 70. When Domitian turned the legal cases over to Nerva, his name would likely be associated with all cases including the backlog of cases of those banished by Nero, Galba, Otho, and Vitellius.

As Edmundson noted, the similarity of the Patmos tradition of Jerome to that Victorinus indicated the possibility of a common source. We know that Jerome researched material for his AD 398 revision of the commentary of Victorinus. He not only corrected Victorinus' Latin but in addition, as Boxall illustrates in his side by side comparison of Jerome's revision versus the original, replaces Victorinus' outlook on Patmos to one as a place of vision. He also, says Boxall, removed some explicit chiliastic passages and added some of his own comments along with some sections from Tyconius.[111]

The "common source" hypothesis of Edmundson helps to explain a seemingly contradictory detail in Jerome's writings which has long puzzled scholars. We know that Jerome completed his *Lives of*

---

[110] George Edmundson, *The Church in Rome in the First Century: An Examination of Various Controverted Questions Relating to Its History, Chronology, Literature and Traditions. Eight Lectures Preached Before the University of Oxford in the Year 1913* (London, New York, and Bombay and Calcutta: Longsman, Green and Co., 1913), 167.

[111] Ian Boxall, op. cit., 48.

Illustrious Men in the fourteenth year of Theodosius, which was in 392.[112] Jerome wrote: "In the fourteenth year after Nero, Domitian having raised a second persecution, he [John] was banished to the island of Patmos, and wrote the Apocalypse."[113]

The following year Jerome completed his *Against Jovinian* and reaffirmed his position that John was banished under Domitian. However, there is a shift in perspective as to when this may have occurred. Jerome now writes:

> John is both an Apostle and an Evangelist, and a prophet. An Apostle, because he wrote to the Churches as a master; an Evangelist, because he composed a Gospel, a thing which no other of the Apostles, excepting Matthew, did; a prophet, for he saw in the island of Patmos, to which he had been banished by the Emperor Domitian as a martyr for the Lord, an Apocalypse containing the boundless mysteries of the future. Tertullian, moreover, relates that he *was sent to Rome*, and that having been plunged in a jar of boiling oil he came out fresher and more active than when he went in.[114]

Notice the italicized words "was sent to Rome" in the above quote. Francis Gumerlock tells us that editors of *Against Jovinianum* beginning in 1564 have changed the original words of Jerome. Gumerlock explains,

---

[112] "You have urged me, Dexter, to follow the example of Tranquillus in giving a systematic account of ecclesiastical writers ... from the time of Lord's passion until the fourteenth year of the Emperor Theodosius." from the Preface of *Lives of Illustrious Men*: Philip Schaff, ed., NPNF2-03. Theodoret, Jerome, Gennadius, & Rufinus: Historical Writings. (New York: Christian Literature Publishing Co., 1892, Reprinted, Grand Rapids, MI: Christian Classics Ethereal Library), 823.

[113] Jerome, *Lives of Illustrious Men*, 9.6.

[114] Philip Schaff and Henry Wace, ed., *Nicene and Post-Nicene Fathers*, Second Series, Vol. 6, *The Principal Works of St. Jerome*, trans. Freemantle (New York: Christian Literature Publishing Co. 1892. Reprinted, Grand Rapids, MI: Christian Classics Ethereal Library), 592. Boxall notes the Latin Text, ed. Migne 184a:247. See Ian Boxall, op. cit., 41.

"Moreover, Tertullian relates that he [John] was sent by Nero into boiling oil." The words "by Nero" (a *Nerone*) are contained in the ancient editions of Jerome's work, including the 1524 edition by Erasmus of Rotterdam. However, in the 1564 edition by Vittori the words "by Nero" were changed to "at Rome" (*Romae*). In that edition a note says that for "'by Nero' as was read previously, from Tertullian himself we have put 'at Rome.' For, this was in the time of Domitian not Nero, and Tertullian himself did not report that it happened 'by Nero' but 'at Rome', there being no mention of Nero." Vittori's change was reproduced in the editions of Vellarsi in 1767 and Migne in the next century.[115]

Amazing! Changing the words of an author allows the original implications of the words to be obscured. The original words of the author show at the very least, in the word of Gentry, the "confounding of two traditions."[116]

The editor in the notes to the 1564 edition justifies his decision to change the words of Jerome based on two tacit assumptions. One assumption is the same assumption that Eusebius made, that the tyrant who banished John was Domitian even though Tertullian does not mention the name of the tyrant.

The second assumption is that the time of Domitian referred to is the time that he was Emperor. However, it could be the time he was temporarily Caesar in AD 70.

The editor of the 1564 edition does note something of importance. He correctly notices that Jerome ties together the *time* of Nero's attempted execution of John to the *time* of Domitian. From the viewpoint of the editor, this is impossible. He then changes the words of Jerome.

What follows below is a hypothesis which accounts for the seemingly contradictory details.

---

[115] Francis X. Gumerlock, *Revelation and the First Century (Preterist Interpretations of the Apocalypse in Early Christianity)*, [Powder Spring, GA: American Vision Press, 2012], 42.

[116] Kenneth L. Gentry, Jr., *Before Jerusalem Fell: Dating the Book of Revelation*, 3rd ed. (Fountain Inn, SC.: Victorious Hope Publishing, 1998, 2010),105.

We noted earlier that it is quite possible that Victorinus believed that John was banished by Domitian in AD 70 and then released by Nerva in the AD nineties. Edmundson hypothesized that Victorinus and Jerome, because of the similarity of their traditions, may have had a common source that tied together the names of Domitian and Nerva without being specific as to when the banishment and release of these prisoners occurred.

In AD 398, Jerome published his revision to the commentary of Victorinus. By the year AD 393, when Jerome wrote his *Against Jovinian,* Jerome may have already uncovered the source hypothesized by Edmundson as Jerome may now have tied the banishment under Domitian to the time period shortly after the suicide of Nero when Domitian was temporarily Caesar.

Authors continually do research and sometimes they discover, what is to them, a new source. A new source may have convinced Jerome to revise his previously held position *as to when* John was banished under Domitian.

Let's take a look at a possible source known to Jerome that is reflected in his AD 398 update of Victorinus' commentary. If the source hypothesized by Edmundson was available to Victorinius and if it was unclear as to which of the two time periods that Domitian banished prisoners that John was banished, then Jerome had a choice to make; just as Eusebius had a choice to make.

If Jerome chose AD 70 for the banishment date of John, this should be visible in his update to Victorinus' commentary and in his later work.

Jerome used sections from Tyconius' work as we noted per Boxall. Tyconius, as we saw earlier, *wrote that Nero was the sixth king.* Although Jerome does not write that Nero was the sixth King, we see that Jerome knew the works of Tyconius which may have influenced him to tie the attempted execution of John to the time of Nero.

Francis Gumerlock tells us that Jerome's revision has the following in the expanded comments:

Moreover, one of the heads slain unto death and his fatal wound was healed, he speaks of Nero. For it is plain that while the cavalry sent by the senate pursued him, he cut his own throat.[117]

In his commentary on Daniel, written just a few years after his update to the commentary of Victorinus, Jerome says (as quoted by Gumerlock):

> "And so there are many of our view point who think that Domitius Nero was the antichrist because of his outstanding savagery and depravity." Domitius was Nero's family name.[118]

The quote linking Nero to the fatal wound which was healed, and the quote linking Nero to the Antichrist, and the portions of the commentary update attributed to Tyconius give us reason to believe that Jerome chose Nero as the persecutor — which in turn implies that Jerome chose the earlier date for the banishment of John under Domitian.

If Jerome did modify his position, then the plunging of John into oil by Nero may have occurred late in AD 67 just months before Nero's suicide and just three years before Domitian was temporarily Caesar. Jerome could have referred to this event and the banishment of John under Domitian in the same section of his writing without contradicting himself. Removing the contradiction is an indication that the earlier date for the banishment of John is the correct choice in understanding Jerome's words.

If the apostles Paul and Peter were executed in AD 67/68 during the Neronian persecution as Church tradition holds and if at around the same time, John had just escaped his attempted execution by Nero, very little time would have passed before the suicide of Nero in June of AD 68. According to Suetonius, Nero was attempting to flee Rome with a fleet shortly before his suicide, but his own soldiers refused to obey orders as he was going to be brought up on charges

---

[117] Gumerlock. op. cit., 131.
[118] Ibid., 123.

before the Senate.[119] Nero began to lose power months before his suicide, beginning with the revolt against his tax policies by governor Julius Vindex of Gaul.[120]

With Nero tied up with associated politics in early AD 68 at the very end of his persecution of Christians, it is probable that John's case would have been put on hold. The suicide of Nero initiated "the year of the four emperors" and the eventual taking over of the cases of banished prisoners by Domitian when he was temporarily made Caesar before the return of Vespasian to Rome.

We have made an argument for the case that both Victorinus and Jerome believed that John was banished by Domitian in AD 70. Jerome, as opposed to Eusebius, saw Nero as the persecuting emperor. Nero is not only the persecuting emperor for Jerome, Nero is the Antichrist. Note again the exact words of Jerome, "And so there are many of our view point who think that Domitius Nero was the Antichrist."

What we see in Jerome's work is a 3 stage development.

1) Prior to January of AD 393, which is the latest date for completion of Jerome's *Lives of Illustrious Men*, Jerome adheres to the position of Eusebius that John was banished by Domitian. Based on Eusebius's *Chronology*, Jerome determines this to be in the fourteenth year after the death of Nero.

2) As discussed above, in AD 394 there seems to be, in the thinking of Jerome, a shift in the timing as to when John was banished under Domitian. After this date Jerome associates the banishment of John under Domitian to AD 70, shortly after the death of Nero.

3) Four years later, in AD 398, Jerome writes his update to the commentary of Victorinus and also writes his commentary on Matthew. We notice a third stage in the development of Jerome's thought in his *Commentary on*

---

[119] C. Suetonius Tranquillius, "The Life of Nero" in *Lives of the 12 Caesars*, trans. Alexander Thompson (London: George Bell & Sons, 1896), par. xlvii.
[120] Ibid., par. xl.

Matthew (20:23). Jerome now adds the word "immediately" to the banishment of John after the attempted execution of John by Nero when Nero had John plunged into burning oil.

In the words of Jerome:

> Although a persecutor did not shed his blood, for they note that he was placed in a vat of burning oil to be martyred and thence proceeded to receive the crown of a Christian athlete and immediately was dispatched to the isle of Patmos.[121]

It seems by AD 398 Jerome believes that John, after suffering the attempted execution by Nero, was immediately banished to the Island of Patmos. This is a change from his previous held position, summarized in stage 2 above, that John was banished by Domitian in AD 70. Nero, for Jerome, was the persecutor and the Antichrist.

My hypothesis is that John was banished by Nero and was at Patmos during Nero's suicide. John was still at Patmos when Domitian temporarily stepped in as Caesar in AD 70. The names of Domitian and Nerva would still be tied together as Edmundson hypothesized.

Eusebius, on the other hand, gives us a detailed argument as to why John was released by Nerva in AD 96 with Domitian as the tyrant. We will take a final look at the choices made by Eusebius in the next chapter.

---

[121] R. Alan Culpepper, *John, the Son of Zebedee: The Life of a Legend* (Columbia, SC: Univ. of South Carolina Press, 1994. Reprinted, Minneapolis: Fortress Press, 2000), 165.

Chapter 6
CENTRALIZED PERSECUTION OF CHRISTIANS AND THE IMPERIAL CULT

What could have been a possible motivation for Eusebius to choose Domitian as the persecuting emperor rather than Nero when he considers the banishment of John under the tyrant?

In the 1990s there was a reassessment of Domitian's reign. Centralized persecution began again after Vespasian, not with the reign of Domitian, but with the reign of Trajan.[122] This centralized persecution continued after the reign of Trajan and intensified under Decius in AD 250 about ten years before Eusebius was born. Decius required Christians to offer sacrifices to the Roman gods. Persecution was renewed under Valerian, and Christians were, under the threat of imprisonment, ordered to worship Roman gods. The most comprehensive persecution attributed directly to the emperor occurred under Diocletian during the lifetime of Eusebius.

Barnes tells us that:

> The first persecuting edict [under Diocletian] was promulgated throughout the Roman Empire. Even Constantius, who mitigated its effects and allowed no executions in his domains, demolished churches. How the law worked in practice can perhaps be seen most clearly in Africa, where Maximian encouraged stricter enforcement. In this edict, Diocletian had provided that the local magistrates and leading men of each city should supervise the suppression of the Christian cult. In one African town, the *curator* arrested a priest, two lectors, and the elders of the congregation and demanded their holy books. When they replied that the absent bishop had the books, the magistrate kept them in custody until the bishop returned. He admitted having Scriptures but refused repeated requests to surrender them for burning. The curator then sent the bishop under escort to Carthage, where the proconsul sentenced him to death.[123]

---

[122] See Pliny to Trajan, Letter X. 96.3. Trajan's reply in Letter X, 97 1-2.
[123] Timothy D. Barnes, *Constantine and Eusebius* (Cambridge: Harvard Univ.

Barnes explains that although the edicts did not specify definite penalties, it assumed normal practices would apply to those who were uncooperative. The normal practice was they that would be executed by the sword or even more brutally. An individual governor could enforce the edict with mildness or with extreme severity. Christians were compelled by force to deny Christ, burn incense, join in the destruction of churches, and burn Scriptures.[124]

> The proconsul of Africa and the *praeses* of Numidia chose the latter course. More than sixty years later, their ferocity was still remembered. The Christians in their provinces could nowhere feel safe, even though they steadfastly avoided pagan temples and altars. By physical force, they were compelled to burn incense, to deny Christ, to join in the destruction of churches, and to consign the holy Scriptures to the flames.[125]

For Eusebius, the persecution of Christians as reflected in his writing was all about imperial Rome. By the time Eusebius began to write, Christianity was still technically not a legal religion. It was not until the time of Constantine and the Edict of Milan that there was tolerance for Christians throughout the Empire, and Christianity became a legal religion. The centralized persecution of Christianity leading into his own day and during his lifetime was a primary concern for Eusebius. By contrast, the persecution under Nero lasted for only three and half years and was simply not as important to Eusebius as the persecution that he wrote about going back to Domitian.

To attribute the banishment of John to Domitian involves the belief that Domitian not only banished Christians but sentenced them to death as well, as was done in the time of Eusebius and under Nero.

However, the sentencing to death and torture of Christians is expressed by Tacitus to have occurred under Nero. In recent scholarship, it is now questioned whether any *centralized persecution* occurred at all under Domitian.

Press, 1981), 23.
[124] Ibid., 23.
[125] Ibid., 23.

It is well known that Domitian regularly banished and executed political opponents and confiscated their property including that of his cousin Flavius Clemens in AD 95. Twelve former consuls were executed by Domitian, and it has been asserted that "probably only his confiscations averted bankruptcy in the last years."[126]

There is, however, little evidence that Domitian banished or executed Christians at all except possibly for the wealth of his cousin Flavius Clemens and Flavius' wife Domitilla. Although Eusebius wrote that Domitilla was banished because she was a Christian, this account is in conflict with the account of Cassius Dio (67:14 1-2) which reports that she was guilty of sympathy for Judaism.

"Externally in certain circles, there has been a radical reassessment of the portrait of Domitian as a megalomaniac demanding worship from his subjects."[127] Thompson expresses doubts that any persecution at all was initiated by Domitian. The misleading portrait is based on a circle of political-writers during the reign of Trajan who were linked with a senatorial aristocracy that were in ongoing conflict with Domitian. The group was headed by Helvidius Priscus, whose father was executed by Vespasian. Domitian "made a clean sweep of the Helvidian coterie, late in his reign, after trying to placate them with high office or the offer of it."[128]

Boxall tells us the:

> *Ascension of Isaiah* seems to know nothing of a persecution under Domitian, despite its allusion to what occurred under Nero (Asc. Isa. 4:3; Knight 1999; 24). However, the internal evidence of Revelation does not suggest a situation of state persecution, while the earlier dating cuts the link with the reign of Domitian. This is not to deny that martyrdom features strongly in the visionary section of the Apocalypse;

---

[126] The execution of the senators for their property is well known. It is written about in the standard encyclopedia:
http:www.britannica.com/biography/Domitian.

[127] Ian Boxall, *The Revelation of Saint John (Black's New Testament Commentary)* [Grand Rapids, MI: Baker Academic. 2009], 12.

[128] Leonard L. Thompson, *The Book of Revelation: Apocalypse and Empire* (New York: Oxford University Press, [1990]1996), 108.

but these are more likely allusions to Nero's past action against Christians in Rome, and visionary anticipations of what Rome will be capable of in the future, than descriptions of present state persecution.[129]

Steven Friesen in his *Imperial Cults and the Apocalypse of John* asserts,

> In fact, the only substantive issue commentators mention regularly in the debate about Domitianic imperial cult policy is the allegation that Domitian demanded to be called Lord and God. Most specialists now hold that this was an exaggeration, if not a fabrication, on the part of Suetonius. Writers from the Domitianic period such as Martial and Statius did not use such forms of address, nor do coins and inscriptions of Rome evince such practices.[130]

Mark Stevens states,

> It is now reasonable to question whether the Domitianic period was a time of excessive divinization of the *princeps*, at least in terms of the emperor's own promotion of his divinity. *If indeed there were any new developments and innovations in imperial cult practice at this time, they are likely to have received their impetus from local elites in the cities of the east, as opposed to it being the result of a centralized policy of cult promotion.*[131]

If Domitian did not banish Christians or throw them into boiling oil in the AD eighties or nineties, then when was John banished?

As we saw earlier, the Muratorian Cannon gives a strong inference as to when John wrote the book of Revelation. John wrote his letters to the seven churches before the death of Paul. In addition, two of the oldest manuscripts of the book of Revelation are the Syriac versions. They give direct evidence that John was banished by Nero.

---

[129] Ian Boxall, *The Revelation of Saint John (Black's New Testament Commentary)* [Grand Rapids, MI: Baker Academic, 2009], 13.

[130] Steven J. Friesen, *Imperial Cults and the Apocalypse of John* (Oxford: Oxford Univ. Press, 2001, 2006), 148.

[131] Mark B. Stevens, *Annihilation Or Renewal? The Meaning and Function of New Creation in the Book of Revelation* (Tübingen: Mohr Siebek, December 31, 2011), 144-145. Emphasis mine.

The heading of the Syriac Philoxenian translation of the book of Revelation prepared by Polycarpus, the chorepiscopus of Philoxenus, bishop of Mabbug, dated to AD 508 [132] reads:

> The Revelation which was made by God to John the Evangelist, in the island of Patmos, to which he was banished by Nero the Emperor.[133]

So why would Eusebius choose the persecution under Domitian in his argument over that of the persecution under Nero?

One reason would be that the centralized persecution against Christianity in his own day led him to believe that the persecution was centralized in the time of Domitian. In addition, there was a major change taking place in the time of Eusebius, namely, Christianity was becoming respectable. According to Timothy Barnes, we do not know exactly when this change took place, but with the Edict of Milan in AD 314, the majority of the empire became Christian. Christianity was respectable.

According to the classicist Barnes, Eusebius projected the Church of his time "back into the first two centuries and assumed that Christian churches had always been numerous, prosperous, and respectable ... Eusebius's picture of the Church before 200 is fundamentally anachronistic."[134] Barnes continues,

> The Ecclesiastical History can be compared not only with the writings which it quotes but with writers whom Eusebius had not read. Eusebius knew the writers of Egypt, Syria, and Asia Minor well . . . He shows no awareness, for example of Athenagoras . . . Of Latin writers Eusebius knew virtually nothing: of Tertullian's voluminous output he had read only the *Apologeticum* in a Greek translation; of Cyprian, only letters to be found in Antioch; of Minucius Felix and Novatian, nothing at all. As

---

[132] Kenneth L. Gentry, Jr., *Before Jerusalem Fell: Dating the Book of Revelation*, 3rd ed. (Fountain Inn, SC: Victorious Hope Publishing, 1998, 2010), 106.

[133] Francis X. Gumerlock, *Revelation and the First Century (Preterist Interpretations of the Apocalypse in Early Christianity)*, [Powder Spring, GA: American Vision Press, 2012], 38.

[134] Timothy D. Barnes, *Constantine and Eusebius* (Cambridge: Harvard Univ. Press, 1981), 142. Emphasis mine.

for the history of the Church in the West, Eusebius reports events in Rome with relative frequency. For Italy and the western provinces, however, his information was meager.[135]

Later Barnes continues:

The earliest Christian writings in Latin, therefore, should not be interpreted (as has traditionally been the practice) within an Eusebian historical framework. They should be allowed to speak for themselves in their own authentic tones. *Tertullian directed his Apologeticum and Ad Scapulam to magistrates in Carthage, not to Roman emperors; he [Tertullian] chose these addressees because in the late second and third centuries the attitude of provincial governors affected most Christians far more immediately and far more directly than the attitude of the emperor. Eusebius was unaware of this basic fact about the persecution of the Christians in the Roman Empire.*[136]

Notice in particular Barnes' comment about the misunderstanding of Eusebius concerning persecution in the perspective of Tertullian. Barnes asserts,

Eusebius does not present the early Church as a hated and persecuted minority gradually attaining security and respectability . . . . he presents persecution as a rare and unusual phenomenon which reflected not any underlying hostility by an established order toward a potentially subversive religion but the machinations of the devil, the moral depravity of a Roman emperor, or the envy of despicable individuals.[137]

In summary, Eusebius brings another supposition to the table. According to Barnes, Eusebius projects the centralized persecution of Christians back into times where persecution should not be attributed — to the moral depravity of a particular emperor. Instead, the persecution should be attributed locally to the provincial governors. In particular, Eusebius has a basic misunderstanding of the writings of Tertullian.

---

[135] Ibid., 143.
[136] Ibid., 142-43.
[137] Ibid., 136.

Eusebius never makes his readers aware that Nerva worked on the cases of banished political prisoners in AD 71 after Domitian's brief reign. Eusebius makes the *choice* to write that John was released after the death of Domitian to fit in with, what we know today, is the unlikely scenario that Domitian himself initiated persecution against Christians.

The case of Eusebius is dependent on an ambiguous statement concerning "the tyrant" combined with an ambiguous statement made by Irenaeus — which is all dependent on what is viewed by Thompson, Friesen, and Stevens and Barnes *as an incorrect statement concerning the centralized persecution under Domitian*. It seems that Eusebius is following what appears to be a pattern for his misuse of sources based on his suppositions.

Gundry noticed the misuse of the words of Dionysius of Alexandria. Another indication that Eusebius misuses the words of his sources is that *Irenaeus himself nowhere ties Domitian with the persecution of John*.

Note the following comment by Ian Boxall:

> Irenaeus, it should be noted, does not himself link the Apocalypse with persecutions under Domitian. Nevertheless, from Eusebius onwards, the issues of dating and persecution have become inextricably linked, with the tradition of a large-scale persecution of Christians under Domitian.[138]

Early date advocates are not surprised. That Irenaeus never associates Domitian with the persecution of John does not prevent Eusebius from building his case upon his perceived centralized persecution of Christians during the time of Domitian.

The most likely Patmos scenario is that John was banished in AD 65 to 67 under Nero to the Island of Patmos and was released by Nerva in AD 71 following the brief reign of Domitian.

---

[138] Ian Boxall, *Revelation: Vision And Insight* (London: SPCK, 2002), 87.

Chapter 7
THE SYRIAC TRADITION, EPIPHANIUS, AND JEROME

The Syriac tradition directly supports the early date for the authorship of Revelation. In the Syriac tradition, the heading of the Syriac Philoxenian translation of the book of Revelation reads:

> The Revelation which was made by God to John the Evangelist, in the island of Patmos, to which he was banished by Nero the Emperor.[139]

We have shown that there are a number of independent extra-biblical traditions that support the straightforward reading of Revelation 17 that Nero was the sixth King, the king who "is" in power when the book of Revelation was written. The commentary of Tyconius, which was available to Jerome, lists Nero as the sixth King. The Muratorian Fragment, dated to about AD 150, gives direct evidence that the book of Revelation was written before Paul's seven letters were completed. This information, also available to Jerome, suggests that the composition of the book of Revelation should be dated to the reign of Nero, as Paul died no later than AD 67/68.[140]

We have given evidence supporting an early date for the Patmos tradition. The banishment of John as described by Clement of Alexandria, Tertullian, and Origen more likely occurred under the reign of Nero rather than under the reign of Domitian.

We have demonstrated, given their common tradition, that both Victorinus and Jerome may have believed that John was banished by

---

[139] Francis X. Gumerlock, *Revelation and the First Century (Preterist Interpretations of the Apocalypse in Early Christianity)*, [Powder Spring, GA: American Vision Press, 2012], 38.

[140] Ibid., 40.

Domitian in AD 70. We can see the common tradition in that both Victorinus and Jerome believed that in the last days Nero will be raised up from hell as the final Antichrist, *under another name*, and will deceive the Jews and Christians.[141] We have given an explanation for why the original words of Jerome attributing the torture of John in boiling oil to Nero were obscured and needlessly removed by editors. We have given evidence to show that Jerome believed that the Antichrist was Nero rather than Domitian. We have given evidence that Jerome may have believed, after AD 388, that John was banished by Nero rather than Domitian to the Island of Patmos.

Jerome had an associate by the name of Epiphanius, who was bishop of Salamis.[142] Epiphanius was born in Palestine in about AD 315 and was perhaps of Jewish parentage. He was the older contemporary of a famous pair, Jerome and Rufinus, both of whom became acquainted with Epiphanius. Jerome was particularly taken with Epiphanius' knowledge of five languages: Hebrew, Syriac, Egyptian, Greek, and Latin.[143]

Epiphanius oddly dates the Patmos episode to the reign of Claudius while the Syriac versions of Revelation dates the banishment of John to the reign of Nero. Boxall tells us that Epiphanius may have confused the names of the two emperors.[144] Hort, in his *Apocalypse*, writes that Epiphanius may have used another of Nero's names.

---

[141] "God will send as a king worthy of those who are worthy of him, namely, the Jews and those who persecute Christ, and he will send him as a Christ such as the persecutors and the Jews deserve. And since he will bear another name, he will also undertake another life, so that they [the Jews] might receive him as the Christ." Footnote 6 states: "The Jews will mistake the antichrist for the expected Christ because he will promote circumcision and the law." William C. Weinrich, and Victorinus, *Latin Commentaries on Revelation* (Downers Grove, IL: IVP Academic, Ancient Christian Texts, 2011), 18.

[142] Ian Boxall, *Patmos in the Reception History of the Apocalypse* (Oxford: Oxford Univ. Press, 2013), 40.

[143] Martin Sprengling's forward to *Epiphanius' Treatise on Weights and Measures: The Syriac Version*. Edited by James Elmer Dean. University of Chicago Press, 1935, vii.

[144] Boxall, op. cit., 40.

Hort explains,

> But as one of his names [i.e., one of Claludius's names] was Nero, so also our Nero was likewise a Claudius, and is often called on inscriptions Nero Claudius or Nero Claudius Caesar. It seems probable therefore that, whatever Epiphanius may have meant, his authority meant and perhaps said Nero.[145]

Given that Epiphanius and Jerome were intimate friends,[146] one could speculate that it is possible that their interaction may have influenced Jerome in some degree to modify his position to the earlier date for the banishment of John to the AD 70 date under Domitian. Good friends often discuss topics of interest to their faith, and it is likely that Jerome and Epiphanius discussed the Syriac viewpoint of Epiphanius. This possible influence may even be seen in AD 388 when Jerome added the word "immediately" to the banishment of John and to the boiling oil incident attributed to Nero. In any case, it seems by AD 388 that both Jerome and Epiphanius may have believed that John was banished by Nero.

A modern author who dates the authorship of Revelation and John's banishment to Patmos early in the reign of Nero, as does the Syriac tradition, is Kym Smith. Both the Syriac tradition and Smith date the return of John from Patmos to a time before the fall of Jerusalem when Nero was still in power.

Smith argues that the book of Revelation was written in AD 62, before the Neronic persecution. He argues not only that Revelation was written early, but that it preceded most of the New Testament. Smith in his *Redating the Revelation*[147] gives a reconstruction of the AD sixties based largely on the book of Acts.

---

[145] Kenneth L. Gentry, Jr., *Before Jerusalem Fell: Dating the Book of Revelation*, 3rd ed. (Fountain Inn, SC: Victorious Hope Publishing, 1998, 2010), 104. "Other scholars who agree with an assessment such as Hort's include Moffat, Guthrie, Robinson, and Mounce, to name a few."

[146] Ibid., 104.

[147] Kym Smith, *Redating the Revelation and …a Reconstruction of the Sixties of the*

Smith argues that John was banished by Nero to Patmos in about AD 61 and received the Revelation in 62. John was released at the end of the reign of Nero.[148]

John, who had gone to Asia sometime after Paul's imprisonment, had already been banished in AD 61. It was about this time in June or July of AD 62 that Paul returned to Ephesus and John received the Revelation.[149] John made two copies. John first sent a copy to Paul in Ephesus.[150] Upon receiving this copy as authentic, Paul then dispatched Silvanus to Rome to deliver Peter's copy.[151]

Peter, convinced of the authenticity of the vision, did not just reply in the affirmative, he penned his first Epistle to "the broader group of churches in 'Pontus, Galatia, Cappadocia, Asia, and Bithynia.'"[152]

Having received his copy early, Paul was able to communicate his answer to John within a week since Ephesus was no more than a two or three-day journey from Patmos if winds were favorable.[153]

In the month or two while they were waiting for Peter's endorsement, both John and Paul wrote their own letters of exhortation. Accompanying Silvanus from Rome was Mark, who would have also been able to confirm the apostle's verification of the Revelation.[154]

> Of immediate concern was Jerusalem and the believers there. Was not that city the 'holy city' whose temple the nations were to trample? Paul

---

First Century, Giving the Context and Completion of the New Testament (Blackwood, South Australia: Sherwood Publications, 2001).

[148] Ibid., 59.
[149] Ibid., 75.
[150] Ibid., 76.
[151] Ibid., 77.
[152] Ibid., 78.
[153] Ibid., 78.
[154] Ibid., 79.

would have dispatched someone to take copies of the Revelation and the three apostles' letters almost as soon as Silvanus returned.[155]

In the spring of AD 64 Paul and his helpers set sail for Rome. There were "some brethren in Puteolie with whom Paul was well acquainted and he would have also spent time with them."[156]

When Paul finally reached Rome, probably in April or May, his first thought was to update Peter.[157]

After two or three months Paul was imprisoned a second time to face Nero. Smith tells us that, unlike his previous trials which involved his appeal to Nero, this trial was for treason. At this point Paul understood that Nero was the Beast of the Apocalypse. Although Paul had been warning believers that the struggle was a spiritual battle, someone who misunderstood reported him to the emperor. Paul was promptly imprisoned and Peter as well, if he were not already in prison. At this time Paul, after first receiving his copy of the Revelation, was deserted by Demas. All those who had come from Asia deserted Paul as well except for Onesiphorus.[158]

Note that in Smith's reconstruction, very few copies of the book of Revelation were made prior to AD 70. John had the book of Revelation republished, with more copies made, during the time of Domitian who was the second persecutor of the Church. This is seen in the account given by Irenaeus that John was seen towards the end of Domitian's reign (or was it the book that was seen?) as John was having more copies of the book of Revelation distributed at that time.

Smith points out that if Revelation was written in the late AD nineties, as some writers believe, the book of Revelation would have benefited those facing the persecution of Domitian little as that persecution was nearly over by then.[159]

---

[155] Ibid., 80.
[156] Ibid., 93.
[157] Ibid., 93.
[158] Ibid., 94.
[159] Ibid., 17.

It is interesting that the Syriac tradition and the position of Smith both agree with the earlier date implied in the Muratorian Fragment. Says Smith,

> The author of the fragment then goes on to list the seven churches which Paul addressed by name. Now the story is confused because there is no doubt that some of Paul's letters preceded the Revelation. Nevertheless, this is a clear reference to the Revelation: the author himself names the Apocalypse as that book in which the seven churches were addressed and John's rule was established. ... At the very least it places the writing of the Revelation in the midst of Paul's epistolary activity, and few would consider that Paul lived past the year 64.[160]

We have shown that arguments given by Eusebius portraying a late date for the banishment of John are based on the *assumption* that the identity of the "tyrant" was Domitian.

According to classicist Timothy Barnes, Eusebius had a fundamental misunderstanding concerning the nature of the persecution of Christians in the early Church at the time of Tertullian. Eusebius incorrectly attributed the persecution of Christians to the emperor rather than to local governors. This basic misunderstanding provided the basis, when combined with his assumption concerning the tyrant, to allow justification for Eusebius to choose AD 96 as the date for the return of the exiles under Nerva rather their return in AD 71.

Although the dominant Patmos tradition is that John was banished by Domitian in the early 80s and released by Nerva in AD 96, I believe that we have shown that the data better fits the hypothesis that John was banished by Nero and was at Patmos when Domitian was temporarily made Caesar by Vespasian in early AD 70. John was then released by Nerva, as tradition holds, not in AD 96 but in AD 71.

A strength of the position expressed by Kym Smith is that it is more consistent with both the Syriac tradition and the Muratorian

---

[160] Ibid., 55.

Fragment as it dates the banishment of John and the authorship of Revelation prior to the death of Paul.

Part II

Topics in Preterism Explained and Defended

Chapter 8
THE OLIVET DISCOURSE AND DOUBLE FULFILLMENT

In his book *Man of Sin* Kim Riddlebarger refers to futurist G. B. Caird's understanding of prophetic perspective, endorses it, and then extends it to the book of Revelation and specifically to Nero. Let's take a look at how Caird develops the meaning of the term "double fulfillment" as metaphoric language.

A metaphor has two parts, vehicle and tenor, where tenor is the original subject and vehicle is what transforms the subject. So when Caird says, as stated in proposition #3 below, that there is a blurring of vehicle and tenor on the part of the prophet, he means that the tenor (the near-term judgment) blurs with the vehicle (the apocalyptic end of the world judgment and the language describing it). The near-term judgment *points* to the final judgment.

As Caird examines the "day of the Lord" passages in the Old Testament, he describes double fulfillment by means of three propositions:[161]

> 1. The biblical writers believed literally that the world had a beginning and will have an end.

In Psalm 102:2-26 we see the creation of the world and the end of the world.

> Of old you laid the foundation of the earth and the heavens are the work of your hands.
>
> They will perish, but you will remain; they will all wear out like a garment.
>
> You will change them like a robe, and they will pass away.

---

[161] G.B. Caird, *The Language and Imagery of the Bible* (London: Gerald Duckworth & Co. 1980), 256.

2. "The prophets regularly used metaphorical end-of-the-world language to refer to what they certainly well knew was not the end of the world."[162]

For example, in Isaiah 13, we read about God's judgment on Babylon. The language sounds as if it was the end of the world.

> Behold, the day of the Lord comes, cruel, with wrath and fierce anger, to make the land a desolation and to destroy its sinners from it. For the stars of the heavens and their constellations will not give their light; the sun will be dark at its rising, and the moon will not shed its light (Isaiah 13:9, 10).

3. As with all other uses of metaphor, we have to allow for the possibility of some blurring of the edges between vehicle and tenor on the part of the speaker.

Caird tells us that in thirteen of the eighteen instances the "day of the Lord" passages in the Old Testament, the "day of the Lord" is said to be imminent or present. Caird states,

> Now these *prophets were not claiming that the contemporary crisis was the day of the Lord* . . . neither did they believe in a succession of days of the Lord . . . . *they were using the term as a metaphor.*[163]

Riddlebarger observes that Caird describes double fulfillment in terms of bifocal vision. With the near vision the prophets foresaw imminent events, and with the long sight that saw the day of the Lord.[164] In the imminent events, *it was the Lord who was to be seen.* The Medes were stirred up by God. They were God's army of judgment. We see the same type of judgment in the book of Revelation.

---

[162] Ibid., 256.
[163] Ibid., 258.
[164] Kim Riddlebarger, *The Man of Sin Uncovering the Truth about the Antichrist* (Grand Rapids, MI: Baker Books, 2006), 73.

The Roman army was sent by God for judgment. Jesus, through the armies of Rome, came in judgment against those who pierced him and against those who rejected him as their Lord.

Caird cites passages from the prophet Joel as an example of a metaphorical Old Testament judgment of God utilizing what Caird call a prophetic camera technique.[165]

> Blow a trumpet in Zion;
>   sound an alarm on my holy mountain!
>   Let all the inhabitants of the land tremble,
>   for the day of the Lord is coming; it is near,
> a day of darkness and gloom, a day of clouds and thick darkness!
> Like blackness there is spread upon the mountains
>   a great and powerful people; their like has never been before,
> nor will be again after them through the years of all generations.
> The earth quakes before them; the heavens tremble.
> The sun and the moon are darkened,
>   and the stars withdraw their shining. (Joel 2: 1-2, 10).

What the prophet Joel is saying here is that the impending judgment would be terrible, so terrible that it would seem *as if* it was the final judgment on the *final day* of the coming of the Lord.

We know that the stars did not literally "withdraw their shining" when the Assyrian armies invaded Israel. The sun and the moon were not literally "darkened." The Lord is coming on the clouds in judgment! — but we don't literally see him in the clouds; we see his sign. Joel says, "Alas for the day! For the day of the Lord is near, and as destruction from the Almighty it comes (Joel 1:15)." We see the Lord in the armies.

In Joel 3:1-2, we see the longer term focus of the metaphor.

> For behold, in those days and at that time, when I restore the fortunes of Judah and Jerusalem, I will gather all the nations and bring them

---

[165] G. B. Caird, op. cit., 259-60.

down to the Valley of Jehoshaphat. And I will enter into judgment with them there, on behalf of my people and my heritage Israel, because they have scattered them among the nations and have divided up my land . . . .

From the perspective of Caird and Riddlebarger, what we see in the book of Joel is a metaphorical judgment. We see both the near-term and the long-term focus of the prophet.

The fall of the Jerusalem in the Olivet Discourse is the near-term focus of a metaphorical judgment. Since Jesus is the greatest prophet, we may substitute the name of our Savior for "prophets" in Caird's quote concerning the prophets. We will then compare the result *to the original words* of Caird for a side-by-side comparison.

> Now **these prophets** were not claiming that the **contemporary crisis** was the day of the Lord, . . . they were using the term as a metaphor.

> Now **Jesus** was not claiming that the **fall of Jerusalem** was the day of the Lord . . . . Jesus was using the term as a metaphor.

An objection to the partial preterist position that it splits the final judgment into two parts does not hold up when viewed in light of this comparison. By looking carefully at Caird's words we see that the prophesied fall of Jerusalem was an impending judgment used in the same manner as it was for the Old Testament prophets when God came on the clouds in judgment. Since the fall of Jerusalem was the "day of the Lord" in a metaphorical sense, the final judgment is not split into two parts.

Verses 29 and 30 of Matthew 24 read:

> Immediately after the tribulation of those days the sun will be darkened, and the moon will not give its light, and the stars will fall from heaven, and the powers of the heavens will be shaken. Then will appear in heaven the sign of the Son of Man, and then all the tribes of the earth

will mourn, and they will see the Son of Man coming on the clouds of heaven with power and great glory.

We see that this language is very similar to the apocalyptic language used by the prophet Joel. However, just as in Joel's prophecy, we do not literally see the sun darkened and the moon no longer giving its light. We do not literally see stars falling from heaven. In the Olivet Discourse, we do not literally see the "Son of Man" in the clouds, *we see his sign*. We see his sign in the destruction of the temple. In the book of Revelation, John's version of the discourse, we see his sign in the sky where we read:

Once more they cried out, "Hallelujah! The smoke from her goes up forever and ever (Revelation 19:3)."

Clouds in the spiritual realm indicate power and glory. In the near-term focus of the *metaphor*, God comes in the clouds of heaven against those who pierced him, not in the clouds of the physical earth. In the first century, every eye saw his sign in the sky (the fall of Jerusalem). It was a public event that "all" in the Roman Empire were aware of. The AD 70 judgment publicly inaugurated the new covenant and was the short-term fulfillment of the Olivet Discourse. However, at the same time it points to the long-term fulfillment at the end of history.

This metaphorical coming in AD 70 *points* to the Day of the Lord. The "sign" of the destruction of Jerusalem points to the final judgment. In the first century it was made publicly visible to all that the Old Testament sacrificial system was removed. The whole Roman world was aware of the fall of Jerusalem and the destruction of the temple. The judgment was not secret! At the end of history, we will see the physical return of Christ.

We can see in the metaphor the "already" but "not yet" of Ridderbos. We *are* "already" a "new creation" with the establishment of the new covenant, but "not yet." The new covenant was publicly made visible in AD 70 and we can "see" the "coming of the kingdom" from that point on. The kingdom is here now! Yet we still pray today for the coming of the kingdom.

The final fulfillment of the kingdom, however, is "not yet." In the Olivet Discourse, the impending destruction of the temple is the near-term contemporary judgment that the first century generation would see fulfilled. The judgment would be so horrible that it would *seem* as if it were the end of the world. However, the destruction of Jerusalem only *points* to the final judgment. The final judgment and the final removal of the curse of sin from creation at the end of history is "not yet." The final judgment takes place in the latter days of history.

From the amillennial perspective, the "latter days" covers the period of time from the birth of Christ to his coming again on the last day of history.

From the amillennial *preterist* point of view, the near-term focus of the metaphor is on "latter days" of the Jewish Age during which the Old Testament sacrificial system was publicly eliminated and the new covenant was established.

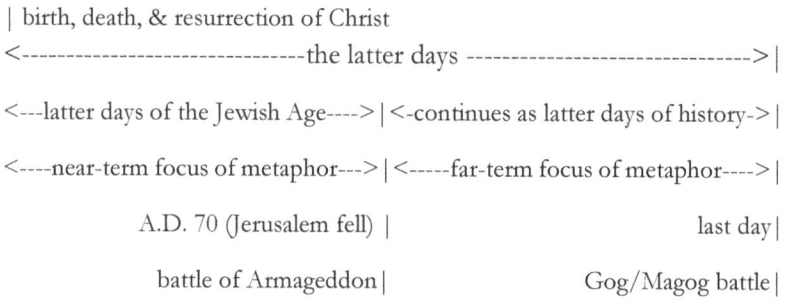

| birth, death, & resurrection of Christ
<--------------------------------the latter days -------------------------------->|

<---latter days of the Jewish Age---->|<-continues as latter days of history->|

<----near-term focus of metaphor--->|<-----far-term focus of metaphor---->|

        A.D. 70 (Jerusalem fell) | last day|

        battle of Armageddon | Gog/Magog battle |

the battle of Armageddon metaphorically points to the battle of Gog/Magog

The far-term focus of the metaphor corresponds to the completion of the "latter days" when Christ will return in judgment at the end of history against his enemies and will "wipe away all the tears" of his followers. By contrast to the near-term focus, the far-term focus of the metaphor Jesus will be physically seen in the clouds by every eye as he returns to earth in the same manner in which he ascended.

In other words, the *meaning* of "the latter days" includes the end of the Jewish age since that is when the new covenant, which was inaugurated with the resurrection of Christ, became publicly visible to the entire world. A Jew, living in the first century, certainly saw the destruction of the temple as the end of the age.

It is interesting to note here that full preterists get lost in the blurring of the edges between vehicle and tenor. They believe that in AD 70, we have the final coming of the Lord.

In Matthew's version of the discourse there is a transition between the near-term and the long-term focus. Gentry claims that Matthew 24: 34-36 is the *transition text* between the near-term focus and long-term focus. The key indicator is the phrase **"Truly, I say to you."** Gentry quotes William Hendriksen's use of the word "truly" (Greek: *amen*). Says Hendriksen in his commentary on Matthew,

> In every case ... in which this word occurs in the New Testament it introduces a statement which not only expresses a truth or fact ... but an *important*, a *solemn* fact, one that in many cases is at variance with popular opinion or expectation or at least causes some surprise.[166]

In Matthew 24:34 after the words "truly I say to you," we read the words "this generation shall not pass away until all these things take place."

Just before verses 34-36 we notice the "coming of Christ," as the near-term focus of the metaphor. Just after verses 34 -36 we again read the same words "the coming of Christ" but with the long-term focus (the final judgment).

Matthew 24:21-35 (short-term focus):

> For then there will be great tribulation, such as has not been from the beginning of the world until now, no, and never will be. And if those days had not been cut short, no human being would be saved . . . For as

---

[166] Kenneth L. Gentry, Jr., *The Olivet Discourse Made Easy* (Draper, VA: Apologetics Group, 2010), 51.

the lightning comes from the east and shines as far as the west, so will be the *coming of the Son of Man* . . . .

"Immediately after the tribulation of those days the sun will be darkened, and the moon will not give its light . . .Then will appear in heaven the sign of the Son of Man . . . **Truly, I say to you**, this generation will not pass away until all these things take place.

Heaven and earth will pass away, but my words will not pass away. Matthew 24:36-37 (long-term focus):

"But concerning that day and hour no one knows, not even the angels of heaven, nor the Son, but the Father only.

For as in those days before the flood they were eating and drinking, marrying and giving in marriage, until the day when Noah entered the ark, and they were unaware until the flood came and swept them all away, so will be the *coming of the Son of Man.*

Gentry covers a number of reasons why these verses 34-36 are transitional. There is a shift from the near-term focus of the metaphor to the far-term focus. He first notes that in verses 27 and 28 we have exactly the same expressions, "the coming of the Son of Man."

I have arranged a portion of his comments in a table so that the metaphor can be easily seen; a table to be studied before talking to the Bertrand Russells of the world who believe that Jesus was a failed prophet.

In the table, we see the "many days" of the near tribulation vs the far-term "that day." We see the "signs to be watched" in the near-term versus "no signs" in the far-term. We see the events that occur in the near time frame that were "fulfilled within a generation" versus the timing of the final return of Christ that "no one knows" except for the father.

Although there will still earthquakes, wars, and rumors of wars in the far-term perspective of the metaphor, they are no longer signs indicating the end is near. If they were signs then Christians would be able, by closely reading those signs, to anticipate when the end will be. However, Jesus said that only the father knows the time of the end!

Table of the metaphorical AD 70 judgment pointing to the end

Verse	Text	Gentry's comments
v 22	If those days had not been cut short, no human being would be saved.	Many **days** of tribulation vs day in the far term.
N v 24	For false christs and false prophets will arise	**Many signs** to be read (fig tree parable) and many false prophets and false christs will appear Instead of looking in the wilderness or in the inner rooms for Jesus, refers to both the far tem physical [167] return and the near-term judgment.
E v 26	If they say to you, "Look, he is in the wilderness," do not go out.	
A		
v 27 **R**	For as the lightning comes from the east…so will be the **coming of the Son of Man.**	The sign of the Son of Man will be as the lightning that comes from the east and shines as far as the west.
T		
E v 29	Immediately after the tribulation of those days the sun will darkened, and the moon will not give its light, and the stars will fall from heaven, and the power of the heaven will be shaken.	Just as Old Testament metaphorical language described the falling of a kingdom or empire; we now have the passing of the Jewish age whose sacrificial system was inhibiting the growth of Christianity.
R		
M v 30	…then will appear in heaven the sign of **the Son of Man.**	The sign of the Son of Man appears in heaven. The sign is the smoking temple and destruction of Jerusalem. The sign proves Jesus is in heaven seated at the right hand of God.

---

[167] Ibid., 102, "His [Jesus] physical return will be visible to all. After all, the original question (24:3) shows the disciples' conflating of the two events: AD 70 and the second advent. Just a few verses later (24:36 ff) Jesus will begin focusing on that more glorious event."

Verse	Text	Gentry's comments
v 31	He will send His angels with a great sound of a trumpet, and they will gather together his elect from the four winds, from one end of heaven to the other.	Jesus sends his messengers,[168] the gospel is joyfully preached (great sound of a trumpet.[169]) throughout the entire world.
T v 34 R A N S v 36 I T I O N TEXT	This generation shall not pass, until all these things are fulfilled. But concerning that day and hour no one knows, not even the angels of heaven nor the Son.	A concluding statement of the near term of the metaphor ending with a time frame that was fulfilled within a generation. "But concerning" indicates a change of subject in the Greek "that day" of the metaphor refers to the final day of the Lord. No one knows the time of his coming except the Father since at this time Jesus has not yet be glorified.
F v 37 A R	For as were the days of Noah, so will be the coming of the Son of Man.	No signs after verse 36 Life is normal like in the days of Noah.
TERM		The final judgment.

---

[168] Thomas Ice and Kenneth Gentry Jr., *The Great Tribulation -- Past or Future? Two Evangelicals Debate the Question* (Grand Rapids, MI: Kregel Academic & Professional, 1999), 63. "The word 'angels' here is translated *angeloi* in Greek. We can translate it "messengers," signifying *human* messengers ... The term does not seem to refer to the supernatural heavenly beings here ... Even if we apply this to angels, however, it would then refer 'to the supernatural power which lies behind such preaching.' Then it would teach that the angels of God attend our faithful proclamation of God's Word."

[169] Gentry, op. cit., 120, "... a symbolic statement announcing the arrival of the ultimate Jubilee Year. With the fulfilling of the old covenant in the person and work of Christ, man's ultimate debt is forgiven: his sin debt to God."

Herman Ridderbos takes the opinion expressed by Gentry that the Discourse refers to the to the Jewish land, at least up to verse 29. Ridderbos asserts, "The eschatolological and particulartistic elements (temple, Judea) are indeed closely and indissolubly connected."[170]

As Ridderbos continues into verse 30, he does accept the translation of the Greek word "gē" here as "earth." Gentry translates "gē" as "land." Keep in mind that a translation often involves interpretation. Ridderbos implies that with the translation of "gē" as "earth," "the signs in heaven can no longer be conceived of as *only* within the boundaries of the Jewish land. And when the sign of the Son of Man is seen, 'then shall all the tribes of the earth mourn.' "[171] However, Ridderbos does say, "The eschatology, as such, is universalistic. But in Matthew and Mark it is *described and viewed* from the particularistic standpoint. Only at the extreme end does the particular merge with the universal."[172]

If the eschatology is *described*, in the words of Ridderbos, as particularistic, is not Gentry's translation of "gē" as land both equally valid and contextually more accurate?

If we keep this specific comment of Ridderbos in mind, I believe the correct interpretation of the passage is that of Gentry, where the smoke from Jerusalem, in the "near term" of the metaphor, is the "sign of the Son of Man." The context of the passage going into verse 29 as noted by Ridderbos "is described and viewed from the particularistic standpoint." I believe that the shift in language here to that which is interpreted by Ridderbos as universalistic is simply a continuation of the metaphoric language that begins in verse 29 where the "sun is darkened" and "the moon will not give its light." We noted the usage of this metaphoric language earlier in the prophecy of Joel. This metaphoric language dramatically brings attention to the end of

---

[170] Herman Ridderbos, *The Coming of the Kingdom*, trans. H. de Jongste, (Philadelphia: P & R Pub. Co., 1962), 496.
[171] Ibid., 496. Emphasis mine.
[172] Ibid., 496. Emphasis mine.

the Jewish Age by *metaphorically* pointing to the final judgment and return of Christ. Jesus has answered the disciples first question of "when will these things be." The fall of Jerusalem would be in their lifetime. "This generation will not pass away until all these things take place." This generation, as even atheist Bertrand Russell notes, refers to the generation that Jesus was addressing. This is why Russell considered Jesus to be a failed prophet. Russell claims that "all these things," specifically the "end of the world," did not happened as described in verses 29-31. Certainly "this generation" does not refer to some future generation thousands of years in the future.

N. T. Wright asserts:

> Isaiah 13.10 and 34.4, quoted in Mark 13.24f. [Mark's Version of the Discourse], speak of the sun being darkened, the stars falling from heaven, and so forth. In their own contexts these passages refer, not to the collapse of the space-time world, but to startling and 'cosmically' significant events, such as the fall of great empires, within the space-time world.[173]

R.T. France, in his commentary on Matthew, criticizes the "natural" understanding that the language of Matthew 24:29-31 refers to the end of the world. Says France,

> The point at which this interpretation most obviously conflicts with that of many readers of the passage is with regard to 24:29-31, which are traditionally understood to relate to the end of the world and the Parousia (even though that word is conspicuously absent from them). I shall argue in the commentary below that this "natural" understanding of the terms used is in fact only natural to those who have been conditioned to it by a long tradition of Christian exegesis, and that in the context of first century Jewish thought it is far from obvious. The "cosmic" language of 24:29 is drawn directly from the OT prophetic

---

[173] N.T. Wright, *Jesus and the Victory of God: Christian Origins and the Question of God, Vol. 2* (Lanham: Fortress Press, 1997), 513.

passages where it functions not to predict the physical dissolutions of the universe but as a symbolic representation of catastrophic political changes within history ... It will mark the end of the old order, to be superseded by the sovereignty of the vindicated Son of Man.[174]

Amillennialist Sam Storms agrees with France. Storms writes:

I agree with R.T. France that Matthew 24:4-35 "is concerned with the destruction of the temple, answering the question 'When' with a clear time-scale summed up in 34, and that the second question about the Parousia only with the new beginning in 24:36."[175]

I believe we have demonstrated that Kenneth Gentry is correct in his view that the transition text is completed in verse 36. After verse 36 we see the far-term focus of the metaphor. Gentry is not alone in his interpretation. In the far-term focus there will be no signs. Certainly, there will be earthquakes and natural disasters until the end of time. They are not, however, signs of the second coming of Christ.

Jesus gives us a parable telling us what to do during his delay. In the parable of the faithful servant and evil servant, the evil servant says in his heart in verses 48-49, "'My master is delaying his coming,' and begins to beat his fellow servants, and to eat and drink with drunkards . . . ."

The faithful servant is active and wise. His activity prevents what happened in the previous parable where Jesus comes like a thief catching the owner of the house unaware.

In Luke's version of the discourse, Jesus also compares life at the end of history to the days of Lot.

---

[174] R.T. France, *The Gospel of Matthew* (Grand Rapids, MI: Eerdmans Publishing Co., 2007), 891.

[175] Sam Storms, *Kingdom Come* (Fearn, Scotland: Mentor Imprint of Christian Focus Pub., 2013), 237.

> Likewise, as it was also in the days of Lot: They ate, they drank, they bought, they sold, they planted, they built; but on the day that Lot went out of Sodom it rained fire and brimstone from heaven and destroyed *them* all. Even so will it be in the day when the Son of Man is revealed. (Luke 17:28-30).

We should not be passively waiting for the coming of the Lord. We should be active! We should be like the faithful servant! We should be, as seen by Vern Poythress, actively involved in redeeming mathematics, science, and culture to the glory of God. We must continue to spread the good news. We must continue making disciples of all the nations:

> baptizing them in the name of the Father and of the Son and of the Holy Spirit, teaching them to observe all things that I have commanded you; and behold, I am with you always, **even to the end of the age**." Amen. (Matt 28:19-20).

The short-term fulfillment of the prophecy is our guarantee of the fulfillment to come of the far-term vision of the prophecy. Jesus was not a failed prophet to those in need of salvation as Bertrand Russell proclaimed. The sureness of the long-term prophecy is demonstrated in the remarkable fulfillment of the near-term prophecy within a generation. Jesus is coming at the end of history to judge the living and the dead.

Although some specific details of exegesis of the discourse differ, both Gentry and Riddlebarger agree, as do I, that the prophecy of Christ's coming in judgment is a metaphorical coming with a near-term and far-term focus.

There is, however, a significant point of disagreement in applying the scope of the term "double fulfillment." Says Riddlebarger:

> Given the fact that double fulfillment can be found in the prophets (Joel, Amos, Isaiah, and Jeremiah) as well as in the Olivet Discourse, this phenomenon is the means through which we should endeavor to

understand the apparently conflicting data in both Testaments regarding an imminent Antichrist (or antichrists) and a future eschatological foe who appears at the time of the end.[176]

To break down the detail, we will divide Riddlebarger's conditional into two parts. Let us first consider the antecedent of the conditional:

Given the fact that double fulfillment can be found in the prophets (Joel, Amos, Isaiah, and Jeremiah) as well as in the Olivet Discourse,

I would agree that this antecedent is a true statement, *if* one restricts the use of the term "double fulfillment" to the metaphorical usage illustrated by Caird in the Old Testament and Olivet Discourse. It should also be noted that nowhere in any of the above examples of metaphorical judgment is there any evidence that *detail in the prophetic near-term focus* points to possible fulfillment in the *same detail* in the far-term focus. The final judgment will have a worldwide scope versus a localized scope. The details of the future fulfillment will be different.

It is questionable as to what specific details of a symbol in the near-term focus apply to possible fulfillment of details in the far-term focus of a metaphorical judgment. Order of events, location, and characteristics of individuals would not be in direct correspondence.

However, in the conclusion of his conditional, Riddlebarger states,

this phenomenon is the means through which we should endeavor to understand the apparently conflicting data in both Testaments regarding an imminent Antichrist (or antichrists) and a future eschatological foe who appears at the time of the end.[177]

---

[176] Kim Riddlebarger, op. cit., 73.
[177] Ibid., 73.

Riddlebarger later specifically applies double fulfillment to Nero.[178] Gentry disagrees that the number of the Beast and its image is a detail that could have a long-term fulfillment. Gentry comments:

> We really stretch credibility if we argue that all the many details of the beast (and why not all of Revelation?) are to be fulfilled in incredible detail again later. The beast himself plays a large and complicated role in Revelation. A careful reading of Revelation shows a whole complex of interrelated, intricately woven themes, personalities, and events all of which would have to find exact fulfillment twice.[179]

The Olivet Discourse does point *metaphorically* to the end of the age at the last days of history. If the book of Revelation is John's version of the Olivet Discourse and we draw a parallel between the near-term battle of Armageddon to the battle of Gog/Magog, *we can only say that "Nero" metaphorically points to "Gog."* The details will be different. The battle of Armageddon is the near-term focus and only *metaphorically points* to end-time battle of Gog/Magog. Some view AD 70 as a microcosm of the final judgment. However, there is just not enough information to support the statement that the symbol of the Beast (Nero) *along with the specific details of this symbol* point to another fulfillment.

Gentry correctly objects to usage of the term "double fulfillment" as used by Riddlebarger.[180] It simply goes beyond the scope of the near-term focus of the metaphor to conjecture that the destruction of the temple may point ahead to another fulfillment or that the number of the Beast may be repeated in another fulfillment.

The destruction of the temple is at the end of Jewish Age — at which time the new covenant is inaugurated. The Beast of Revelation is specific to the first century. The events of AD 70 may foreshadow

---

[178] Ibid., 173.

[179] Kenneth L. Gentry, Jr., *Perilous Times* (Texarkana, AZ: Covenant Media Press, 1999), 133.

[180] Kim Riddlebarger, op. cit., 173.

events preceding the final return of Christ. However, they will not be repeated in detail. The future events will be different, involving a worldwide conflict with a different cast of characters and characteristics.

The great tribulation and battle of Armageddon are past events. The coming battle of Gog/Magog ends with the final destruction of the forces of evil with Satan being thrown into the fiery pit. The battle will be a worldwide conflict that will bring us to the end of history and a new beginning — a final redemption of creation culminating in the new heavens and the new earth.

The book of Revelation does specifically tell us the name of the leader of the forces of evil allied with Satan at the time of the end. His name is Gog.

Chapter 9
REVELATION IS JOHN'S VERSION OF THE OLIVET DISCOURSE

James Stuart Russell considers the book of Revelation to be John's version of the Olivet Discourse. There are many parallels.

At the beginning of the book of Revelation in verse 7 we read:
Behold, he is coming with the clouds, and every eye will see him, even those who pierced him, and all tribes of the earth will wail on account of him.

Let us compare this passage to Matthew 24:30 of the Olivet Discourse.

Then will appear in heaven the sign of the Son of Man, and then all the tribes of the earth[181] will mourn, and they will see the Son of Man coming on the clouds of heaven with power and great glory.

Every eye, every person across the entire Roman empire knew of the destruction of the temple. This destruction *points* to the final coming of Christ when every eye *will* literally see him. "Near-term" judgment in the book of Revelation is specifically mentioned against those who pierced him. Christ is bringing his wrath against those who crucified him, specifically against those who say they are Jews but are

---

[181] Kenneth L. Gentry, Jr., *Before Jerusalem Fell: Dating the Book of Revelation*, 3rd ed. (Fountain Inn, SC: Victorious Hope Publishing, 1998, 2010), 128. Gentry points out the word "earth" in the English translation can also equally as well be interpreted as a specific land. The context here is the twelve tribes, not the whole earth. Israel is known as the tribes of the Promised Land. In Joshua 1:2 we read: "Now therefore arise, go over this Jordan, you and all this people, into the land that I am giving to them, to the people of Israel."

not. In Matthew 27:25-26 it is recorded:

> And all the people answered, "His blood be on us and on our children!"... and having scourged Jesus, delivered him to be crucified.

Ultimately, it was those who claimed to be Jews but were not who take the blame for crucifying Jesus. The Romans crucified Jesus via their legal system. However, Peter and the apostles make it clear that the Jews who rejected Jesus are to blame.

In Acts 5:29-30 we read:

> But Peter and the apostles answered, "We must obey God rather than men. The God of our fathers raised Jesus, whom you killed by hanging him on a tree.

Luke 19:43-44 says:

> For the days will come upon you, when your enemies will set up a barricade around you and surround you and hem you in on every side and tear you down to the ground, you and your children within you. And they will not leave one stone upon another in you, because you did not know the time of your visitation.

Revelation 1:7 tells us that Jesus is coming against those who pierced him. We see the slain lamb, who is also the Lion from the tribe of Judah (Rev. 5:5-6), taking the scroll from him who sits on the throne.

> And between the throne and the four living creatures and among the elders I saw a Lamb standing, as though it had been slain ... And he went and took the scroll from the right hand of him who was seated on the throne (Revelation 5:6-7).

Christ came in judgment in AD 70. The "near-term" coming of Jesus was in the glory of the Father just as the Old Testament judgments were.

> Fall on us and hide us from the face of him who is seated on the throne, and from the wrath of the Lamb, for the great day of their wrath has come, and who can stand? (Revelation 6:16-17).

The seals of judgment are ready to be opened by the Lamb, the Lion from the tribe of Judah. The tribes of the land mourn.

There are two other accounts of the Olivet Discourse besides the one we considered previously in Matthew.

In Mark's and Luke's account of the Olivet Discourse, we notice some remarkable parallels to the book of Revelation.

We will give a mapping for each of the seven seals and the trampling of Jerusalem to passages in the Olivet Discourse similar to those given by Boxall.[182] There are many clear correspondences. The seals are John's overview of the book of Revelation. We also know that the remarks of Jesus in the Discourse are directed specifically at those who rejected him (Mark 13:30).

> *The First Seal* of the scroll is broken (the false christ appears):
> And I looked, and behold, a white horse! And its rider had a bow, and a crown was given to him, and he came out conquering, and to conquer. (Revelation 6:2)
> *Discourse* (the false christ's appear):
> And he said, "See that you are not led astray. For many will come in my name, saying, 'I am he!' and, 'The time is at hand!' Do not go after them (Luke 21:8). See also Mark 13:6.[183]

---

[182] Ian Boxall, *The Revelation of Saint John (Black's New Testament Commentary)* [Grand Rapids, MI: Baker Academic, 2009], 106.

[183] Josephus tells us that a number of false christs appeared during the Jewish War beginning in AD 66. Josephus relates that even earlier, in the time Felix was procurator, thirty thousand followed an Egyptian prophet into the wilderness. Four hundred of the people were killed and two hundred captured when Felix ordered

The Second Seal is broken (the second rider appears bringing war): And out came another horse, bright red. Its rider was permitted to take peace from the earth, so that people should slay one another, and he was given a great sword (Revelation 6:3,4).
Discourse: (wars and rumors of wars):
And when you hear of wars and rumors of wars, do not be alarmed. (Mark 13:7). And when you hear of wars and tumults, do not be terrified (Luke 21:9).

The Third Seal is broken (the third rider appears bringing famine): And I looked, and behold, a black horse! And its rider had a pair of scales in his hand (Revelation 6:5). In verse six we see that the famine will be severe.
Discourse: There will be great earthquakes, and in various places; there will be famines (Mark 13:8).

The Fourth Seal is broken (the fourth rider appears bringing death): And I looked, and behold, a pale horse! And its rider's name was Death, and Hades followed him. And they were given authority over a fourth of the earth, to kill with sword and with famine *and with pestilence* and by wild beasts of the earth (Revelation 6:7-8).[184]
Discourse: There will be great earthquakes, and in various places famines and pestilences. And there will be terrors and great signs from heaven (Luke 21:11).[185]

The Fifth Seal is broken (souls of the martyrs are seen under the altar): I saw under the altar the souls of those who had been slain for the word of God and for the witness they had borne (Revelation 6:9).

---

his soldiers to attack the Egyptian and those with him. See Josephus, *Jewish War*, Book ii, Chapter 13, Sections 4,5. Also see *Jewish Antiquities*, Book xx, Chapter 8, Section 6.

[184] Emphasis added is mine. Pestilence is added to famine after the third seal.

[185] Josephus reports terrible famine during the siege of Jerusalem. *Jewish Antiquities*, Book xx, Chapter 2, Section 5. *Jewish War*. Book v, Chapter 10, Section 3 and book vi, Chapter 3, Sections 3,4.

Discourse: You will be delivered up even by parents and brothers and relatives and friends, and some of you they will put to death. You will be hated by all for my name's sake (Luke 21:16-17).

The Siege of Jerusalem is prophesied. Jerusalem *will* be trampled.
Revelation, The Trampling of Jerusalem: do not measure the court outside the temple; leave that out, for it is given over to the nations, and they will trample the holy city for forty-two months (Revelation 11:2).
Discourse, The Trampling of Jerusalem: For there will be great distress upon the earth and wrath against this people. They will fall by the edge of the sword and be led captive among all nations, and Jerusalem will be trampled underfoot by the Gentiles, until the times of the Gentiles are fulfilled (Luke 21:23-24).

The Sixth Seal is broken (Day of the Lord is described in apocalyptic language):
I looked, and behold, there was a great earthquake, and the sun became black as sackcloth, the full moon became like blood, and the stars of the sky fell to the earth as the fig tree sheds its winter fruit when shaken by a gale. The sky vanished like a scroll that is being rolled up, and every mountain and island was removed from its place (Revelation 6:12-14).
Discourse (Day of the Lord is described in apocalyptic language): But in those days, after the tribulation, the sun will be darkened, and the moon will not give its light, and the stars will be falling from heaven, and the powers in the heavens will be shaken. And then they will see the Son of Man coming in clouds with great power and glory. (Mark 13:24-25).

The Seventh Seal is broken (There is a silence in heaven, an interlude).
The first six seals take us up to the Day of the Lord. with the breaking of the seventh seal in Revelation 8 and then a number of recapitulations leading to the Day of the Lord, including a final recapitulation leading to the Day of the Lord in Revelation 19:1-3 where we read:

After this I heard what seemed to be the loud voice of a great multitude in heaven, crying out,

> "Hallelujah!
> Salvation and glory and power belong to our God,
>   for his judgments are true and just;
> for he has judged the great prostitute
>   who corrupted the earth with her immorality,
> and has avenged on her the blood of his servants."

Once more they cried out,

> "Hallelujah!
> The smoke from her goes up forever and ever."

Discourse: (coming of the Son of Man in Matthew 24:30):
Then will appear in heaven the sign of the Son of Man, and then all the tribes of the earth will mourn, and they will see the Son of Man coming on the clouds of heaven with power and great glory.

The sign of the Son of Man from the Discourse is the smoke from Jerusalem which goes up forever and ever.

In both the Olivet Discourse and in the book of Revelation, there are portrayals of wars, persecution, famine, and death. Rebellions broke out throughout the empire.

The events of the first six seals and Mark 13:20-30 take us all the way up to the near-term fulfillment of the discourse with the siege and fall of Jerusalem.

In Revelation 20 we read about the final destruction of Satan. In Mark 13:32 we read: "But concerning that day or that hour, no one knows, not even the angels in heaven, nor the Son, but only the Father. Be on guard, keep awake. For you do not know when the time will come."

Just as there was near-term prophecy and far-term prophecy in the Olivet Discourse, there is near-term prophecy and far-term prophecy in the relating of the same truths in the book of Revelation. The book of Revelation is John's version of the Olivet Discourse.

Chapter 10
RECAPITULATION AND THE GOG/MAGOG BATTLE

We noticed in chapter eight, the Olivet Discourse and Double Fulfillment, that the judgment of AD 70 is viewed by some as a microcosm of the final judgment. So it would not be surprising if the *language* describing the fall of Jerusalem would be similar to the *language* describing the battle just prior to the final judgment.

The disagreement as to whether or not the battle of Armageddon is future or past has much to do with whether or not the interpreter sees the battle of Gog/Magog as a recapitulation of the battle of Armageddon. Amillennialists see only one battle on the eschatological calendar. It follows that if the battle of Armageddon is future, then it must be the same battle as the battle of Gog/Magog. Amillennialists who believe that the battle of Armageddon is past, see two different battles separated by the millennium.

Amillennialists see the battle of Gog/Magog taking place after the millennium and take note that in the description of this battle there is emphasis on its universality. Nations from the whole earth follow Satan in their opposition to the Saints:

> ... Satan will be released from his prison and will come out to deceive the nations that are at the four corners of the earth, Gog and Magog, to gather them for battle; their number is like the sand of the sea (Revelation 20:7-8).

All Christians believe that this will be the final battle although some believe that the battle will be a spiritual one only. The language of this final battle indicates that the final conflict will involve the entire world. The question comes up about the language used in the description of the battle of Armageddon.

There are similarities in the language used in the description of the battle of Armageddon and the final battle. Does this mean the battles described are the same battle?

Greg Beale believes they are the same battle. Kenneth Gentry believes they are two different battles. Beale believes the key to understanding that the two battles are the same battle is the phrase *"all the nations of earth."*

All the nations of earth gather together for the last battle against the Saints. Beale believes that "all the nations" gathering together for both the battle of Armageddon and Gog/Magog is an indication that they are the same battle. For Kenneth Gentry, "all the nations" gathering together for the battle of Armageddon refers to the nations surrounding Israel. The language is hyperbolic. The battle of God/Magog, however, is global.

Which is it? The same battle being described from a different perspective, or two different battles with some similarities in symbolism from Ezekiel and Zechariah? To answer this question, we will examine these Old Testament passages suggested by Greg Beale. Beale observes:

> after the announcement of coming judgment, John sees a vision of the judgment itself. He observes that "the beast and the kings of the earth and their armies have been gathered to make war;" which essentially duplicates the wording used in 16:14 and 20:8 to describe the prelude to the last battle of history.[186]

In AD 70 the battle was at Jerusalem, and in Zechariah we see the Great Day of the Lord identified with the city of Jerusalem.

---

[186] G. K. Beale, *The Book of Revelation (The New International Greek Testament Commentary)* [Grand Rapids, MI: Wm. B. Eerdmans Publishing Co., Reprint edition (1999), 2013], 967.

Behold, a day is coming for the Lord, when the spoil taken from you will be divided in your midst. For I will gather all the nations against Jerusalem to battle . . . . (Zechariah 14:1-2).

The words "all nations" in Zechariah 14 quoted above, according to Gentry, are hyperbole. The book of Zechariah contains both metaphor and hyperbole. "All nations" or "every nation" is used in Scripture at times in a hyperbolic sense even in texts which are not prophetic. We read for example in Act 2:5 that "Now there were dwelling in Jerusalem Jews, devout men from every nation under heaven." These were the nations surrounding Israel politically and socially.

Gentry believes that the phrase "all the nations" quoted from Zechariah refers to the Roman armies in AD 70, which were made up not only of soldiers from what we know as Italy but of soldiers from the conquered provinces. Not only did Agrippa II march from Judea with Vespasian against Jerusalem, Arab leaders did as well. Historically, Israel was dominated by Babylon, Persia, and Greece. The Lord came to Jeremiah "when Nebuchadnezzar king of Babylon and all his army, with all the kingdoms of the earth that were under his dominion and all the peoples, were fighting against Jerusalem and against all its cities" (Jer. 34:1). Later, Cyrus, king of Persia, said, "The LORD, the God of heaven, has given me all the kingdoms of the earth (Ezra 1:2)." Rome conquered these nations that surrounded Israel. The provinces of Rome extended to Europe, Asia, and Africa.

The people of conquered provinces thought of themselves as nations. The Jews did as well. Caiaphas, the high priest, said that "it is better for you that one man should die for the people, not that the whole nation should perish." The apostle Paul thought of the provinces of Rome as nations. In Romans 16:26 he says, "but [the gospel] has now been disclosed and through the prophetic writings has been made known to all nations."

"The whole passage [Zechariah 14] - as it often is with prophecy - is a mingling of literal and figurative prophetic allusions."[187]

The thought of the temple being rebuilt in Zechariah's day would have been applied by the disciples who heard the Olivet Discourse to the destruction of the temple in AD 70.

Gentry remarks that even the dispensationalist author J. Dwight Pentecost admits:

> ... that the disciples who heard the Olivet Discourse would naturally have applied Zechariah 14 to the A.D. 70 destruction of the Temple. But then, he says, such involves a confusion of God's program for the Church with that for Israel.[188]

The Day of the Lord language of the Olivet Discourse refers metaphorically to the end of the Jewish Age *and* the end of history. The end of the Jewish Age is the end of the sacrificial system and the inauguration of the new covenant. At the end of history, the new heavens and new earth are the fulfillment of the kingdom that shall never end. The Old Testament prophets, however, saw the first coming of Christ and his final coming at the end of history as one event. The New Testament writers saw their present age as being in the last days of the old covenant. The last days also refer to the establishment of the new covenant, which will culminate with the new heavens and new earth in the last day of history. That final age has not yet arrived; it is still to come.

With the Olivet Discourse in mind we will consider verses 3-5 of Zechariah 14:

> Then the Lord will go out and fight against those nations as when he fights on a day of battle. On that day his feet shall stand on the

---

[187] Kenneth L. Gentry, Jr., *He Shall Have Dominion* (Tyler, TX: Institute for Christian Economics, 1992), 470-471.
[188] Ibid., 471.

Mount of Olives that lies before Jerusalem on the east, and the Mount of Olives shall be split in two from east to west by a very wide valley, so that one half of the Mount shall move northward, and the other half southward.

In Zechariah 14 it is the Lord who fights for Israel. It is not the feet of Jesus that stand on the Mount of Olives. The reference to Jesus is in Zechariah 13, when the Shepherd is struck. In Zechariah 14 it is the Lord whose feet stand on the Mount of Olives. "The feet of the Lord" is figurative just as it is in Micah 1:3 where the judgment of God is seen through the Assyrian army. Micah wrote: "For behold, the Lord is coming out of his place, and will come down and tread upon the high places of the earth. And the mountains will melt under him, and the valleys will split open."

Gentry draws an Old Testament comparison:

> The Lord will fight for His true people "as when he fought in the day of battle" (v. 4). The Lord's feet standing on the Mount of Olives and His fighting for His people need be no more literal than other such references of the Lord's fighting for Israel in the Old Testament. The language is similar to that in Joshua 10:14, 42 and 23:3, where the Lord "fought for Israel." In Joshua, these references indicate His providential favor in Israel's victory and deliverance, not His corporeal presence.[189]

What does "that day" refer to in verse 4 of Zechariah quoted above? We see the answer in Revelation 21. I like McKenzie's exposition here.[190] In Revelation 21 we see that it is not physical Jerusalem but the New Jerusalem from which flows the living waters.[191] John 7:37-39 tells us that:

---

[189] Ibid., 471-72.

[190] Duncan McKenzie, *The Antichrist and the Second Coming: A Preterist Examination, Vol. 1* (Maitland, FL: Xulon Press, 2009), 283-85.

[191] Ibid., 283-84.

> On the last day of the feast, the great day, Jesus stood up and cried out, "If anyone thirsts, let him come to me and drink. Whoever believes in me, as the Scripture has said, 'Out of his heart will flow rivers of living water.'" Now this he said about the Spirit, whom those who believed in him were to receive, for as yet the Spirit had not been given, because Jesus was not yet glorified.

We see in Zechariah 14 that "on that day" the Lord is fighting for the bride.

> On that day there shall be no light, cold, or frost. And there shall be a unique day, which is known to the Lord, neither day nor night, but at evening time there shall be light. On that day living waters shall flow out from Jerusalem, half of them to the eastern sea and half of them to the western sea. It shall continue in summer as in winter (Zechariah 14: 6-8).

The life-giving waters do not flow from physical Jerusalem but are symbolic of the life-giving properties of the Holy Spirit.

We see the life-giving properties of living water withheld from those who are not part of the New Jerusalem[192] in Zechariah 14:16 - 17 which says:

> Then everyone who survives of all the nations that have come against Jerusalem shall go up year after year to worship the King, the Lord of hosts, and to keep the Feast of Booths. And if any of the families of the earth do not go up to Jerusalem to worship the King, the Lord of hosts, there will be no rain on them.

It is worth taking note of McKenzie's comment on the above passage:

---

[192] Ibid., 284.

To take verses 16-19's statement about the nations of the world going up to Jerusalem to celebrate the Feast of Tabernacles in a literal physical sense is grossly misguided. It should be noted that Jesus taught just the opposite. He said the time was coming (and was already beginning) when people would no longer worship in Jerusalem.[193]

The living waters flow through Jesus in the new covenant. Jesus said to the woman at the well, ". . . but whoever drinks of the water that I will give him will never be thirsty again. The water that I will give him will become in him a spring of water welling up to eternal life . . . the hour is coming when neither on this mountain nor in Jerusalem will you worship the Father (John 4:13-21)."

The Lord is fighting for his true people, the remnant. The Lord is fighting for the New Jerusalem bride in the battle of Armageddon. In Revelation 16:14 John alludes to Ezekiel's "that day" when the Lord gathers the nations against Jerusalem.
Revelation 16:14 -16:

> For they are demonic spirits, performing signs, who go abroad to the kings of the whole world, to assemble them for battle on the great day of God the Almighty. ("Behold, I am coming like a thief! Blessed is the one who stays awake, keeping his garments on, that he may not go about naked and be seen exposed!") And they assembled them at the place that in Hebrew is called Armageddon.

Armageddon is Hebrew for the mountain of Megiddo. Revelation 16:16 does not say that the battle was fought at Armageddon: Revelation tells us only that the kings of the earth gathered their forces there. McKenzie quotes Arthur Ogden on Megiddo:

---

[193] Ibid., 284.

Josephus [The Jewish War, 5, 1, 1] tells us that when Titus left Egypt with orders from his father to subdue the Jews that he returned "to Caesarea, having taken a resolution to gather all his other forces at that place." Bear in mind that Caesarea was within sight of Mt. Carmel, the mountain of Megiddo, and that those armed forces coming from the northern regions must pass through Megiddo before reaching the appointed place of gathering. Titus stayed in the regions around Caesarea until most of the forces from the north arrived, and then moved on to Jerusalem for the battle of the great day of God Almighty.[194]

John also uses the imagery of the Gog/Magog battle from Ezekiel. This imagery is alluded to by John for both the battle of Armageddon and the end-time battle of Gog/Magog after the millennium. The sacrificial feast after the battle is described in Ezekiel 39.

In Ezekiel 39:17-18 we read:

"As for you, son of man, thus says the Lord God: Speak to the birds of every sort and to all beasts of the field, 'Assemble and come, gather from all around to the sacrificial feast that I am preparing for you, a great sacrificial feast on the mountains of Israel, and you shall eat flesh and drink blood. You shall eat the flesh of the mighty, and drink the blood of the princes of the earth — of rams, of lambs, and of he-goats, of bulls, all of them fat beasts of Bashan.

In Revelation 19:17-18 after the vision of the fall of Babylon and judgment on the great prostitute, John describes the aftermath of the battle of Armageddon. This is a clear allusion to the Gog/Mag battle described in Ezekiel.

In Revelation 19:17-18 we read:

Then I saw an angel standing in the sun, and with a loud voice he called

---

[194] Ibid., 321.

to all the birds that fly directly overhead, Come, gather for the great supper of God, to eat the flesh of kings, the flesh of captains, the flesh of mighty men, the flesh of horses and their riders, and the flesh of all men, both free and slave, both small and great."

In our exposition of the Olivet Discourse we noted that there is both a short-term and a long-term fulfillment of the prophecy of Jesus.

The Olivet Discourse is not an apocryphal writing with dragons and beasts with heads and horns, but a straightforward prophecy with figurative language. The short-term fulfillment in the Olivet Discourse is the fall of Jerusalem and the long-term fulfillment is judgment at the end of history. The "Day of the Lord" has its short-term fulfillment in the fall of Jerusalem and long-term fulfillment in the final judgment. If the book of Revelation is John's version of the Olivet Discourse, we would expect to see similar language for both.

Battles and judgments are activities. John, Gentry reminds us, compares two other activities in Revelation to a single source in Ezekiel, whereas in the book of Revelation they are clearly distinct. The activity is measurement.

The temple is *measured* with a measuring rod like a staff in Revelation 11:1-2, and the New Jerusalem is measured with a measuring rod of gold in Revelation 21:15. The imagery for both measurements is found in Ezekiel 40:5 as a single measurement where the measurement of a wall of Jerusalem is done with a measuring reed.

The activities of taking measurements in Revelation are clearly distinct, yet they have a single common source in Ezekiel. So the fact that two battles occur in Revelation both referencing the same source in Ezekiel is not enough to show the battles are identical. However, only one exception is needed logically to show that the battles are not identical.

There is a clear exception. Satan was bound at the beginning of Revelation 20 after the battle of Armageddon and then unbound after the millennium before the Gog/Magog battle.

The binding of Satan corresponds to the beginning of the millennium. A point of dispute among amillennialists is when the binding of Satan took place.

Saint Augustine believed that the binding of Satan began during the ministry of Christ when he said, in Matthew 12:28-29:

> But if it is by the Spirit of God that I cast out demons, then the kingdom of God has come upon you. Or how can someone enter a strong man's house and plunder his goods, unless he first binds the strong man? Then indeed he may plunder his house."

Says Augustine,

> It was then for the binding of this strong one that the apostle saw in the Apocalypse "an angel coming down from heaven, having the key of the abyss, and a chain in his hand. And he laid hold," he says, "on the dragon, that old serpent, which is called the devil and Satan, and bound him a thousand years."[195]

In John 12:30-31 the voice from heaven is heard just after the triumphal entry. Jesus responds: "This voice has come for your sake, not mine. Now is the judgment of this world; now will the ruler of this world be cast out."

We see from above two passages that Satan was bound beginning with the public ministry of Christ. The voice which had come for the sake of the disciples proclaimed that Satan would "now" be cast out with the coming death and resurrection of Christ.[196]

---

[195] Philip Schaff, ed., *NPNF 1-02. St. Augustin's City of God and Christian Doctrine* (New York: The Christian Literature Publishing Co., 1890. Reprinted Grand Rapids, MI: Christian Classics Ethereal Library), 690.

[196] Some amillennialists, following Saint Augustine, believe the binding of Satan

In Revelation 12:10-12 we notice a parallel passage to John 12:30-31:

> And I heard a loud voice in heaven, saying "Now the salvation and the power and the kingdom of our God and the authority of his Christ have come, for the accuser of our brothers has been thrown down, who accuses them day and night before our God. And they have conquered him by the blood of the Lamb and by the word of their testimony, for they loved not their lives even unto death. Therefore, rejoice, O heavens and you who dwell in them! But woe to you, O earth and sea, for the devil has come down to you in great wrath, because he knows that his time is short!"

We note that the time was short for Satan when he was cast down from heaven just before his defeat in the crucifixion and resurrection of Christ. This is the same time referred to in Revelation 12:12.

There is no indication that Satan is bound when Christ comes on the White Horse in Revelation 19:11 to lead the final battle against the Beast and the false prophet in the battle of Armageddon. The time for Satan is short! Satan is then defeated and the Beast and false prophet are cast into the lake of fire.

In the verses immediately following Revelation 19, Revelation 20: 1-3, we read the verses alluded to by Saint Augustine:

> Then I saw an angel coming down from heaven, holding in his hand the key to the bottomless pit and a great chain. And he seized the dragon, that ancient serpent, who is the devil and Satan, and bound him for a thousand years, and threw him into the pit, and shut it and sealed it over him, so that he might not deceive the nations any longer, until the thousand years were ended. After that he must be

---

began with the public ministry of Jesus, while others believe that Satan was not fully bound until the death and resurrection of Christ.

released for a little while.

Now the length of time is one-thousand years. The time is no longer short.

The binding of Satan with the destruction of the Beast and false prophet is the public manifestation of what already happened in AD 30, the binding of Satan with the death and resurrection of Christ. The last major barrier to the spread of the gospel was removed with the elimination of the sacrificial system. The saints who cried out "how long before you judge and avenge our blood"[197] were vindicated with the judgment against "those who pierced him."[198]

It is not until after the Gog/Magog battle that Satan is destroyed — cast into Hell. When Satan is cast into Hell, *the beast and the false prophet are already there* (Rev. 20:11). The Gog/Magog battle is after the millennium, whereas the battle of Armageddon is before the millennium. They are two different battles.

---

[197] Revelation 6:10.
[198] Revelation 1:7.

Chapter 11
NERO IS THE BEAST

And the beast was given a mouth uttering haughty and blasphemous words, and it was allowed to exercise authority for forty-two months. It opened its mouth to utter blasphemies against God, blaspheming his name and his dwelling, that is, those who dwell in heaven. Also it was allowed to make war on the saints and to conquer them. And authority was given it over every tribe and people and language and nation (Revelation 13: 5-7).

The persecution of Nero began about the middle or latter part of Nov. A.D. 64, at Rome. It ended with the death of Nero, which was on the ninth of June, A.D. 68, for on that day Galba entered Rome and was proclaimed emperor. Here again is 3+ years or 1260 days with sufficient exactness; for the precise time of forty-two months expires about the middle or end of May, and Nero died in the first part of June.[199]

Gentry tells us that at times corporate Rome is referred to as the Beast and at other times Nero is referred to as the Beast. We use the same language today when we refer to the President of the United States and at other times to the United States. When some refer to the Patient Protection and Affordable Care Act, they refer to the federal statute as "Obama Care," referring to it as his statute, although it is a federal statute. He did sign the bill. As another example, a well-known tweet by Ryan Liza, Washington correspondent for the New Yorker, reads "Countries bombed: Obama 7, Bush 4."[200]

Revelation 13:18 (NASB):

Here is wisdom. Let him who has understanding calculate the

---

[199] Kenneth L. Gentry, Jr., *Before Jerusalem Fell: Dating the Book of Revelation*, 3rd ed., (Fountain Inn, SC.: Victorious Hope Publishing, 1998, 2010), 254.
[200] Jon Greenberg, "Lizza says Obama has bombed more nations than Bush," politifact.com/punditfact/statements/2014/sep/25/ryan-lizza/lizza-says-obama-has-bombed-more-nations-bush/

number of the beast, for the number is that of a man; and his number is [a]six hundred and sixty-six.

Footnotes: a. Revelation 13:18 One early ms reads 616

Not only is Nero the sixth King, but from the name "Nero" the number 666 can be calculated. Some idealists place emphasis on fact that the number seven symbolizes completeness while the number six is one less. The number 6 falls one short of the perfection of the number 7 and 666 would indicate coming up short of 7 three times over (if the original source is not 616). This symbolic interpretation, although having merit, cannot alone be the full interpretation. It cannot be ignored the number "is that of a man."

The number is "six hundred and sixty-six," not three sixes. The practice used by the Hebrews in the literation of numbers and letters is known as gematria. In Greek and Hebrew there were no Arabic numbers as we know them today but letters of the Greek or Hebrew Alphabet. For example, in Greek, the letter "alpha" was both the letter "a" and the number 1. The letter "beta" was both the letter "b" and the number 2. The letter gamma was both the letter "g" and the number 3. The letter "theta" would be both "q" and 9. The next letter after "theta" would be "iota" which would be both "i" and 10. The letter "nu" was both the letter "n" and the number 50, the letter omega was both the letter "o" and the number 800 and so on. The numeric value of both the Hebrew "n" and the Greek "n" was 50.

What is interesting here is not only that Nero can be encoded as 666, but rather *how* the name of the emperor in its Greek spelling, Neron Caesar, is encoded. If "Nero" is encoded directly from the Greek, the number is (50 + 5 + 100 + 800) = 955. If "Neron" is encoded directly from the Greek, the number would be fifty more. (50 +5 + 100 + 800 + **50**) = 1005. If "Nero" is encoded from the Hebrew "nrw," the number for "Nero" would be 256 and "nrwn" would be 50 more because of the additional letter "n." The total would be 306. The Hebrew language *has no vowels*.

A Jew of the first century would know the Greek spelling of the name of the Roman emperor since it was imprinted on the Neronian coins of the era and bore the inscription: ΝΕΡΩΝ ΚΑΙΣΑΡ (transliterated as *NERON KAISER*). He would also know its Hebrew spelling. To arrive at the correct solution, the Greek spelling of Nero Caesar (*Neron Kaisar*) would first be transliterated into Hebrew by the person trying to solve the puzzle. He needs to begin with נרון קסר (*nrwn qsr*). It is *only* when a person, trying to solve the puzzle, starts with the Hebrew letters that the numeration totals give the desired result. If we start with the Greek letters, as we saw above, we will not arrive at 666. However, "nrwn" which is (50 + 200 +6 +50) plus "qsr" which is (100 + 60 + 200) gives a total of 666. (50 + 200 + 6 + 50) + (100 + 60 + 200) = 666.

A Roman who lived during the time of Nero and who understood the Greek but not Hebrew, would not likely be able make the proper decoding. It would, in fact, be impossible, unless he knew the Hebrew letters that were the starting point for solving the puzzle. So, 666 is the encoding of Nero in Hebrew while the book of Revelation was written in Greek. This is a very simple, but effective, method of double encoding that would baffle someone not knowing the correct starting point. There is a change of alphabet via transliteration AND a conversion of each transliterated Hebrew letter to a numerical value. The resulting values must then be added. There is some degree of complexity when attempting to solve the riddle. However, it is also a matter of knowing that one must start with the Hebrew transliteration of Neron Kaisar.

As mentioned above, a Jew living at the time of Nero would only have to look at a Roman provincial coin to see an image of Nero's face. To a large degree, Roman coinage is specific to a geographical area, and its inscriptions changed over time, depending who the local ruler was and who was in charge in Rome. According to the Roman Provincial Coinage Project at the University of Oxford, these coinages [RPC] were struck for use in a single province that was probably under Roman provincial or imperial control.[201]

Minting of provincial coinage was not only dependent on who was in power, but also on the popularity of a specific event or person a coin was minted to commemorate. Once a particular official fell into disgrace, a new coin would be minted. An event important to the Roman empire would also prompt the minting of a new coin.

One particular Neronian Roman coin shows Agrippina (Nero's mother) facing Nero. The coin is Neronian. Agrippina had the power when Nero was young, and that power is reflected on the coin. However, once Nero no longer wanted to listen to his mother, he had her killed and that coin was no longer minted.

A new coin, celebrating Nero's first wife, Octavia, was no longer minted after Nero divorced her and then had her beheaded in AD 62. Nero sent the head of Octavia to Poppaea Sabina, with whom he was having an affair. He married Poppaea twelve days later. Tacitus tells us that Octavia was a virtuous wife. A new coin was minted in honor of Poppaea. A link to a JPEG of a Nero and Poppaea Billion Tetradrachm of Alexandria minted in AD 64/65 is given in the footnote below.[202]

Poppaea, while she was with child, quarreled with Nero over his spending too much time at the chariot races. Nero responded by kicking her in the abdomen. Poppaea died from the injury. Suetonius claims Nero kicked her in a "fit of rage" while Tacitus says that Nero's kick was a "casual outburst." There was a coin of her minted posthumously in AD 65.

Provincial coinage was of lower quality than imperial coinage and tended to be minted for shorter periods of time. For this reason, however, they are important historically for dating purposes.

---

[201] Roman Provincial Coinage Online, University of Oxford, rpc.ashmus.ox.ac.uk/intro/whatisrpc/.

[202] Wildwinds, http://wildwinds.com/coins/sear5/s2002.html#milne_223

See page v of this book for a photo, from my personal collection, of a bronze quarter denomination coin that was common in Judea from 63 AD to 68 AD. The spelling on the coin for the name of the emperor is NERON KAIZAR (English transliteration from the Greek letters).

The obverse of the coin reads ΝΕΡΩΝ ΚΑΙΣΑΡ ΣΕΒΣΤΟΣ. Hendin notes this type of coin was struck in three different denominations. According to Gentry, the book of Revelation was written in the mid-sixties. The three denominations of the coin were minted in the mid-sixties.

There is also the provincial coinage in Syria where Nero's name was imprinted as "Neron" as shown in the Judean coin referenced above. We see, for example, the "NERON KAISAR SEBASTOS" spelling. This coin is a Silver Tetradrachm of Nero, minted in Antioch, AD 61 - 63.[203]

Note that the coinage mentioned above is Roman Provincial Coinage (RPC). Provincial bronze coinage was exclusive to the province where it was minted. Imperial coinage, on the other hand, was usually imprinted with "Nero Caesar" in Latin letters. If the starting name for the calculation were the Latin, "Nero," rather than the Greek, "Neron," then the result of the algorithm would give a number that is fifty less.

A strong piece of evidence showing that the calculation starting with the Hebrew is the correct method, is that there is a well-known textual variant that shows the number as 616, rather than 666. The number is 50 less than 666. This variant is listed as a footnote in the RSV version quoted above. The transliteration of the Latin name Nero Caesar into Hebrew would be "nrw qsr." The "n" is missing. $(50 + 200 + 6) + (100 + 60 + 200) = 616$. A fragment from *the oldest* surviving copy of the New Testament has the number of the Beast of Revelation 13 as 616.[204]

---

[203] Mantis, http://numismatics.org/collection/1956.127.2284. RPC 1.4185.
[204] Joe Kovacs, World Net Daily, "666 Wrong Number of Prophetic Beast?"

As noted by Kenneth Gentry, the reason the variant exists seems to be that a scribe in the first century who knew the solution to the puzzle was a Latin copiest who may have been more familiar with the later "Nero Kaiser" rendering of Nero's name.[205] The solution in the mind of the copiest would begin with the Latin version of name. This would transliterate into the Hebrew as "nrw qst" which would give the result of 616. He then began to change to 616 in his copies, believing that 666 was an incorrect result of the computation. The point is, the existence of the variant implies that the scribes knew that the Beast of Revelation was Nero. If it turns out at some future date that the original number written by John was 616, the opposite argument could be applied. The existence of the variant implies that the scribes believed that Nero was the Beast.

The existence of the variant seemed to baffle Irenaeus more than a hundred years later. He seemed unaware of the solution. There is, however, some recent research by Francis Gumerlock which indicates that Irenaeus was aware of a solution of to the puzzle. Although the solution was arrived at by a different calculation, the solution known to Irenaeus was the name "Nero." We will consider this research at the end of this chapter.

Irenaeus wrote:

> this number [666] being *found* in all the most approved ancient copies. . . . I do not know how it is that some have erred following the ordinary mode of speech, and vitiated the middle number [L] in the name, deducting the amount of fifty from it, so that instead of six decads they will have it that there is but one.[206]

World Net Daily, http://www.wnd.com/2005/05/30211/ (accessed April 11, 2016).

[205] Kenneth L. Gentry, Jr., Kenneth. *Perilous Times* (Texarkana, AZ: Covenant Media Press, 1999), 128.

[206] Philip Schaff, ed., *ANF01. The Apostolic Fathers with Justin Martyr and Irenaeus* (Reprinted Grand Rapids, MI: Christian Classics Ethereal Library), 1374.

What today is the most widely accepted solution was first published by C.F.A. Fritzsche in the "Annalen der gesammten theol. Liter., I. 3. Leipzig" in the year 1831.[207] There were four other German rationalists who simultaneously came up with the same solution. To me, as a teacher of mathematics, it is not surprising that it took this long for the solution to be rediscovered, although Gumerlock convincingly argues a solution was known to Irenaeus. The solution to the puzzle, like many other mathematical puzzles, is easy to see in hindsight, *once* the solution is arrived at.

There is an important issue concerning the dating of the book of Revelation centering around the words, "approved ancient copies," in the above quote from Irenaeus. To consider this issue we will digress momentarily from the solution of the puzzle to the dating of Revelation.

It seems it was a matter of dispute as to which of the two numbers 616 or 666 was the correct number. To resolve the dispute, an appeal had to be made to the "most approved ancient copies."

If the book of Revelation was written almost in his time, then it seems that it should not be necessary to appeal to "ancient copies" to resolve the dispute. Since an appeal was made to ancient copies, we need to ask some questions. How old were the ancient copies as opposed to the copies in use?

These copies, however, are still not the originals. How old are the original letters John wrote? Gentry argues that "ancient copies" implies several generations as the book of Revelation had to be repeatedly copied and distributed through a number of cycles of scribes.[208] However, just a couple of paragraphs later, as written in the standard rendering of Irenaeus, "[the vision] was seen by John almost in his own time."

So what was it? Was the vision recently seen almost in his own

---

[207] Philip Schaff and David Schaff, *History of the Christian Church*, Vol. 1 (New York: Charles Scribner's Sons, 1910), 846.

[208] Gentry, op. cit., 58-59.

time or were there ancient copies of the book of Revelation that could be appealed to?

Irenaeus knew that the solution to the 666 puzzle involved gematria. However, he was unaware that one must start with the value of the Hebrew letters. Irenaeus, when searching for a solution to the puzzle with only the value of the Greek letters, came up with three candidates: "Evanthas," "Latenios," and "Teitan" with the most likely being "Teitan." The point is, Irenaeus knew there was a computation involved. There is one final piece of evidence that a Hebrew transliteration is the correct approach to the puzzle.

We notice another use of gematria combined with a Hebrew transliteration which at the same time identifies Nero with the Beast in Chapter 13 of Revelation.

The name for the Beast given in Chapter 13 of Revelation is directly linked to the Beast from the sea. The Greek word for beast (*therion*), transliterated in Hebrew letters (*trywn*), also adds up to 666. Nero is the face of the Beast that claimed lordship. His face is also on Roman coins.

There have been two primary objections to identifying 666 with the name of Nero. The first is that the identification of Nero seems to be unknown to the early church fathers. Until recently no modern author that I am aware of has claimed that Irenaeus made any identification of 666 with the name of Nero. No "idealist" writer does so. William Hendricksen does not, Riddlebarger does not, and Beal does not.[209] Certainly no dispensational writer does so. Gentry does not. No preterist author that I am aware of does so. Then in 2006, Gumerlock wrote his insightful article in the *Westminster Theological Journal* in which he argues that Irenaeus knew the name "Nero" was identified by some as the solution behind the "spurious" number

---

[209] G. K. Beale, *The Book of Revelation (The New International Greek Testament Commentary)* [Grand Rapids, MI: Wm. B. Eerdmans Publishing Co., Reprint edition (1999), 2013], 20.

616.[210] Irenaeus, it seems, knew that the name "Nero" was a solution to the puzzle.

The first commentator to write on the meaning of 666 in the book of Revelation was Irenaeus. We noted above that a fragment of *the oldest* surviving copy of the New Testament gives the number of the Beast of Revelation 13 as 616. This fragment discovered at the Egyptian city of Oxyrhynchus is dated to about AD 300.[211]

According to Ellen Aitken, a professor of early Christian history at McGill University, "scholars have argued for a long time over this, and it now seems that 616 was the original number of the beast."[212] In other words, it can be *argued* that 616 was the original number and not 666. The 616/666 dispute in the time of Irenaeus was no small dispute.

According to Daniel B. Wallace, Executive Director of the Center for the Study of New Testament Manuscripts:

> It may well have been Irenaeus' input that caused scribes to alter the text to 666 if 616 was in the exemplar that they used. But the point here is that one cannot simply appeal to the earliest manuscript and assume that the case is settled.[213]

David Parker, professor of New Testament Criticism and Paleography at the University of Birmingham in England, "points out

---

[210] Francis X. Gumerlock, "Nero Antichrist: Patristic Evidence for the use of Nero's Naming in Calculating the Number of the Beast (Rev 13:18)," *Westminster Theological Journal*, 68.2 (Fall 2006): 358.

[211] Joe Kovacs, World Net Daily, "666 Wrong Number of Prophetic Beast?" World Net Daily, http://www.wnd.com/2005/05/30211/ (accessed April 11, 2016).

[212] Ibid.

[213] Religion News Blog, "Daniel B. Wallace responds to article on 'the number of the Beast,'" Religion News Blog, http://www.religionnewsblog.com/11139/daniel-b-wallace-responds-to-article-on-the-number-of-the-beast (accessed April 10, 2016).

the possibility that 616 was considered by the second century church father Irenaeus who rejected it."²¹⁴

The 616 number appeared to have been circulated widely enough to make an appeal to ancient copies necessary in order to resolve the dispute. Gumerlock gives us historical evidence in the *Liber* that there were portions of the early church that accepted 616 as the correct number and rejected 666.

Francis Gumerlock gives a translation of paragraphs 614 - 620 of the AD 438 version of the *Liber genealogus* (*Book of Genealogy*) which uses the letters of Nero's name in calculating the number of the Beast. The *Liber genealogus*, Gumerlock explains, is a chronology written in Latin by an unknown African Donatist. The first version was written in AD 405, and there are four slightly different versions written in the years 427, 438, 455, and 463. The Liber lists persons and events in chronological order from Adam and Eve to the fifth century of the Christian era and makes use of the genealogies in the OT and the genealogies in Matthew and Luke. In addition, the Liber makes use of lists of Persian and Roman kings, dictators, and emperors. Some of the other sources identified by Gumerlock include the Chronicle of Hippolytus and a recension of Victorinus's Commentary on Revelation.²¹⁵

What is of interest is that in this same section of paragraphs that shows solutions from a recension of Victorinus, we also see the solution that gives 616 calculated from the name "Nero." This seems to be the only known patristic writing which equates the name of Nero to 616. Gumerlock tells us that "as far as contemporary scholarship stands, no patristic texts, not even the twenty or so patristic commentaries on Revelation, extant in whole or in fragments, suggest the name of Nero for identifying the number of the Beast."²¹⁶ This immediately brings to mind the 616/666 dispute in the time of

---

²¹⁴ Ibid.
²¹⁵ Gumerlock, op. cit., 350.
²¹⁶ Ibid., 349.

Irenaeus. In paragraph 615 we notice that the copy of Revelation used by the author of the *Liber* contains the number 616 rather than 666.[217]

Although the calculation is different than what today is believed to be the correct solution, the method may be considered by those who see Nero as the Beast to be a vestige of an earlier method. The author of the Liber considers 'Nero' to be the correct solution and *outright rejects all solutions that calculate to give the number 666*. He also claims to have an ancient source that gave the "superior way of thinking."[218] Another known vestige noted by Gumerlock is "the seventh or eighth-century *Commemoratorium de Apocalypsi Johannis Apostoli*. Commenting on Rev 13:18, it says, 'The number of his name is understood according to the Hebrew language' (CCSL 107:221)."[219]

Irenaeus viewed the versions of Revelation using 616 instead of 666 as corrupted with an "erroneous and spurious number." Gumerlock argues that since Irenaeus informs us that some found a name "hit upon by themselves" of "him who is to come," Irenaeus knew exactly what that name was.

One reason for Irenaeus not revealing this name may be that he believed that the name was based on a corrupted number. Another is that Irenaeus does not favor an interpretation that favors a Roman emperor. Irenaeus did, however, know this name arrived at by these Christians that used the 616 number. Gumerlock gives a strong argument that it is "*likely* that Irenaeus knew exactly what that name was."[220] It seems to be more than a coincidence that the Donatist author not only utilizes a calculation that links the number of the Beast to Nero but in addition utilizes the 616 number which was the center of the dispute.

Another objection to identifying the name of Nero with 666, as noted by Greg Beale, is that one must start out with a "defective

---

[217] Ibid., 359.
[218] Ibid., 359.
[219] Ibid., 359.
[220] Ibid., 358.

Hebrew spelling of qsr without a *yodh* after the *qoph*, a spelling that some argue is attested to in one of the Judean scrolls and in the Talmud . . . Jastrow gave examples only of spellings with the *yodh*"[221]. In other words, the punctuation is incorrect.

However, argues Bauckham, the fact the Greek word for beast as shown above also yields 666 gives us a reason for the defective spelling.

Bauckham contends:

> As Peake pointed out, the abnormal spelling could be accepted if we assume that John had some other reason for wanting the sum to come to 666 . . . . But, in fact, that the defective spelling was used for Nero himself has now been shown by a papyrus document in Aramaic from Murabba'at, which is dated in the second year of Nero Caesar.[222]

The reason is that the word for beast, as noted above, also adds up to 666. John, contends Bauckham, is employing an isopsephism. There is a numeric equality between the two words. Isopsephisms are used not only in Roman gematria, but in Jewish exegesis as well.[223]

Bauckham concludes, "The gematria does not merely assert that Nero is the Beast: it demonstrates that he is."[224]

Nero represented corporate Rome. John tells us that the Beast would suffer a mortal wound but would then recover. We know that Revolution broke out against Rome in various places in the empire. As the revolts spread throughout the empire, the Jews started their own rebellion in AD 66. The Jews achieved some early victories against the Romans, and Nero had to dispatch Vespasian, Rome's best General, in the spring of AD 67. Vespasian employed a scorched earth policy, putting down all opposition on the way to Jerusalem.

---

[221] Beale, op. cit., 719.
[222] Richard Bauckham, *The Climax of Prophecy: Studies on the Book of Revelation* (Edinburgh: T. & T. Clark, 1993), 388.
[223] Ibid., 386.
[224] Bauckham, op. cit., 389.

With Judea in ruins, Vespasian encircled Jerusalem. However, during the siege of Jerusalem, Nero committed suicide and Rome went into further turmoil. There was a series of short-lived emperors and a year of civil war.

As reported by Tacitus:

> I am entering on the history of a period rich in disasters, frightful in its wars, torn by civil strife, and even in peace full of horrors. Four emperors perished by the sword. There were three civil wars; there were more with foreign enemies; there were often wars that had both characters at once.[225]

In AD 69 Rome was on the verge of collapse. The Roman legions of Egypt declared Vespasian the Emperor on July first, and those in Judea on July third. Vespasian left the siege of Jerusalem in the hands of his son Titus. Vespasian's troops took Rome on December 20 of AD 70, and on the twenty-first of December, full powers were conferred on him.[226]

In AD 70, Rome minted a new bronze coin. It shows Vespasian helping the goddess Roma, who represents corporate Rome, back to her feet.[227] John's prophecy came true. Nero was the Beast who was the face of the Roman Empire. The Roman Empire survived a mortal wound when Nero committed suicide. Vespasian was the new resurrected face of the Beast. The corporate beast is itself "an eighth."

---

[225] Cornelius Tacitus, *The History of Tacitus*, trans. Alfred John Church and William Jackson Brodribb (London: Macmillan and Co., 1873), 1.

[226] Barbara Levick, *Vespasian*, (London: Routledge, 1999), 15.

[227] Ibid., 191. Plate 16 Obv. Vespasian laureate. Rev. Vespasian extending hand to raise kneeling Roma; behind, Minerva; ROMA RESVRGE(N)S S.C.: 'Rome rising again'. (Aes, Rome, 70). The Ashmolean Museum, by permission of the Visitors.

Chapter 12
NERO REDIVIVUS

A primary reason that the majority of scholars today opt for the late date for the authorship of Revelation is the Nero redivivus myth. The myth began with rumors that Nero came back to life and was temporarily in hiding after his suicide in June of AD 68.

The logic traditionally used is that Revelation is written to a Church in crisis because of persecution. Nero and Domitian are the two candidates for the persecutor. The Nero redivivus myth rules out Nero as a candidate. Therefore, the Revelation was written during the reign of Domitian.[228]

The prevailing framework utilized when interpreting Revelation is that the author of Revelation was aware of this myth and based his symbolism of the Beast upon it. Even most preterist scholars date the book to AD 69, just after the suicide of Nero. The notable exceptions are Kenneth Gentry, R.C. Sproul, and possibly Keith Mathison. They believe that what is recorded in Revelation is not only a prophecy of the suicide of Nero, but in addition, is a prophecy of the subsequent recovery of the Roman empire from the wound of Nero's suicide. I will defend the point of view that what we see in the book of Revelation 13 and Revelation 17 is prophecy that was shortly to be fulfilled.

We will consider the origin of the *redivivus* myth and its development in history. We will note references to the myth in the Sybilline books as well as in Apocalyptic literature and then compare these extra-biblical sources to Scripture and note more than one inconsistency if the time frames are equivalent. We will consider Gentry's interpretation of Revelation 13 and 17 where the mortal wound of the Beast was healed.

---

[228] Keith Mathison, *From Age to Age, The Unfolding of Biblical Eschatology* (Phillipsburg, N.J: P & R Pub. Co., 2009), 644.

The groundwork for the rapid spread of the redivivus myth was laid even before Nero committed suicide by his own sword.

Suetonius tells us that:

> Astrologers had predicted to Nero that he would one day be repudiated. ... Some of them, however, had promised him the rule in the East, when he was cast off, a few expressly naming the sovereignty of Jerusalem, and several the restitution of all his former fortunes.[229]

Certain aspects of what were to become the myth apparently were widespread well before Nero committed suicide in June of AD 68 and must have had an influence on its development. The seeds of the Nero Redivivus myth were "firmly planted early in his reign and well-watered by the deluge of tyranny that he unleashed in the later years of his reign."[230]

In the words of Suetonius:

> He [Nero] died in the thirty-second year of his age ... Some, however, were not wanting, who for a long time decked his tomb with spring and summer flowers. Sometimes they placed his image upon the rostra, dressed in robes of state; at another, they published proclamations in his name, as if he were still alive, and would shortly return to Rome, and take vengeance on all his enemies.[231]

Pretenders who took advantage of the developing myth were soon to appear. However, it was not only pretenders but emperors who did not object being called Nero. Otho followed Galba in the year of the four emperors. Suetonius attributes the following to Otho upon returning to his palace after presenting himself to the Senate:

---

[229] Kenneth L. Gentry, Jr., *Before Jerusalem Fell: Dating the Book of Revelation*, 3rd ed. (Fountain Inn, SC: Victorious Hope Publishing, 1998, 2010), 307.

[230] Ibid., 305.

[231] Suetonius, *The Lives of the Twelve Caesars: Nero*: 57.

When in the midst of the other adulations of those who congratulated and flattered him, he was hailed by the common herd as Nero, he made no sign of dissent; on the contrary, according to some writers, he even made use of that surname in his commissions and his first letters to some of the governors of the provinces.[232]

The same could be said of Vitellius. He "imitated [Nero] closely, and greatly pleased the public by offering sacrifices to Nero's spirit in the Campus Martius, making all the priests and people attend."[233] One could view Otho or Vitellius as living in the adulation of Nero. Each could be considered taking on the persona of Nero.

Assume for a moment that John utilized the Nero redivivus myth in his development of his symbol of the Beast. Also assume that John wrote *before* Nero committed suicide. We know that the "seeds" of the myth were very widespread before Nero's death, as repudiation of Nero was foretold by the Astrologers, and in addition, the myth was almost immediately utilized by the pretenders who were to follow. We could argue that these "seeds" would have been sufficient enough for John "- either as a knowledgeable citizen, but especially as an inspired prophet! - [to] have discerned such an early expectation in these as pre-indicators pointing his readers to the man Nero."[234] This is enough, says Gentry, to "render the *Nero redivivus* myth virtually useless as a tool to establish a late date for Revelation."[235]

At least three different look-alike pretenders attempted to take power over a twenty-year period. The third look-alike appeared about twenty years after the death of Nero, during the reign of Domitian about AD 88/89 when Suetonius was young. According to Suetonius, the look-alike received support from the Parthians. Suetonius continues:

---

[232] Gentry, op. cit., 308.
[233] Ibid., Gentry from Weigall's book, *Nero*.
[234] Ibid., 306.
[235] Ibid., 307.

Vologesus, king of the Parthians, when he sent ambassadors to the senate to renew his alliance with the Roman people, earnestly requested that due honour should be paid to the memory of Nero; and, to conclude, when, twenty years afterwards, at which time I was a young man, some person of obscure birth gave himself out for Nero, that name secured him so favourable a reception from the Parthians, that he was very zealously supported, and it was with much difficulty that they were prevailed upon to give him up.[236]

The second pretender appeared during the reign of Titus. In the notes of his *History* Tacitus records:

The armies of Parthia were all but set in motion by the fraud of a counterfeit Nero. Zonaras says, "In his reign (the reign of Titus), there appeared the false Nero, an Asiatic, whose name was Terentius Maximus. He resembled Nero in face and voice, and he was also a harp-player. He found some adherents in Asia Minor, and then, proceeding to the Euphrates, largely increased their number. At last he fled to Artibanus, king of the Parthians. This Prince, who had some cause of quarrel against Titus, received him, and made preparations for securing his return to Rome."[237]

The first false Nero appeared during the brief reign of Galba and was probably the most troublesome. About the time Vespasian and Mucianus were joining forces in the East, the report spread that a man appeared in form and face in likenesses to Nero and was also a musician, as was Nero. He was both a singer and lyre-player. His name was unknown. The imposter attracted an army of deserters and put to sea.

Pappano first cites the ancient historian Zonaras and then adds a comment:

---

[236] Suetonius, *The Lives of the Twelve Caesars: Nero*:5.
[237] Cornelius Tacitus, *The History of Tacitus*, Notes on Book I, trans. Alfred J. Church and William J. Brodribb (London: Macmillan and Co., 1873), 210.

"that after causing a disturbance throughout Greece he set sail with his followers for the military stations in Syria. Syria had been since the beginning of the Empire the most strongly garrisoned and most important of the eastern provinces." Thus the control of its military forces meant control of the entire East, a long step toward the purple. Viewed in this light, Zonaras' account fits logically into the story and may be accepted as probable at least. Relentless storm-winds, however, made the final decision and carried the expedition to the island of Cythnus.[238]

This "Nero" recruited a number of unskilled troops at this island. However, Calpurnius Asprena, who was assigned the provinces of Galatia and Pamphylia by Galba, was en route to the provinces with an escort from the fleet and put into port at Cythnus. The pretender happened to be there. Calpurnius stormed his ship and he was killed. The body of the pretender was sent to Asia and then to Rome. "Everywhere the corpse excited wonder by some unexplained quality of eyes and hair - probably their resemblance to those of the real Nero - and a certain '*torvitas vultus.*' "[239]

It did not take long for the rumor spread that Nero had come back to life to take vengeance on his enemies.

It took years for the Nero redivivus myth to dissipate. This rumor is considered by many to be a source for the following passage written by John in Revelation 13:1, 3, 12, 14b:

> And I saw a beast rising out of the sea, with ten horns and seven heads, One of its heads seemed to have a mortal wound, but its mortal wound was healed, and the whole earth marveled as they followed the beast . . . . It [the land beast] exercises all the authority of the first beast in its presence, and makes the earth and its inhabitants worship the first beast,

---

[238] Albert Earl Pappano, "The False Neros," *The Classical Journal* 32, no. 7 (Apr., 1937): 388.

[239] Ibid, 389. "Torvitas vultus" or "Fiercensss of gaze;" Pappano cites Henderson as seeing this quality in the extant busts of Nero.

whose mortal wound was healed . . . . telling them to make an image for the beast that was wounded by the sword and yet lived.

In other words, it is believed that after the suicide of Nero, the author of Revelation used the Nero redivivus myth as a basis for this symbolism in Revelation. If the symbolism was based on the Nero redivivus myth, then the earliest the book of Revelation could have been written would be after the suicide of Nero.

Smalley, for example, suggests that "the book emerged just before the fall of Jerusalem to Titus."[240] However, most scholars take the point of view that even a later date would be more appropriate as they see a gradual development of the Nero redivivus myth in Revelation. This historical approach to Revelation was developed by Wilhelm Bousset in the late 1890s.

The major work of Wilhelm Bousset was *A History of the Belief in Christ from the Beginnings of Christianity to Irenaeus*. The introduction to the fifth edition of his book contains an introduction by Rudolph Bultmann. Bultmann gives credit to Bousset for his own understanding of the literature of the New Testament by comparing early Christianity with other religions. Bousset published his commentary on Revelation, *Die Offenbarung Johannis*, in the late 1890s.[241]

Bousset claims that the origin of the Antichrist in the book of Revelation is to be found in the dragon of Babylonian mythology. The woman of Revelation 12 is close to the iconography of Isis, the "mistress of heaven." Bousset contends that the author of Revelation sees the church of his own time in a mortal struggle with the Roman Empire, the Beast, Satan incarnate. Domitian, according to Bousset is Nero redivivus, the Antichrist.

---

[240] Steven S. Smalley, *The Revelation of John: A Commentary on the Greek Text of the Apocalypse* (Downers Grove, IL: InterVarsity Press, 2005), 3.

[241] William Baird, *History of New Testament Research, Vol. Two: From Jonathan Edwards to Rudolf Bultmann*. (Minneapolis: Augsburg Fortress Press, 2003), 248.

Bousset gives an account of the gradual development of the *Nero redivivus* myth that he sees in the book of Revelation. Nero, Bousset argues, was not immediately thought of as the Antichrist but only as Nero in league with the Parthians for the overthrow of Rome. The Christian redactor (the editor of the sources) then advances a stage - Nero becomes the Antichrist. By comparing the Sybilline books, we can see that this change did not emerge until the end of the first century.

There are two beasts. One is the "beast from the sea," and the other is the Beast from the land of Palestine. They are in league together against Christ. The references to the worship of the images of the Beast possibly came from some false prophet who encouraged the Jews to tolerate the worship of the emperors. *The book of Revelation, after the section on the seven vials, is the Jewish Apocalypse, which pictured the overthrow of Rome by Nero redivivus and the Parthians*, the supernatural birth of the Messiah, and his reservation in heaven until the time comes for him to appear in the clouds.[242]

The parallels to the Sybilline book five show, Bousset argues, that portions of the book of Revelation should be dated to a time period in the AD 90s. In addition to the Sybilline books, Jewish Apocalyptic literature also includes the books of *4 Ezra* and *2 Baruch*. Both *4 Ezra* and *2 Baruch* are non-historical (historical fiction) books that were written after the fall of Jerusalem in AD 70.

Despite the historical parallels, however, the description of the wounded head of the Beast and the recovery given in Revelation 13 are not compatible with the *Nero redivivus* myth. As noted by Minear, the *Nero redivivus* myth itself does not show a strengthened Roman Empire when the mortal blow was healed. It was just the opposite.

Now there is little evidence that the rumored resuscitation of Nero actually had any such effects. It did not induce either Roman citizens or

---

[242] J. H Wilkinson, "Bousset's Die Offenbarung Johannis," *The Critical Review of Theological and Philosophical Literature*, Vol. 8 (1898): 301-05.

Christians "to follow the beast with wonder." It did not enhance the seductive worship of the dragon, nor did it aid the dragon in his deadly war against the saints. In fact, the legend of Nero's pending return from Parthia was considered a threat to the empire and the line of emperors.[243]

In addition, the Nero redivivus myth went through several stages and took time to develop. In the literature in which the myth is developed, the *temple was already destroyed*. Books four and five of the Sibylline oracles contain material predicting the return of Nero and condemning Rome for destroying the temple.

Two of the central oracles show that the fifth Sibylline Oracle was composed shortly after the destruction of Jerusalem. Collins states that:

> the bitterness of complaint about the temple and the deeply pessimistic character of the book suggest that at least the central oracles, contained in vss 52 - 100, 111 - 178, 179 - 285, and 286 - 434, were written not long after the destruction of the temples both of Jerusalem and of Leontopolis.[244]

The books of *4 Ezra* and *2 Baruch* were written during the same period of time as the Sibylline Oracles. The destruction of the temple is also the subject of both books. *4 Ezra* contains a series of visions where Ezra carries on a dialogue with an angel. The books are a type of historical fiction. *4 Ezra* begins with the mourning over the destruction of Jerusalem and the pollution of the holy vessels while the later chapter details the fate of the Roman Empire. *2 Baruch* is similar. Baruch, the scribe of Jeremiah, also uses the Babylonian

---

[243] Paul S. Minear, "The Wounded Beast", *The Journal of Biblical Literature*, 72.2 (June 1953): 97.

[244] John J. Collins, *Sibylline Oracles of Egyptian Judaism* (Missoula, Montana: Society of Biblical Literature and Scholars' Press for the Pseudepigrapha Group. Dissertation Series, Number 13., 1974), 94.

captivity as its background and refers to the destruction of Jerusalem. In both accounts the destruction of Rome is prophesied.

Nero committed suicide in June of AD 68, the first pretender did not appear until AD 69, and Jerusalem fell in AD 70. Based on these dates there would be little time for the myth to develop before the fall of Jerusalem. In the Sybilline oracles, in 4 Ezra, and in 2 Baruch, the Nero redivivus myth is presented with a backdrop of Jerusalem's fall. However, in the book of Revelation, the *temple is described as still standing*. Not only is the temple still standing, Nero is the Beast.

With the temple described as still standing and Nero described as the Beast, it is more likely that what John is writing in the book of Revelation is a prophecy that Nero, the first great persecutor of the early church, will be slain by the sword.

Gentry notes that the manner of Nero's death corresponds with the prophecy of Revelation 13:10, 14 (NASB):[245]

> If anyone is destined for captivity, to captivity he goes, if any one kills with the sword, with the sword he must be killed. Here is the perseverance and the faith of the saints.
>
> And he deceives those who dwell on the earth because of the signs which it was given him to perform in the presence of the beast telling those who dwell on the earth to make an image to the beast who had the wound of the sword and has come to life.

Gentry continues:

> In the context of speaking of the beast, John gives encouragement to those whom the beast was presently afflicting. "Here is the perseverance and faith of the saints," i.e., that the beast who slays by the sword would also be slain by the sword.[246]

---

[245] Gentry, op. cit., 217-18.
[246] Ibid., 218.

Just as Christ prophesied the destruction of the temple within a generation in the Olivet Discourse, the mighty angel gave a vision in Revelation to John that prophesied the suicide of Nero, with dark days ahead for Rome, and its temporary recovery. The Beast who slays by the sword would also be slain by the sword. "But its mortal wound was healed, and the whole earth marveled as they followed the beast."

Nero died. Rome was resurrected through Vespasian. However, it was the corporate beast which had received the mortal wound. It was the corporate beast that was resurrected. With Rome on the verge of collapse, Vespasian brought Rome, the corporate beast, back to life.

Gentry brings the following parallels to our attention in Revelation 17:8 and 17:11.[247]

Revelation 17:8	Revelation 17:11
The beast that was and is not is about to come up out of the abyss to go to destruction	The beast that was and is not is himself an eighth and he goes to destruction

Gentry points out that it is the corporate beast itself that is "an eighth," that is resurrected, and that represents the remaining Roman emperors. Christ was resurrected on the eighth day. The Satanic corporate beast mimics Christ's death and resurrection.

Ultimately, it is not Domitian, *Nero redivivus*, who goes to destruction, it is corporate Rome itself.

---

[247] Ibid., 302.

Chapter 13
THE TEN KINGS AND LOCAL PERSECUTION

And the ten horns that you saw are ten kings who have not yet received royal power, but they are to receive authority as kings for one hour, together with the beast. These are of one mind, and they hand over their power and authority to the beast . . . They will make war on the Lamb, and the lamb will conquer them . . . . they and the beast will hate the prostitute. They will make her desolate and naked, and devour her flesh and burn her up with fire, for God has put it into their hearts to carry out his purpose by being of one mind and handing over their royal powers to the beast, until the words of God are fulfilled. And the woman that you saw is the great city that has dominion over the kings of the earth." (Revelation 17:12-18).

The ten kings will receive royal power and "give their power to the beast." In other words, they are local rulers that serve the Beast and are empowered to act on his behalf. They are the allies of the Beast. They are believed to be, according to Jay Adams[248] and other partial preterists, the local governors of the Provinces of Rome. These local governors controlled legions in their province, administered justice, and levied and collected taxes.

Greg Beale also recognizes that the ten kings represent local allies, although in the final battle of history:

"the ten horns ... ten kings" in 17:12 -14, all . . . refer to the allies of the beast in fighting against the Lamb and God in the final battle of history. Furthermore, the OT background of the image of "kings of

---

[248] Jay Adams, *The Time is at Hand* (Woodruff, SC: Timeless Texts, [1966], 2004), 78.

the earth committing immorality" with the whore (cf. 17:2, 18:3, 9) also has them turning against her and destroying her.[249]

James Stuart Russell believed that the ten kings are commanders of local allies of Vespasian. These allies could be local rulers like Agrippa II or local military commanders. He believed the number ten to be a symbolic number.

This symbol, says Russell:

> ... signifies the auxiliary princes and chiefs who were allies of Rome and received commands in the Roman army during the Jewish war. We know from Tacitus and Josephus that several kings of neighbouring nations followed Vespasian and Titus to the war. Allusion has already been made to some of these auxiliaries: Antiochus, Sohemus, Agrippa, and Malchus. There were no doubt others, but it is not incumbent to produce the exact number of ten, which, like seven, appears to be a mystic or symbolic number.[250]

It is interesting that we have both Agrippa[251] from Judea and the Arabs giving their support to Vespasian and Titus.

> He [Titus] found in Judaea three legions, the 5th, the 10th, and the 15th, all old troops of Vespasian's. To these he added the 12th from Syria, and some men belonging to the 18th and 3rd, whom he had withdrawn from Alexandria. This force was accompanied by twenty cohorts of allied troops and eight squadrons of cavalry, by the two kings Agrippa and Sohemus, by the auxiliary forces of king Antiochus, by a strong

---

[249] G. K. Beale, *The Book of Revelation (The New International Greek Testament Commentary)* [Grand Rapids, MI: Wm. B. Eerdmans Publishing Co., Reprint edition (1999), 2013], 878.

[250] James S. Russell, *The Parousia: A Critical Inquiry into the New Testament Doctrine of Our Lord's Second Coming* (London: Daldy, Isbister [1878], 2008), 502.

[251] See Appendix F for more on Agrippa II.

contingent of Arabs, who hated the Jews with the usual hatred of neighbours.[252]

Although I believe that Russell is likely correct in interpreting the number ten as symbolic, it is interesting to note that there were ten senatorial provinces[253] when Caesar Augustus changed the republic into a monarchy and reorganized the government in AD 14 when John was about eight years old.

One interpretation would be that the senatorial governors are *representative of the local power* of Rome but are also symbolic on a wider scale. The persecution of Christians began locally in Judea with the Jews in league with the local Roman authorities and then spread throughout Asia Minor as the Word of God spread.

We read in Acts 13:47-50:

> For so the Lord has commanded us, saying, "I have made you a light for the Gentiles, that you may bring salvation to the ends of the earth." And when the Gentiles heard this, they began rejoicing and glorifying the word of the Lord, and as many as were appointed to eternal life believed. And the word of the Lord was spreading throughout the whole region. But the Jews incited the devout women of high standing and the leading men of the city, stirred up persecution against Paul and Barnabas, and drove them out of their district.

"They will make war on the Lamb." Persecution followed Christians from Judea all the way to Rome. It is possible that John literally had the local governors in mind when he wrote about the ten kings in Revelation.

---

[252] Cornelius Tacitus, *The History of Tacitus,*. trans. Alfred J. Church and William J. Brodribb. (London: Macmillan and Co., 1873), Book V. Ch. 1, 210.

[253] See Appendix D for more information on the ten provinces and the literal interpretation of the ten kings of Revelation.

The local governors were not, early on, aware of the differences between Christianity and the Jewish religion and initially treated Christians as a Jewish sect. The governors of Judea who were appointed by the Roman senate were in a political working environment with local Jewish leadership and at first aided the Jews in persecuting the Christians simply as a favor which was expected to be returned.

The Jewish Levitical leadership is the prostitute of Revelation who tried to manipulate Rome. The primary example from Scripture is the crucifixion of Jesus. However, in the end, Rome directly persecuted Christians and turned on the Jews when it was clear that the Jews were rebelling against the Empire.

One of the religious customs was the cult of Emperor worship, which was a grass roots movement dating all the way back to Alexander the Great, who received divine honors as did his Ptolemaic successors. This was continued under Julius Caesar. Thomas Slater writes:

> The Roman imperial cult began in Asia in the first century BCE. Dio Cassius writes that early in Augustus's principate Roman citizens in Asia were required to worship Julius Caesar and the goddess Roma, while the provincials were required to worship Augustus and the goddess Roma.[254]

The imperial cult was practiced throughout Asia and in most eastern regions of the Roman Empire. Cities competed for the privilege of being declared *neokoros,* an official center for the imperial cult, by the senate and the emperor. Ephesus had a cult to Roma and Julius Caesar and later added a temple to Tiberius.

An Ephesian coin from the reign of Nero depicts Nero on the observe. The reverse of the coin portrays the proconsul of Asia along

---

[254] Thomas B. Slater, "On the Social Setting of the Revelation to John," *New Testament Studies*, Vol. 44, Issue 02 (April, 1998): 252.

with a temple, with four columns in front and six on the side, bearing the words "of the neokorate Ephesians." The coin is dated to AD 65/66 because the image on the reverse was of the proconsul Marcilius Acilius Aviola, who was in service at that time.[255]

Christians who denied these local religious traditions were an affront to the pagan Asian social community. The persecution by the imperial cult was a localized persecution throughout Asia with ties to the local governors.

The ten kings not only aligned themselves militarily with Rome, they persecuted the Christians locally and ultimately turned on the harlot.

---

[255] Steven J. Friesen, *Twice Neokoros: Ephesus, Asia, and the Cult of the Flavian Imperial Family* (Leiden: Brill Academic, 1993), 53.

Chapter 14
THE TEMPLE WAS CLEARLY STANDING

Then I was given a measuring rod like a staff, and I was told, "Rise and measure the temple of God and the altar and those who worship there, but do not measure the court outside the temple; leave that out, for it is given over to the nations, and they will trample the holy city for forty-two months. And I will grant authority to my two witnesses, and they will prophesy for 1,260 days, clothed in sackcloth." (Revelation 11: 1-3).
…and their dead bodies will lie in the street of the great city that symbolically is called Sodom and Egypt, **where their Lord was crucified** (Revelation 11:8).

Gentry first notes that the events of Revelation 11:8 take place in the holy city. We can identify the holy city as Jerusalem, since we see in verse eight of the same section that it is the city where Jesus was crucified. It is critical to note here that the great city where the Lord was crucified is a geographically symbolic location pointing to what once was a holy city.

Because the Jews rejected Jesus, says Gentry,

through spiritual metamorphosis the once "holy city" has been transformed into an unholy "Egypt" and "Sodom."[256]

"Egypt" and "Sodom" are symbolic terms describing a *geographical* location. We know that the Herodian temple is located in Jerusalem, so the temple which is located in Jerusalem is still standing at this time.

---

[256] Kenneth L. Gentry, Jr., *Before Jerusalem Fell: Dating the Book of Revelation*, 3rd ed., (Fountain Inn, SC.: Victorious Hope Publishing, 1998, 2010), 170.

Gentry observes that there is a clear correspondence between Luke 21:24 and Revelation 11:2.[257]

Revelation 11:2 reads:

> but do not measure the court outside the temple; leave that out, for it is given over to the nations, and they will trample the holy city for forty-two months.

In Luke 21:24, Jesus predicted the fall of Jerusalem and its subsequent trampling and in Revelation 11:2 *that trampling still has not yet begun.* "They *will trample* the holy city for forty-two months." The temple is still clearly standing when John wrote the book of Revelation. Gentry states "Here the correspondences are so strong, they bespeak historical identity rather than mere accidental similarity."[258]

Gentry quotes five scholars whom all contend that Jerusalem was standing. One of the five, Fredrick Dusterdieck, states:

> It is sufficient for chronological interest, that prophecy depends upon the presupposition that the destruction of the Holy City had not yet occurred .... This testimony of the Apoc., which is completely indisputable to an unprejudiced mind, can still be misunderstood only with great difficulty.[259]

John A. T. Robinson in his groundbreaking book *Redating the New Testament* writes:

> One of the oddest facts about the New Testament is that what on any showing would appear to be the single most datable and climactic event of the period - the fall of Jerusalem in AD 70 - is never once mentioned

---

[257] Ibid., 176.
[258] Ibid., 176.
[259] Ibid., 165.

as a past fact . . . [T]he silence is nevertheless as significant as the silence for Sherlock Holmes of the dog that did not bark.[260]

There was no "striking silence" when we considered the *Nero Redivivus* myth and noted the mention by John Collins of the bitter complaint given in fifth Sibylline Oracle concerning the destruction of the temple. In the books of *4 Ezra* and *2 Baruch,* we noticed their mourning over the destruction of Jerusalem and the pollution of the holy vessels. In the book of Revelation, during the same purported time of authorship, the destruction of the temple is still future.

The Temple was clearly standing.

---

[260] Ibid., 166-167.

Chapter 15
OBJECTION FROM THE POINT OF VIEW THAT THE TEMPLE IS SYMBOLIC

Riddlebarger references Caird who contends that if John wrote the book of Revelation before the destruction of the Herodian temple, it would mean the armies of Titus, which occupied the outer court for three and a half years, must leave the inner court and altar undefiled per John's vision.[261]

Of course, this is not what happened historically. The temple was totally destroyed. John's metaphors of the outer court and the inner sanctuary, it is suggested, are then ignored as well. It is claimed that if the temple had already been destroyed, the passage would make more sense. The time of the Gentiles (or trampling) would *already be underway* because the outer court was presently being trampled while the heavenly temple is protected by God. In addition, measurements taken by John when instructed to measure the temple by the angel do not reflect the historical temple in Jerusalem at all. They in fact, fit the heavenly temple described in Ezekiel. The temple, it is claimed, is symbolic.

The argument, however, that draws a parallel between the measurements of a heavenly temple as given in Ezekiel's vision and the measurements given in the book of Revelation, does not apply. Gentry reminds us that the context is different. In the book of Ezekiel, it is made clear that the temple was already destroyed and that

---

[261] Kim Riddlebarger, *The Man of Sin: Uncovering the Truth about the Antichrist* (Grand Rapids, MI: Baker Books, 2006), 182.

the context is in the rebuilding of the future second temple.[262] In Revelation there is no indication that the Herodian temple is destroyed and there is no indication anywhere in the book of Revelation that a future third Temple will be constructed.

In addition, the context of the text in Revelation before and after the measurement of the temple is that it is on earth. A heavenly location of the temple is also questionable because the threat of the Gentiles against at least part of the temple is difficult to envisage if the temple is in heaven.

Gentry tells us "the proper understanding of the passage requires a mixture of the figurative-symbolic and the literal-historical."[263] This is not uncommon in Scripture (e.g., 2 Kgs. 21:12-13; Amos 7:8-9; Isa. 34:11, Lam. 2:8; Rev. 18:9-10).[264]

Not all writers agree that the measuring of the Temple is for preservation, although this is the majority viewpoint. The logic traditionally involved is that since the unmeasured part is trampled, the measured part is protected.[265] The text, however, does not explicitly say the measured part is protected. Although texts can be cited indicating that measurement is positive, texts can also be cited indicating that measurements are taken before destruction.[266]

In 2 Kings 21:12-13 we read:

> therefore thus says the Lord, the God of Israel: Behold, I am bringing upon Jerusalem and Judah such disaster that the ears of everyone who hears of it will tingle. And I will stretch over Jerusalem the measuring line of Samaria, and the plumb line of the house of Ahab, and I will

---

[262] Kenneth L. Gentry, Jr., "The Temple Problem for Revelation's Dating," Postmillennialism, http://www.postmillennialism.com/the-temple-problem-for-revelations-dating/ (accessed April 11, 2016).
[263] Kenneth L. Gentry, Jr., *Before Jerusalem Fell: Dating the Book of Revelation*, 3rd ed. (Fountain Inn, SC: Victorious Hope Publishing, 1998, 2010), 174.
[264] Ibid., 175.
[265] Matthijs Den Dulk, "Measuring the Temple of God: Revelation 11.1-2 and the Destruction of Jerusalem," *Journal of New Testament Studies* Vol 54, no. 3, (05 June 2008): Cambridge Journals Online, 438.
[266] Ibid., 438.

wipe Jerusalem as one wipes a dish, wiping it and turning it upside down.

In 2 Samuel 8:2 David measures out two lengths of cord for those to be put to death and one length of a cord for those to be saved.

An indication that judgment is impending is that the staff used to measure is a *kalamos* which signifies authority. It is used to judge.[267]

It could be that the temple is measured because it is under the jurisdiction of God and marked specifically for destruction. This is the clear historical result that the whole world saw. The Temple and its sacrificial system are forever gone. The outer court is left to the jurisdiction of the Gentiles to trample.

In the words of Den Dulk:

> The command to measure is intended to convey to John's audience that the initiative for the temple's destruction was God's and that therefore, there can be no talk of a victory of the Gentiles over the God of Israel. Even though the Gentiles trample the holy city they can do so only for a limited period of time and only because they were given the warrant to do so by God himself.[268]

Gentry views the measuring of the Temple for the preservation of its innermost aspects, i.e., the altar and the worshipers within (Rev 11:1). The outer court is not measured; it is cast out.[269]

Gentry explains,

> This seems to refer to the inner-spiritual idea of the Temple in the new covenant era that supersedes the material Temple of the old covenant era. Thus, while judgment is about to be brought upon Israel, Jerusalem, and the literal Temple complex, this prophecy speaks also of the preservation of God's new Temple, the Church (Eph. 2:19ff.; 1 Cor. 3:16;19; 2 Cor. 6:16; 1 Pet. 2:5ff.) that had its birth and was originally

---

[267] Ibid., 440.
[268] Ibid., 438-439.
[269] Gentry, op. cit., 174.

headquartered at Jerusalem (Luke 24:47; Acts 1:8; 8:1; 15:2). Notice that after the holocaust, *the altar is seen in heaven* (Rev. 11:18), whence Christ's kingdom originates (John 18:36; Heb. 1:3) and where Christians have their citizenship (Eph. 2:6; Col 3:1,2).[270]

Both the altar and the worshipers are preserved. There were worshipers present when John was instructed to measure the temple.

However, the above objection, that "the time of the Gentiles would already be underway" because the outer court was *presently* being trampled when John wrote these words is flawed. In describing the trampling, John uses the *future* tense.

In Rev 11:2, John uses the future tense in the statement "they *will* trample the holy city for forty-two months." The statement made supporting the symbolic only view that "the outer court was *presently* being trampled" comes into direct conflict with the words of John, because, when John was instructed to measure the Temple, he wrote the words "they *will* trample." The words were a prophecy, just as they were in Luke.

Some claim that a figurative interpretation of the temple as the Church is based on the view that Rev. 11:1-2 is a fragment of a hypothesized zealot oracle spoken during the last days of war against Rome, before the Romans entered the temple. As the Romans overran the outer court, the zealots were forced to retreat to the inner courts. The zealots took their refuge in the inner courts believing that they would be persevered from destruction.

R. H. Charles says that the first two verses of Revelation 11:

> are a fragment, as Wellhausen was the first to recognize, of an oracle written before 70 A.D. by one of the prophets of the Zealot party in Jerusalem, who predicted that, though the outer court of the Temple

---

[270] Ibid., 174.

and the city would fall, the Temple and the Zealots who had taken up their abode within it would be preserved from destruction.[271]

Charles believes that John then reworked this Zealot prophecy so that now "the temple of God is ... the spiritual temple of which all the faithful are constituent parts."[272] In this context, the temple is to be understood for protection, not of the Herodian temple, but of the Church sent to witness before a hostile world.

Caird takes this argument one step further. Caird, writing of this thesis which goes back to Wellhausen, claims that "John could not have intended these words [Rev. 11:1-2] to be taken figuratively unless someone else had previously used them in their literal sense."[273] This would be a "theological" argument for the late date of the authorship of Revelation. In other words, one cannot interpret the temple figuratively unless there is a literal object, person, or event that existed or occurred before AD 70 that is being referred to.

In response to this position, however, Boxall says:

> Yet the opening verses, no less than the rest of the chapter, make good symbolic sense, and do not require a hypothetical prophetic oracle as their source. The expectation that the Gentiles would oppress God's people, as they had done again and again throughout history, including recently in Rome during the reign of Nero, would have been quite possible for a Christian apocalyptic seer, even before Rome's destruction of the physical Temple in Jerusalem. Indeed, the language echoes that of Daniel 8:10 -14, which speaks of the trampling of God's sanctuary for 'two thousand and three hundred evening and mornings' (i.e. about three and a half years or forty-two months; cf. Isa. 63.18; Ps. 79.1); Daniel is a book which, as we have seen, played a crucial role in John's visionary awareness.[274]

---

[271] R. H. Charles, *A Critical and Exegetical Commentary on the Revelation of St John*, Vol. 1 (Edinburgh: T. & T. Clark, [1920], 2000), 274.
[272] Ibid., 274.
[273] Ian Boxall, *Revelation: Vision And Insight* (London: SPC,. 2002), 97.
[274] Ibid., 97.

Boxall continues:

> It may well be that events in Jerusalem in the late 60s had some impact upon what John (rather than a hypothetical zealot prophet) saw; but this need not require us to date his finished symbolic product to a much later date. Indeed, if Revelation 11 as a whole were written after the destruction of Jerusalem, why is the reader told in John's visionary account, contrary to historical fact, that only 'a tenth of the city fell' (11.13)?[275]

Finally, as noted earlier, there is a parallel between Luke 21:24 and Rev 11:2:

Luke 21:24 | Revelation 11:2

Gentiles = nations

trampled underfoot = tread under foot[276]

According to Gentry, the context of Luke demands a literal Jerusalem besieged by literal armies which lead to AD 70. John's Revelation and Luke's Gospel use the same language and refer to the same events. In *both* Luke 21:24 and Revelation 11:2, the temple is standing.

---

[275] Ibid., 97-98.
[276] Gentry, op. cit., 176.

Chapter 16
MATHISON ON WHY PRETERISM IS ESSENTIALLY CORRECT

There are four basic interpretative approaches to the book of Revelation; the futurist approach, the historicist approach, the idealist approach, and the preterist approach. The preterist approach is that most, though not all, of the prophecies of the book of Revelation were future when given but fulfilled in AD 70. The futurist approach is that the fulfillment of *all* prophecy after the fourth chapter of Revelation is still in our future.

A fifth approach, notes Mathison, has also emerged which is eclectic in nature, combining strengths of the four primary approaches. The eclectic approach is found in the writing of George Ladd, Gregory Beale, Grant Osborne, and Vern Poythress.

An excellent article about why a preterist approach is essentially the correct approach versus the others is written by Reformed theologian Keith A. Mathison. Mathison is Professor of Systematic Theology at Reformation Bible College in Sanford, Florida, and a published contributor at Ligonier.[277]

In his article, which is an excerpt from his book *From Age to Age*, Mathison makes a key criticism of the idealist position. He quotes Richard Bauckham to explain what he sees as the most serious problem with this position.

Bauckham draws the following conclusion regarding the idealist position:

---

[277] Keith Mathison, "The Preterist Approach to Revelation —The Unfolding of Biblical Eschatology," Ligonier.com, http://www.ligonier.org/blog/preterist-approach-revelation-unfolding-biblical-eschatology/ (accessed April 7, 2016).

Thus it would be a serious mistake to understand the images of Revelation as timeless symbols. Their character conforms to the contextuality of Revelation as a letter to the seven churches of Asia. Their resonances in the specific social, political, cultural and religious world of their first readers need to be understood if their meaning is to be appropriated today.[278]

Mathison explains,

Not only does the idealist approach tend to ignore the historic specificity demanded by its [the book of Revelation] character as a letter, it also tends to ignore the hermeneutical implications of its character as a prophecy. The Old Testament prophets used highly figurative and symbolic language, but they used this language to speak of *real historical nations and specific impending historical judgments*. Writing his own prophetic book, John does the same.[279]

In other words, the idealist may at times ignore the real historical nations, events, or armies behind a first-century symbol. Secondly, the idealist may ignore the prophetic nature of an *impending* judgment, that is, judgment that is to take place shortly. The judgment that was shortly to take place involving images of the Beast and the harlot must be meaningful to the first-century audience that John was prophesying to.

Mathison then gives the end result of the idealist approach:

The idealist approach to the text of Revelation often appears to be more akin to an application of the text than an interpretation of the author's original intended meaning.[280]

---

[278] Keith Mathison, *From Age to Age, The Unfolding of Biblical Eschatology* (Phillipsburg, N.J: P & R Pub. Co., 2009), 650.
[279] Ibid., 650.
[280] Ibid., 651 (footnote #14).

Let us consider an example. Preceding and during World War II, Adolph Hitler was someone who was considered by many to be the Antichrist. His treachery and cruelty in some respects exceeded even that of Nero. However, is it the Hitler of the time of World War II or the "Hitler" of each generation that John prophesied will continually arise? Or is there one prophesied final Antichrist that will arise just before the end of time? Is it even a prophecy if in each generation a monstrously evil person is recognized by many to have the characteristics of the Beast?

It is critical to understand that when God revealed the symbols of the book of Revelation to John, he did so in a way that *they would be meaningful to John and his first-century audience*. This is an underlying *assumption* of the historical-critical method. To go beyond this and claim that the symbolism should be *directly* applied to each succeeding generation as prophecy introduces another assumption. Mathison correctly tells us, I believe, that this process is an application of the text.

The book of Revelation was written to be meaningful to its first-century audience. It was written *to* them in their particular historical setting.

There are idealists who do pay more attention to the real historical nations, judgments, and armies behind the symbols than others. One of them is Kim Riddlebarger. Riddlebarger places himself in "the Dutch Reformed school" of thought.[281] We will consider some of Riddlebarger's key arguments. We will compare his ideas to those of Mathison and Gentry.

Before getting into the interpretation of passages from Scripture concerning the end-times, we should make sure we are on the same page with some basic definitions.

---

[281] Kim Riddlebarger, *A Case for Amillennialism: Understanding the End Times* (Grand Rapids, MI: Baker Books, 2003), 31.

Part III
ESCHATOLOGICAL POSITIONS

Chapter 17
DEFINITIONS

Eschatology:

> The study of the teachings in the Bible concerning the end times.

End Times:

> The end of history culminating with the return of Christ and the preceding events.

The Binding of Satan (Rev 20:1-3):

> Then I saw an angel coming down from heaven, holding in his hand the key to the bottomless pit and a great chain. And he seized the dragon, that ancient serpent, who is the devil and Satan, and *bound him for a thousand years*, and threw him into the pit, and shut it and sealed it over him, so that he might not deceive the nations any longer, until the thousand years were ended.

Millennium:

> The 1000 year period when Satan is bound.

Satan's Little Season (Rev 20:7, 8):

> And when the thousand years are ended, Satan will be released from his prison and will come out to deceive the nations that are at the four corners of the earth, Gog and Magog, to gather them for battle.

Gog and Magog Battle:

> The final battle before the return of Christ. Satan will deceive the nations (Magog) who are led by Gog against the saints and the beloved city.

Resurrected Body:

> When Christ returns, the bodies of both the saints who have died and those who are still alive will be transformed into perfect, eternal bodies in the likeness of Christ's resurrected body.

Rapture:

> Living believers receive their resurrected bodies as they meet Christ in the air at his second coming. There are two basic views as to the timing of the rapture. 1)At the end of history. 2) Before the great tribulation.

Premillennialist:

> One who believes that Christ will return secretly before the millennium.

Postmillennialist and Amillennialist:

> One who believes that Christ will return after the millennium which is currently being realized.

Futurist:

> One who believes that the book of Revelation was written after AD 70. He believes that all prophecy in the book of Revelation beginning with chapter four has a fulfillment which is future to us.

Partial Preterist:

> One who believes that the book of Revelation was written prior to AD 70. He believes that most prophecy in the book of Revelation was fulfilled near-term in AD 70 with the fall of Jerusalem, although some prophecy is still to be fulfilled.

Chapter 18
THUMBNAIL SKETCH OF ESCHATOLOGICAL POSITIONS

Amillennial and postmillennial - the millennium and the end times.

Traces back historically to Origen, later to Tyconius and Saint Augustine.

> The millennium, *symbolized* by one thousand years, begins with the ministry of Christ and ends with Satan's Little Season. Satan is bound during the millennium in that he can no long deceive the nations. At the end of Satan's Little Season, the Gog and Magog battle will begin. The wicked will be destroyed with fire from heaven followed by the return of Christ, the resurrection of all who have died, and the final judgment. The new heaven and new earth are then created.

Premillennial dispensational - the millennium and the end times.

Traces back historically to Darby and the Plymouth Brethren in the early 1800s.

> Christ will secretly return either just before or just after the beginning of a period of tribulation known as the great tribulation. At this return of Christ the saints will be raptured (those who are alive) or resurrected (those who have previously died). The first of two Gog and Magog battles will begin either just before or just after the rapture followed by the battle of Armageddon. Christ will return a second time, destroy all of the wicked, and bind Satan for a thousand years (the millennium). No one will be left on earth except for those who repented and turned to Christ during the great tribulation.
>
> Those who were previously resurrected will then join those still living on earth for the millennium. The millennium will include at least a ceremonial return to the sacrificial system at a

third Jewish temple that was built before the great tribulation. During the millennium Christ will rule with David from Jerusalem.

Near the end of the millennium, Satan's Little Season will begin and will then culminate with the Gog/Magog conflict. Gog and his followers will be destroyed by fire from heaven. The wicked will be resurrected along with those who accepted Christ during the great tribulation and have died either during the tribulation or during the millennium. The final judgment will then take place. Satan and his followers will be thrown into hell forever. The new heaven and new earth are then created.

Historic premillennial - the millennium and the end times.

Traces back historically to Papias, Justin Martyr, and Irenaeus.

Great apostasy and tribulation will occur before Christ's return. The church will go through the tribulation. Christ then establishes his millennial reign on earth during which period Satan is bound. At the end of Satan's Little Season, the Gog and Magog battle will begin. There will be one resurrection and judgment at the end of history. The new heaven and new earth are created.

Progressive dispensational - the millennium and the end times.

Recognizing there are connections between the church and the prophecies made to Israel about a new covenant, changes were made to the 1909 Scofield Bible notes and are reflected in the newer notes of 1967 and 1985. In history, there is still a distinction between Israel and the church.

According to Steve Gregg:

> The dispensationalists postulate two distinct "gospels" for two different dispensations. Jesus, they say, preached the "gospel of

the kingdom" to Israel (Mark 1:14), while Paul preached the "gospel of grace" to the Gentiles.[282]

This version of dispensationalism does not see the church as separate and distinct in the future coming kingdom. In the future kingdom all will be equally united to Christ by the Holy Spirit. Christ will still rule politically while ruling the nations but at the same time will bring the spiritual realities of the church to both Jew and Gentile. The pre-tribulation rapture and the rebuilding of a third temple are retained in progressive dispensationalism.

---

[282] Steve Gregg, "Is Dispensationalism Indispensable?" *Christian Research Journal* 35, no. 04 (2012).
Reprinted, http://www.equip.org/article/dispensationalismindispensable/.

Chapter 19
THE DISPENSATIONAL HERMENEUTIC VERSUS THE HISTORIC PROTESTANT HERMENEUTIC

Both Reformed and Dispensational theologians have very similar Hermeneutics. Both groups take into consideration literary devices such as similes, metaphors, and hyperbole when interpreting texts.

Both take into consideration historical context. They both interpret Scripture in the light of the grammatical rules of Hebrew or Greek. Both construct theological concepts inductively by studying numerous individual texts in Scripture and then generalizing. Both interpret the Scripture literally at times and symbolically at times.

Dispensationalists desire to interpret all of Scripture, including the apocryphal books, literally whenever possible. They also recognize a distinction between Israel and the church which, they maintain, is based on a literal approach that they desire to consistently take.

Dispensationalist Charles Ryrie tells us that if we do an inductive study of the words "Church" and "Israel" in the New Testament, the word "Israel" does not mean the "Church," and the word "Church" does not mean "Israel." With an inductive study of the words, the claim is, that we are not superimposing a theological generalization on a text and we let the text speak for itself within its own context.[283]

Ryrie tells us, that in the New Testament, "national Israel continues with her own promises and the Church is never equated with a so-called 'new Israel.'"[284] "Israel" is made up of the "literal" descendants of Abraham.

However, is it a true statement that in the New Testament the word "Israel" does not mean the church? Clearly there was the nation

---

[283] Charles Ryrie, *Dispensationalism Today* (Chicago: Moody Press, 1965, 1967, 1968), 96.
[284] Ibid., 140.

of Israel, however, there was also the *true* Israel, the remnant who obeyed God. We are told in the New Testament:

> For not all who are descended from Israel belong to Israel, and not all are children of Abraham because they are his offspring, but through Isaac shall your offspring be named." This means that it is not the children of the flesh who are the children of God, but the children of the promise are counted as offspring (Romans 9:6-8).

Paul does distinguish between believing Jews and believing Gentiles in Romans 9-11. However, the context is that despite different origins, there is only one promise. Paul tells us that in the Old Testament, not all who were Israel were descended from Israel. There was a small group of Jews that were faithful to God and would receive the promises of God. Isaiah, call them the remnant (Isaiah 10:20).

Paul tells us God's promises have not failed. He tells us that "the promise comes by faith" (Rom. 4:16). This faithful remnant within national Israel was preserved by God's grace. *The promises made to Abraham were fulfilled in Jesus.* When Jesus walked the earth, those who followed him were the faithful remnant, the true Israel. Those who rejected him, though they were physically Jews, were not true Israel.

Those who followed Jesus, true Israel, were initially Jews. Peter's sermon on the Day of Pentecost was to a *Jewish* audience. These Jews were the ones who initially formed the church. Later believing Gentiles were added to the one body of believers made up of both Jews and Gentiles.[285] The true Israel of the Old Testament, the remnant, became the church. It is literally true that "true Israel" is the church.

The New Testament tells us who the "true Israel" is. The New Testament tells us how to interpret the Old Testament. When the eunuch in the book of Acts was reading the prophet Isaiah, Philip asked him if he understood what he was reading. When the eunuch

---

[285] Keith Mathison, *Dispensationalism: Rightly Dividing the People of God?* (Phillipsburg: P&R Pub., 1967, 1995), 39-40.

told Philip that he did not, Philip sat beside him and beginning with Isaiah told him the good news about Jesus. It was only then that the eunuch understood what he was reading.

The Old Testament prophets spoke of the coming new covenant in terms of the tabernacle, the temple, the nation of Israel, the festivals, and the throne of David, which were shadows of what was to be fulfilled in Jesus Christ, the true temple and the true vine. The Old Testament tells us about David and Moses and other Old Testament heroes of faith that are referred to in the New Testament as types. We read in 1 Corinthians 10:1-4:

> For I do not want you to be unaware, brothers, that our fathers were all under the cloud, and all passed through the sea, and all were baptized into Moses in the cloud and in the sea, and all ate the same spiritual food, and all drank the same spiritual drink. For they drank from the spiritual Rock that followed them, and the Rock was Christ.

The New Testament is the fulcrum for interpreting the Old Testament. The classic example is that of John the Baptist. The Jews were looking for Elijah, literally to be the forerunner of the Messiah. They asked John if he was Elijah and he said that he was the voice of one crying in the wilderness. Even the disciples of Jesus were confused as to whether or not John the Baptist was Elijah. Jesus had to directly tell them.

> And the disciples asked him, "Then why do the scribes say that first Elijah must come?" He answered, "Elijah does come, and he will restore all things. But I tell you that Elijah has already come, and they did not recognize him, but did to him whatever they pleased. So also the Son of Man will certainly suffer at their hands." Then the disciples understood that he was speaking to them of John the Baptist (Matthew 17:10-13).

If a New Testament writer spiritualizes Old Testament prophecy in a nonliteral manner, the Old Testament should be interpreted in the same manner the New Testament writers. If there is a dispute on interpreting the book of Revelation and the book of Daniel, the book of Revelation is the final arbitrator. We must interpret Old Testament prophecy in the way the writers of the New Testament do. The New Testament must determine the way in by which Old Testament and the end times are to be interpreted.

Chapter 20
AMILLENNIAL AND POSTMILLENNIAL REFORMED ESCHATOLOGY

Both view the millennium as a period of time beginning with the ministry of Christ and ending with the second coming of Christ at the end of history. The amillennial point of view is that the millennial reign of the resurrected Christ along with the saints, who are in the intermediate state, *is in heaven* (Revelation 20:4-6). The purpose of the book of Revelation from the amillennial perspective is to show us that we are "more than conquerors." In this life we have trouble seeing that we are "more than conquerors" as we go through persecution that we face. The postmillennial point of view is that the coming of the kingdom of God is on earth.

In both the amillennial and postmillennial points of view, as the Word of God spreads across the globe, the duty of a Christian is to work for the redemption of the various aspects of life (education, politics, science, etc.) to the glory of God. In both positions we can see the "already – not yet" of Reformed theologians first noted by Geerhardus Vos[286] and expanded by Herman Ridderbos. "For by grace you have been saved through faith," says the apostle Paul. When one becomes a Christian, one immediately has eternal life *but not yet* as we will not have a resurrected body until the Last Day. The kingdom of God on this earth is *already here and now,* "but not yet" fully redeemed, although we gratefully work for the renewal of all things.

We see in 2 Cor. 5:17 that we are part of that new creation now:

---

[286] Geerhardus Vos, *The Pauline Eschatology* (Princeton University Press, 1930). Reprinted, Phillipsburg, New Jersey: Presbyterian and Reformed Publishing Co., 1979), 38.

> Therefore, if anyone is in Christ, he is a new creation. The old has passed away; behold, the new has come.

We will, however, *not yet see* the final renewing of creation take place until heaven and earth are united together in the new heaven and earth:

> And not only the creation, but we ourselves, who have the firstfruits of the Spirit, groan inwardly as we wait eagerly for adoption as sons, the redemption of our bodies (Romans 8:23).

Hoekema says:

> The kingdom of God, therefore, is to be understood as the reign of God dynamically active in human history through Jesus Christ, the purpose of which is the redemption of God's people from sin and from demonic powers, and the final establishment of the new heavens and the new earth. It means that the great drama of the history of salvation *has been inaugurated, and the new age has been ushered* in .... The kingdom is established by God's sovereign grace, and its blessings are to be received as gifts of that grace. Man's duty is not to bring the kingdom into existence, but to enter it by faith, and to pray that he may be enabled more and more to submit himself to the beneficent rule of God in every area of his life.[287]

In other words, the new age and the old age of evil are at this moment commingled. We live in this age, but are not of this present evil age. The age to come exists right now side by side with the present age of evil. The end of the evil age *has* already in principle happened! It happened with the resurrection of Christ! There were TWO ages that ended with the sacrifice of Christ. The Jewish Age with its sacrificial system is gone, and the present evil age has already in principle been destroyed.

---

[287] Anthony A. Hoekema, *The Bible and the Future* (Grand Rapids, MI: Wm. B. Eerdmans Pub. Co., [1979], 1994)., 45.

We must not put Christ to the test, as some of them did and were destroyed by serpents, nor grumble, as some of them did and were destroyed by the Destroyer. Now these things happened to them as an example, but they were written down for our instruction, on whom the end of the ages has come. (1 Corinthians 10:9-11).

The events associated with the old covenant were written for our instruction, and its end, the "end of the ages", came with the sacrifice made by Christ and his resurrection. The new covenant was inaugurated. However, the *final* fulfillment is NOT YET!

The expectation of the postmillennialist is that Christ shall have dominion over land and sea, and we, over time, will see the majority of the inhabitants of the earth serving Christ before the end of the millennium. This optimism, however, is not limited to the postmillennial perspective.

The expectation of the amillennialist is that we should optimistically work toward the redemption of all of life. However, along the way we will experience persecution due to a world which has forgotten God. This persecution will increase in the Last Days and will culminate in the battle of Gog and Magog at the end of the millennium. Christ will return to a world in which the majority of mankind will have ignored or forgotten God.

> For as were the days of Noah, so will be the coming of the Son of Man. For as in those days before the flood they were eating and drinking, marrying and giving in marriage, until the day when Noah entered the ark, and they were unaware until the flood came and swept them all away, so will be the coming of the Son of Man (Matthew 24:37-38).

Amillennial and Postmillennial Reformed History

Abraham Kuyper, who founded the Free University of Amsterdam in the late 1800s, is considered the founder of the Dutch Reformed school of thought and the first to use the term "amillennial" or "realized millennialism." Kim Riddlebarger, in his book *A Case for Amillennialism,* places himself in the Dutch Reformed school of thought that includes writers such as Geerhardus Vos, Herman Ridderbos, Anthony Hoekema, and Meredith G. Kline.[288]

In the Christian theological tree there is the "Dutch Reformed" branch on which Kim Riddlebarger places himself. In addition, there is a second branch or line of thought in the Dutch Reformed tradition. This second line of thought also started in the Netherlands at the Free University of Amsterdam founded by Abraham Kuyper. This second line of thought is known as postmillennialism. It is a modern postmillennialism which is distinctively Calvinistic.

After the death of Kuyper, a Christian philosophy known as presuppositionalism was developed at the Free University of Amsterdam.[289] In the United States, Cornelius Van Til used presuppositionalism as the basis for his apologetics, his defense of the Christian faith. One of his better-known students, Greg Bahnsen, is best known for his exposition of Van Til's apologetic. Bahnsen is also known as an early date advocate for the book of Revelation. Greg Bahnsen and his well-known student, Kenneth Gentry, developed an orthodox Reformed approach to postmillennialism.

A strong advocate of Reformed postmillennialism is Gary DeMar. DeMar continually works to bring a uniquely Christian perspective to the areas of culture and politics.[290] This wonderful perspective is also shared by amillennialists from Abraham Kuyper to modern day writers such as Cornelius Van Til, John Frame, and Vern Poythress.

---

[288] Kim Riddlebarger, *A Case for Amillennialism: Understanding the End Times* (Grand Rapids, MI: Baker Books), 31.

[289] All human thought systems have basic presuppositions or assumptions. Mathematics, for example, has basic assumptions from which we develop theorems. Presuppositionalists looks at the basic presuppositions or assumptions of systems of thought as a method to gain insight into that thought system. See Greg Bahnsen, *Van Til's Apologetic* (Phillipsburg, New Jersey: P & R Pub. Co., 1998), 446-447 for Van Til's definition as given by Greg Bahnsen. Also see Appendix B.

[290] DeMar says "It is the duty of believers to apply God's Word to every area of life, to bring all things under the Crown Right of Jesus Christ seeking the transformation of our culture." See americanvision.org/about/statement-of-faith/.

Chapter 21
REFORMED VIEW OF THE OLD TESTAMENT LAND COVENANT

A primary difference in the eschatologies of those who come from a covenantal background versus those from a dispensational one has been the role of Israel in the end-times. Covenantal theologians dating as far back as Saint Augustine have maintained that Israel has a place in the end-times only as a race of people and not as a nation. From Augustine to John Calvin and Martin Luther, this has been the eschatological point of view of those who believe that the unfolding of the redemptive plan of God is through the covenants he made with his people. Dispensationalists from Thomas Ice and John Walvoord to Kay Arthur see the birth of modern day of Israel as an end-time fulfillment of the land covenant that God made to the children of Israel in the Old Testament.

> Remember his covenant forever, the word that he commanded, for a thousand generations, the covenant that he made with Abraham, his sworn promise to Isaac, which he confirmed to Jacob as a statute, to Israel as an everlasting covenant, saying, "To you I will give the land of Canaan, as your portion for an inheritance. (1 Chronicles 16:15-18).

Covenantal Reformed theologians maintain that the land covenant has been expanded through Christ, so now the land promised to the children of God is the entire earth.

> Now the promises were made to Abraham and to his offspring. It does not say, "And to offsprings," referring to many, but referring to one, "And to your offspring," who is Christ. ... And if you are Christ's, then you are Abraham's offspring, heirs according to promise (Gal 3:16, 29)
> .
> We read is Psalm 24:1, "The Earth is the Lords." The entire earth belongs to Christ. Every square inch of land on the earth is now Holy

Land. Anywhere a believer in Christ lives on this earth is land that now is Holy Land. Here we again see the "Already – not Yet" of Herman Ridderbos. All the earth is now Holy, but "not Yet", as the full earthly consummation of the kingdom of God will not fully be fulfilled until we live on the "new earth."

Hoekema argues that many passages in the Old Testament that dispensationalists interpret as belonging to the millennium actually refer to the new heaven and earth. Hoekema refers to Isaiah 11:6-10, where the *New Scofield Bible* heading for verses 1 through 10 reads, "Davidic kingdom to be restored by Christ: its character and extent." In other words, dispensationalists see the interpretation as a description of the millennium. In verses 6-10 we see we see a captivating description of this new world:

> The wolf shall dwell with the lamb,
>   and the leopard shall lie down with the young goat,
> and the calf and the lion and the fattened calf together;
>   and a little child shall lead them.
> The cow and the bear shall graze;
>   their young shall lie down together;
>   and the lion shall eat straw like the ox.
> The nursing child shall play over the hole of the cobra,
>   and the weaned child shall put his hand on the adder's den.
> They shall not hurt or destroy
>   in all my holy mountain;
> for the earth shall be full of the knowledge of the Lord
>   as the waters cover the sea.

Hoekema asks:

> But why should it be thought of as giving a picture of the millennial state? Does it not make even better sense to understand these words as a description of final new earth? As a matter of fact, the words "the earth shall be full of the knowledge of the Lord as the waters cover the

sea" are not an accurate description of the millennium, for during the millennium there will be those who do not know or love the Lord, some of whom will be gathered together at the end of the thousand years for a final onslaught against the camp of the saints.[291]

The land promise will be "literally" fulfilled on the "new earth."

Just as the people of God in the Old Testament era were restricted mostly to the Israelites but in the New Testament are gathered in from all the nations, so in the Old Testament times the inheritance of the land was limited to Canaan, whereas in New Testament times the inheritance is expanded to include the entire earth."[292]

*However, **today** the land promise is "already-not yet."*

To understand how a modern Christian Jew may feel about the expansion of the land covenant, put yourself into his position with the following analogy. In this analogy, your father is a very rich man. He tells you that the house you have lived in since you were a child is your inheritance. He is giving you that house. You live in this house and over the years have many fond memories. You remember how your father tucked you into bed at night and told you how much he loves you. You get married, and you, along with your family, live in the house for a number of years. However, you disobey your father and have to leave your house. It is years later. Someone else lives in your house. You are brought some good news. In addition to the house you lived in, your father owns every house in the city. Your father tells you are forgiven for your misdeeds and now every house in the city is your inheritance! Would you not have a longing to live in that original house that you loved?

---

[291] Anthony A. Hoekema, *The Bible and the Future* (Grand Rapids, MI: Wm. B. Eerdmans Pub. Co., [1979], 1994), 203.

[292] Ibid., 278.

As Riddlebarger notes, even if the land promise has been fulfilled, it is remarkable that Jews have returned to their homeland. That the Jews have gathered together to a large degree in one place requires an explanation. Riddlebarger tells us that the answer is given to us by Paul in Romans 11.[293]

Many Reformed thinkers follow the Augustinian view that God is done with Israel as a nation prophetically; God's plan of Redemption was completed once and for all through the sacrifice of Christ. There will never be a return to the Old Testament sacrificial system. The land covenant with Israel was not only fulfilled, it was expanded. With many covenantal theologians there has been an acceptance of the view that the formation of the modern day nation of Israel has no prophetic significance.

Could, however, the grafting of the Jews back into the true vine (Christ) include, in God's mysterious providence, a return of the Jews to the Hold Land? Amillennialist Kim Riddlebarger believes so and so does partial preterist Duncan McKenzie. If Riddlebarger and McKenzie are correct, how does the return of the Jews relate to the current conditions in the Middle East and the current possibility of the Gog/Magog battle? We will take a closer look at the details of their respective positions and well as the position of Kenneth Gentry.

---

[293] Kim Riddlebarger, *A Case for Amillennialism: Understanding the End Times* (Grand Rapids, MI: Baker Books, 2003), 244.

Part IV
Israel and the End Times

Chapter 22
ISRAEL AND PROPHECY

According to futurist Thomas Ice, co-founder of the Pretribulation Institute, a key prophetic event that has already been fulfilled in the past was the formation of modern Israel nearly seventy years ago.

> The fact that the modern state of Israel was reconstituted in 1948 is historical verification that God is preparing the world for Tribulation events.[294]

Thomas Ice would consider the coming battle of Gog/Magog to be a tribulation event. As presented in this view popularized by Hal Lindsey, the tribulation is a series of end-time events that begin with a secret rapture of Christians who are instantly removed out of this world and out of the coming worldwide disasters, famine, suffering, and war. The rapture is an end-time event where each living Christian receives an eternal resurrected body in the likeness of Christ's resurrected body.

Since Ice believes the battle of Gog/Magog of the book of Daniel is still to be fulfilled, a question for dispensationalists is whether to place the Gog/Magog battle before the rapture or after the rapture. Ice places the Gog/Magog invasion just after the beginning of the tribulation. Tim LaHaye and Joel Rosenberg place the battle of Gog/Magog just before the tribulation. The importance of this battle has been brought to the foreground in recent books and videos.

These authors, who promote an end-time view known as dispensationalism, believe the battle of Gog/Magog is on the horizon

---

[294] Ice, Thomas. Gentry Jr., Kenneth L. *The Great Tribulation-Past or Future?*, Kregel Academic & Professional. 1999, 119.

now and is to be shortly followed by the rapture. The other possibility is that the rapture will occur first followed by the Gog/Magog invasion of Israel.

The Gog/Magog battle has become a focal point of current dispensational eschatology. In 2006, Joel Rosenberg wrote a New York Times bestselling book named *Epicenter*[295]. A video documentary[296] was released in 2007 along with special features including interviews with world leaders and theologians. In 2008, an update of the bestseller followed — *Epicenter 2.0: Why the Current Rumblings in the Middle East Will Change Your Future*.[297] In 2015, a novel entitled *The Third Target*,[298] a political thriller on the Middle East, was published. All of these publications depict the current political upheaval in the Middle East which dispensationalists believe may lead the world to the Gog/Magog conflict of the end-times. The great Calvinist preacher John MacArthur recently wrote an article entitled *Why Every Calvinist Should Be a Premillennialist*.[299] He believes that Calvinists should adopt the dispensationalist point of view concerning Israel and the end-times.

Is the formation of modern Israel a fulfillment of prophecy that will soon lead to the Gog/Magog battle of the end-times and the great tribulation? Do current political conditions in the Middle East make a Gog/Magog invasion a real possibility in the immediate future? How should a Christian view the increasing threat of radical Islam?

---

[295] Joel Rosenberg, *Epicenter: Why the Current Rumbling in the Middle East Will Change Your Future* (Carol Stream, IL: Tyndale House Pub., 2006).

[296] *Epicenter*, DVD, hosted by Joel Rosenburg (Carol Stream, IL: Tyndale House Pub., 2008).

[297] Joel Rosenberg, *Epicenter 2.0: Why the Current Rumbling in the Middle East Will Change Your Future* (Carol Stream, IL: Tyndale House Pub., 2008).

[298] Joel Rosenberg, *The Third Target* (Carol Stream, IL: Tyndale House Pub., 2015).

[299] John MacArthur, "Why Every Calvinist Should be a Premillennialist," Grace to You, http://gty.org/Downloads/PDF/macarthur_on_future_israel.pdf (accessed April 7, 2016).

We will spend some time focusing in on the Gog/Magog battle of the end-times and the place of Israel in the end-times from a practical theological point of view.

When the book of Revelation was written is of critical importance as to how one interprets the book.

If the book of Revelation was written after the fall of Jerusalem in AD 70, then much of the prophecy contained in the book is still to be fulfilled thousands of years later. We call this the futurist position. This would mean that most of the prophecies of the book of Revelation, beginning with chapter four, would be of little significance to the Christians living in the first century.

However, the book of Revelation is written as if the members of the newly born church of the first-century needed immediate comfort and direction — or they would perish!

We can only understand the book of Revelation if we understand this context. The book of Revelation starts with these words in Revelation 1 verse 1 (NASB):

> The Revelation of Jesus Christ, which God gave Him to show His servants — things which **must shortly take place**.

If the book of Revelation was written in AD 65 - 67, then most of its prophecies were fulfilled in the fall of Jerusalem in AD 70. The great tribulation is past and the Gog/Magog battle will not occur until after the millennium.

Chapter 23
R.C. SPROUL, JAMES STUART RUSSELL, AND DUNCAN MCKENZIE

Duncan McKenzie is a partial preterist whose perspective is based on James Stuart Russell's, *the Parousia*, first published in 1879. The following comments that R.C. Sproul make concerning James Stuart Russell and full preterism, I believe, should also apply to Duncan McKenzie. In 1999, Sproul wrote a foreword to a new edition of Russell's book. In his foreword Sproul says:

> In this [Olivet] discourse Jesus predicts the destruction of the temple, the destruction of Jerusalem, and the dispersion of the Jews, all of which took place in AD 70. The uncanny accuracy of these predictions is embarrassing to higher critics . . . . [they] grant that Jesus' prophecy of Jerusalem's destruction was correct, they insist that his predictions at the same time, in the same context . . . were incorrect . . . . Russell's work is valuable chiefly for his analysis of the time-frame references of New Testament prophecy and his understanding of the main reference to the parousia. What are the "last days" of the New Testament? . . . . I am persuaded that, in the main, Russell is essentially correct. I do not endorse his work entirely because I think he goes too far, as does "full preterism." . . . . Russell's book has forced me to take the events surrounding the destruction of Jerusalem far more seriously than before, to open my eyes to the radical significance of this event in redemptive history.[300]

---

[300] James S. Russell, Foreword by R. C. Sproul, *The Parousia: The New Testament Doctrine of Our Lord's Second Coming*, new ed. (Grand Rapids, MI: Baker Books, [1887], 1983, 1999), vii - x.

McKenzie frequently cites Reformed partial preterist theologians such as R.C. Sproul, Kenneth Gentry, and Keith Mathison. McKenzie agrees with Reformed theologians that the millennium does not span a literal time period of one thousand years and begins in AD 70.

McKenzie identifies himself as a premillennialist. He agrees with dispensationalists that the rapture occurs *before* the millennium, so he is premillennial. In contrast to traditional dispensationalist theologians, however, he believes that the rapture has *already* occurred, since the millennium began in AD 70. McKenzie believes that beginning in AD 70 each believer immediately receives his resurrection body at death. There no longer is an intermediate state.

> Since AD 70, those who die that are not in the Lamb's Book of Life end up in the lake of fire (Rev. 20:15; 21:24 -27), while those who die in the Lord after AD 70 inherit rewards (Rev. 14:8 -13).[301]

According to McKenzie, the last event that will happen after the millennium is that Satan will be thrown into the fiery pit.

I believe that both the dispensationalist and premillennial preterist positions are in error. *There is only one resurrection. There is only one judgment of the living and the dead.* That resurrection occurs at the end of history and coincides with the second coming of Christ. There was no rapture in AD 70 and there will be no secret rapture in the future. A Christian does not, as most full preterists claim, receive a resurrected body immediately upon death. There will be a public visible "rapture" in the last day of history when Christ returns to judge the living and the dead. An amillennialist, however, usually prefers not to use the term "rapture" which is not found in Scripture. The phrase "to judge the living and the dead," in the Apostles' creed comes from 2 Tim 4:1: "Christ Jesus, who is to judge the living and the dead."

---

[301] Duncan McKenzie, *The Antichrist and the Second Coming: A Preterist Examination, Vol. 1* (Maitland, FL: Xulon Press, 2009), 135.

The judgment of God on Jerusalem in AD 70 was not an invisible judgment any more than the Old Testament judgments of God. The judgment in AD 70, which literally ends the Jewish age with the destruction of the temple, was *visible to the entire Roman world*. There were probably very few people anywhere in the Roman world at that time who did not know about the destruction of the temple and the fall of Jerusalem. It was a metaphorical "Day of the Lord" judgment that points to the final Day of the Lord at the end of history. It is a metaphorical judgment just like the Old Testament "Day of the Lord" judgments. The AD 70 judgment publicly inaugurates the new covenant. *It is the short-term fulfillment of the Olivet Discourse. At the same time, it points to the long-term fulfillment.* The long-term fulfillment is the physical appearance of Jesus on the clouds of glory at the end of history to bring judgment to the wicked and to remove the curse of sin in the renewal of creation with the new heavens and the new earth.

I believe that the historical-redemptive preterist position sheds light the role of Israel in the end-times and can account for the unprecedented attack on the authority of the Word of God, along with the corresponding increase in the evil we see in the world today.

I do believe, however, that there is a dispensational argument concerning the place of Israel in the end-times that must be a part of the discussion. Dispensationalists pay particular attention to the Old Testament patriarchs and Old Testament prophecy. They have a love for the people of Israel. I believe this love is biblical. God has a love for the people of Israel. This love for Israel in seen in Romans 11. We will take note of the dispensational argument as presented by Duncan McKenzie for the role of Israel in the end-times and show its similarities to the position of Kim Riddlebarger.

Riddlebarger tells us that the answer to this problem [the place of Israel in the end-times] was supplied to us by Paul in Romans 11.[302]

---

[302] Kim Riddlebarger, *A Case for Amillennialism: Understanding the End Times* (Grand Rapids, MI: Baker Books, 2003), 244.

Chapter 24
ROMANS 11 AND THE FULLNESS OF THE GENTILES

Together, we will examine the meaning of the words "all Israel" and the phrase "until the fullness of the Gentiles has come in" from Romans 11 as viewed by *Reformed theologians* Herman Ridderbos, Eric Alexander, Keith Mathison, and Kim Riddlebarger. We will then refocus the meaning of the words as applied to Israel in end-time prophecy in view of the work of Duncan McKenzie. McKenzie makes a compelling case for the dispensational argument on the fullness of the Gentiles.

In chapter 9 of Romans Paul expresses his sorrow for the unbelief, of his kinsmen, for "to them belong the adoption, the glory, the covenants, the giving of the law, the worship, and the promises. To them belong the patriarchs, and from their race, according to the flesh, is the Christ, who is God over all, blessed forever." He then dispels any notion that God did not keep his promise or that God's Word is not trustworthy.[303] "For not all who are descended from Israel belong to Israel." God has been faithful to the "true" Israel, the remnant. But has God cast off ethnic Israel altogether?

The apostle Paul has more than an academic interest in the question from verse 1 of Romans 11.[304]

> I ask, then, has God rejected his people? By no means! For I myself am an Israelite, a descendant of Abraham, a member of the tribe of Benjamin. God has not rejected his people whom he foreknew.

---

[303] Herman Ridderbos, *Paul: An Outline of His Theology*, trans. by John Richard DeWitt (William B. Eerdmans Publish Co., [1975], Paperback 1997), 356.
[304] Alexander, Eric. "Israel and the End Times", (The End? Finding Hope in the Millennial Maze:1999 National Conference), MPEG, http://www.ligonier.org/learn/conferences/orlando_1999_national_conference/israel-and-the-end-times/ (accessed April 8, 2016).

Paul offers himself and other Christian Jews as proof[305] that God has not cast out ethnic Israel. God, in his providence, has a place for Israel. Paul then goes on in verse 15:

> For if their rejection means the reconciliation of the world, what will their acceptance mean but life from the dead?

Now the rejection of Israel is not final. We note in verse 23:

> And even then, if they do not continue in their unbelief, will be grafted in, for God has the power to graft them in again.

"How will they be grafted in?" The answer to this question comes from Galatians 6. "Israel's election is an election of grace and that for Israel, too, therefore, there is no other way than that of faith."[306]

There is no special way of salvation for anyone. There is only one way. With this in mind we come to verse 25, where Paul says:

> I do not want you to be unaware of this mystery, brothers: a partial hardening has come upon Israel, until the *fullness of the Gentiles has come in*. And in this way *all* Israel will be saved.

Alexander, in his exposition of Romans 11,[307] says that the explanation of John Calvin here, in extending the word Israel to mean *all* the people of God as the church ("the remnant" or "true Israel"), is so obvious that it is anti-climactic. It is almost a tautology in that this would just restate what is already clear.

Since the entire focus of the passage is on the Jews as a people we need to consider what the words "all Israel" mean here. Alexander suggests that the word "all" is used here in the same manner as the

---

[305] Kim Riddlebarger, *A Case for Amillennialism: Understanding the End Times* (Grand Rapids, MI: Baker Books, 2003), 186.
[306] Herman Ridderbos, op. cit., 360.
[307] Eric Alexander, op. cit.

newspaper headlines "All London Greets Churchill" shortly after World War II. The word "all" means a very large number of people but not every single person. What we can expect to see is an extraordinary work of the Holy Spirit in the end times. Not every Jew but a large unprecedented number of Jews will come to Christ.

Mathison comments:

> In verses 7-10 [Romans 11], Paul explains that while a remnant of Israel has obtained salvation, "the rest were hardened" (11:7). It is important to remember that "the rest" who "were hardened" is a reference to Israel according to the flesh (9:3), the Israel Paul prays may be saved (10:1).
>
> In 11:11, Paul asks and answers a very significant rhetorical question: "I say then, have they stumbled that they should fall? Certainly not!" But who are "they"? *This has to be a reference to Israel according to the flesh, the Israel that stumbled over Christ, the Israel who were hardened – in other words, Israel as a people.* It cannot be a reference to the remnant of Israel who have been saved by faith in Christ, because the remnant did not stumble. From verse 11 onward, Paul speaks of this hardened people of Israel.
>
> ... They were broken off because of unbelief (v. 20), but if *they* do not continue in unbelief, they will be grafted back in (v. 23).
>
> ... There is also good reason to believe that the "Israel" in verse 26 is the same as the "Israel" in verse 25.[308]

Mathison seems to be saying that the text requires us to view Israel in the flesh as people of the Jewish race who occupied a specific geographical area in the first century. These people were not the remnant. They were those who had rejected the Christ. This is the key point of the argument for McKenzie.

---

[308] Keith Mathison, *The Eschatological Times Text of the New Testament, When Shall These Things Be? A Reformed Response to Hyper-Preterism,* ed. Keith A. Mathison (Phillipsburg, NJ: P & R Pub., 2004), 198-200.

McKenzie quotes and then endorses the comments of Mathison *with the understanding that hardened/physical Israel refers to ethnic Jews in a specific geographical area with a Jewish government.* McKenzie continues:

> This distinction between the remnant of Israel versus the majority of Israel that were hardened/ blinded is crucial. It was not just the remnant that would be saved; eventually all Israel (i.e., hardened physical Israel) would be brought back into relationship with God ... If Paul was simply teaching that the rest of the remnant of Israel was about to be saved, that would not be much of a mystery. If he was saying that God had hardened physical Israel in the first century so he could have mercy on them at a later time, it is an amazing mystery.[309]

I too believe that we are witnessing, today, an extraordinary work of the Holy Spirit. An unprecedented number of Jews are coming to Christ today. McKenzie suggests that what we see today, in this extraordinary work of the Holy Spirit, will ultimately be more than a general increase in the numbers of Jews turning to Christ worldwide. There *will be* a dramatic increase in the number of Jews turning to Christ *within the physical land of Israel* as well as in the world as a whole, *although this will not happen fully until after the Gog and Magog battle.* McKenzie suggests that it is an amazing mystery of prophetic significance that Israel is a nation again in our times.

Ridderbos, Riddlebarger, Mathison, and Alexander all address "how" the end-time extraordinary work of the Holy Spirit will happen. There is no special way of salvation for anyone. There is only one way. The "when" is addressed by the phrase, argues McKenzie, "A partial hardening has come upon Israel *until the fullness of the Gentiles has come in.*"

We now get to the dispensational hypothesis for the "when" that is defended by McKenzie. We shall later see that his hypothesis *is not far* from the perspective of Riddlebarger. Before stating his claim,

---

[309] Duncan McKenzie, *The Antichrist and the Second Coming: A Preterist Examination*, Vol. 2 (Maitland, FL: Xulon Press, 2012), 472.

however, McKenzie attempts to show that the "until the fullness of the Gentiles has come in" quoted above (Romans 11) and the "until the times of the Gentiles are fulfilled" in the words of Jesus in Luke 21:24, both have the same *time reference*.

This time period is an indefinite extended period of time. McKenzie claims that there is a correlation between the phrase "fullness of the Gentiles" given in Roman 11 and the "times of the Gentiles" of Luke 21:24.

This claim is not unreasonable. In addition to dispensational scholars who take this position, it seems that Mathison takes this point of view as well.

Mathison notes that in the Olivet Discourse (Luke 21), Jesus words "until the times of the Gentiles are fulfilled" seem to set a time limit to this new exile.[310] Mathison suggests that these words mean that Israel is not cast off permanently. He then mentions in a footnote (#63)[311] that "the Apostle Paul develops this theme in greater detail in Romans 11."

McKenzie next claims the time period of the "times of the Gentiles" in Luke 21:24 (by implication also the "fullness of the Gentiles" referred to in Romans 11) is a time period of indefinite length.

There is, however, a problem for the argument that McKenzie is developing. Luke 21:24 of the Olivet Discourse, is a clear parallel to Revelation 11:1, 2. Kenneth Gentry interprets Revelation 11:1,2 to mean that Jerusalem is trampled by the Romans for forty-two calendar months, which is a definite period of time.

---

[310] Keith Mathison, *From Age to Age, The Unfolding of Biblical Eschatology* (Phillipsburg, N.J: P & R Pub. Co., 2009), 419.
[311] Ibid., 419.

Luke 21:24 ------------>	---------> Revelation 11:1, 2
Trampling until the times of the Gentiles are fulfilled.	42-month trampling of Jerusalem, an indefinite period of time?

The Romans besieged the city of Jerusalem from the Spring of AD 67 to September of AD 70 (42 calendar months). The Romans besieged Jerusalem, trampled Jerusalem for 42 months, and then Israel is scattered to the nations.

According to Jesus in Luke 21:24:

> They will fall by the edge of the sword and be led captive among all nations, and Jerusalem will be *trampled underfoot* by the Gentiles, *until the times of the Gentiles are fulfilled.*

Revelation 11:1-2:

> Then I was given a measuring rod like a staff, and I was told, "Rise and measure the temple of God and the altar and those who worship there, but do not measure the court outside the temple; leave that out, for it is given over to the nations, and *they will trample the holy city for forty-two months.*

McKenzie is aware of Gentry's interpretation. McKenzie says,

Some will disagree with my interpretation; they would say that Luke 21:24 is simply referring to the fact that the Romans would be allowed to trample Jerusalem for a period of time (Rev. 11:2). At the conclusion of this time, Israel would be dispersed into the nations. Verse 24, however, implies that the trampling of Jerusalem by the Gentiles would be subsequent to the Jews' AD 70 dispersion.[312]

---

[312] Duncan McKenzie, *The Antichrist and the Second Coming: A Preterist Examination*, Vol. 2 (Maitland, FL: Xulon Press, 2012), 480.

McKenzie, to support his point of view, notes that the word "trodden" refers to the oppression and contempt which always follows a conquest and simply remarks that the trampling is subsequent to the dispersion. However, since Revelation 11:1, 2 is a parallel passage to Luke 21:24, the argument could be made in response to McKenzie that the time period of the "times of the Gentiles" in Luke 21:24 is the identical forty-two calendar month time period that the Roman siege of Jerusalem fulfilled. There is no indication that trampling takes place after the conquest. The context of Luke 21:20-24 may even be suggesting this.

The key exegetical question can now be posed. Is this one of the cases in Scripture where the short-term, literal interpretation of forty-two months also has a longer-term, spiritual fulfillment where the grafting in of the Jewish people back into the true vine would be the longer term fulfillment based on Romans 11?

Mathison makes the case that the forty-two months in Revelation 11:1-2 may refer to an indefinite period of time as Luke 21:24 seems to. Mathison notes that in Daniel 7:25, "times, times, and half a time" is considered to be an indefinite period of time:[313]

> He shall speak words against the Most High, and shall wear out the saints of the Most High, and shall think to change the times and the law; and they shall be given into his hand for a time, times, and half a time.

The forty-two months is sometimes described as "1260 days" (Rev 11:3) and sometimes as "a time, and times, and half a time" (Rev 13:5). If all three designations are all interchangeable, says Mathison, then the time period of forty-two months may be symbolic of an indefinite period of time.

---

[313] Keith Mathison, *From Age to Age, The Unfolding of Biblical Eschatology* (Phillipsburg, N.J: P & R Pub. Co., 2009), 475.

McKenzie believes this indefinite period of time ended with the birth of the State of Israel. Since the Jews now occupy a large portion of Jerusalem, the city is no longer trampled. Trampling implies total domination. Total domination is no longer the case. The Jews controlled much of the city of Jerusalem in 1948 and gained greater control of the city in 1967. McKenzie concludes that the spirit of the fulfillment of the prophecy was in 1948.

Since 1967, control of the Temple Mount has been back in the hands of the Muslims. The Muslims will never willingly give up control of the Mount.

McKenzie notes that years ago, before the Jews returned to Jerusalem, some commentators believed that God would never allow this return to happen. If the Jews did return, then they would build a third temple and would then re-institute animal sacrifices, which would be an abomination. Who could have envisioned back then the fragmented city we see today where the temple could not be built?[314]

Reformed scholar, Kim Riddlebarger, portrays a similar position on the birth of modern Israel, except that he sees the birth of Israel as a nation simply in relation to a possible large conversion of ethnic Jews to Christ. The Jews living in Israel are located in a single country. This, contends Riddlebarger, falls within God's mysterious providence referred to in Romans 11 rather than the fulfillment of the Abrahamic covenant.[315]

It should be pointed out that Gentry does believe in the possibility of an end-time conversion of a large number of Jews to Christ, as does Eric Alexander and Kim Riddlebarger. This would be a conversion of the Jews as a race of people, not as a nation. This is the traditional Reformed viewpoint.

McKenzie next proceeds to his hypothesis which we will pose as a question: *Could it be that the time period of the millennium is the same time period as the "time of opportunity" for the Gentile nations?*[316] McKenzie

---

[314] Duncan McKenzie, op. cit., 505.
[315] Kim Riddlebarger, *A Case for Amillennialism: Understanding the End Times* (Grand Rapids, MI: Baker Books, 2003), 244.
[316] Duncan McKenzie, op. cit., 482.

interprets "times of the Gentiles" or "fullness of the Gentiles" of Romans 11:25 to mean "the time of opportunity of the Gentiles."[317]

Riddlebarger makes a similar statement when referring to the end of the age, all Israel, and the fullness of the Gentiles. Riddlebarger notes that although not all amillenarians agree as to a future for ethnic Israel, many believe that a large number of Jews will come to Christ once the fullness of the Gentiles comes in and that *this will be a sign or "harbinger of the end of the age."*[318]

McKenzie illustrates his proposed parallel between the two time periods with the diagram[319] shown below:

Luke 21:24:
The time (of opportunity) of
the Gentile nations: AD 70 --1948

Rev. 20:1-3:
Satan bound for the millennium [320] so he cannot deceive
the Gentile nations: AD 70 --1948?

If these two periods coincide, says McKenzie:

it helps to illuminate the phrase "the times of the Gentiles." The phrase does not mean that no more Gentiles would be saved after the Jews came back to the land. Rather, it means that the Gentiles' time of opportunity – the time when Satan was bound during the millennium in his ability to deceive the Gentile nations – would be over when the

---

[317] McKenzie, op. cit., 481-482.
[318] Riddlebarger, op. cit., 192-193. Emphasis mine.
[319] McKenzie, op. cit., 482.
[320] Reformed theologians following the interpretation of Saint Augustine in his *City of God*, believe that the binding of Satan began during the ministry of Christ (Matthew 12:28-29). Gentry believes that the apostle John sees the binding of Satan in AD 70 as the public manifestation, seen by the whole world, of what already had begun in the ministry of Jesus. Note: footnote is mine.

Jews came back to the land in 1948.[321]

Although there are differences, the viewpoints of Riddlebarger and McKenzie are similar. The key, however, to understanding the place of Israel in the end-times is not that Jews are returning to their homeland in fulfillment of an irrevocable land covenant. Rather, the birth of the modern nation of Israel relates to Romans 11 and the providence of God where the Jews as a people are being grafted back into the true vine.

---

[321] McKenzie, op. cit., 482-483.

Chapter 25
SATAN'S LITTLE SEASON AND THE GOG/MAGOG INVASION

The key to understanding that the millennium may have ended in 1948 from the perspective of McKenzie is found in Revelation 20:7-8, in the gathering of the nations together for the Gog and Magog battle. The focus of Satan at that time will be on gathering the nations for this specific conflict.

> And when the thousand years are ended, Satan will be released from his prison and will come out to deceive the nations that are at the four corners of the earth, [by way of][322] Gog and Magog, to gather them for battle; their number is like the sand of the sea.

We see the source of the imagery that John uses for the Gog and Magog invasion in Ezekiel 38 and Ezekiel 39.
Ezekiel 38:8, 16:

> After many days you will be mustered. In the latter years you will go against the land that is restored from war, the land whose people were gathered from many peoples upon the mountains of Israel, which had been a continual waste.

> You will come up against my people Israel, like a cloud covering the land. In the latter days I will bring you against my land, that the nations may know me, when through you, O Gog, I vindicate my holiness before their eyes.

---

[322] Interpretative phrase added by McKenzie to explain what he believes is the proper way to read the text.

Ezekiel 39:27-28:

> When I have brought them back from the peoples and gathered them from their enemies' lands, and through them have vindicated my holiness in the sight of many nations. Then they shall know that I am the Lord their God, because I sent them into exile among the nations and then assembled them into their own land. I will leave none of them remaining among the nations anymore.

Revelation 20:7-10 is the only place in the book of Revelation where the Gog/Magog invasion is mentioned. There is only one Gog/Magog invasion. McKenzie argues that the invasion prophesied in Ezekiel 38-39 is still future and is the same invasion as the Gog/Magog battle prophesied in Revelation 20. The Gog/Magog invasion in the book of Revelation is future. It falls outside of the apocalyptic time-frame of the book of Revelation, namely, that "the time is near."

McKenzie lists the modern names of the countries with the exception of Roash, which he leaves out due to the uncertainty of its identification.

The names of the countries are: Russia (Magog), Turkey (Meshech and Tubal, Gomer, and Togarmah), Iran (Persia), Ethiopia/Sudan (Cush), and Libya (Put).[323]

What is NOT necessary as a prerequisite for the Gog and Magog invasion per McKenzie?

It is not necessary for Israel to possess its original boundaries, as this already has been fulfilled in Joshua. Joshua 21:43-45:

> Thus the Lord gave to Israel all the land that he swore to give to their fathers. And they took possession of it, and they settled there. And the

---

[323] Duncan McKenzie, *The Antichrist and the Second Coming: A Preterist Examination*, Vol. 2 (Maitland, FL: Xulon Press, 2012), 501.

Lord gave them rest on every side just as he had sworn to their fathers. Not one of all their enemies had withstood them, for the Lord had given all their enemies into their hands. Not one word of all the good promises that the Lord had made to the house of Israel had failed; all came to pass.[324]

It is not necessary for the temple to be rebuilt, as Christ is the new temple. It is not necessary for Israel to occupy the Temple Mount.

It is not necessary for the Israelites to subdue the Palestinian state for a time of peace to come to Israel. Rather, a Palestinian state coexisting with Israel would meet that requirement. All that is needed is a covenant of peace.[325]

In addition, from the Reformed point of view, the argument could be made that none of the above explanation by McKenzie is necessary since the land covenant has not only been fulfilled; it has been expanded. Every square mile on this earth is now Holy unto the Lord.

It is likely, however, that the Gog/Magog battle described by Ezekiel is a past event.

Kenneth Gentry recognizes that John's source for his imagery is Ezekiel 38 and 39, but he does NOT recognize the invasion described in Ezekiel as the same invasion as the one described in Revelation.

William Hendriksen viewed the prophecy to be fulfilled in the days of Antiochus Epiphanes, historically one of the most bitter enemies of the Jews. Hendriksen mentions that tribulation under Antiochus, although severe, was of very brief duration. This, say Hendriksen, makes "it well adapted to foreshadow the brief final tribulation which will occur at the close of our present dispensation."[326] In addition, says Hendrisken, the "onslaught could serve as an excellent symbol of the final struggle of the godless world

---

[324] Ibid., p. 503.
[325] Ibid., p. 503, 504.
[326] William Hendriksen, *More Than Conquerors: An Interpretation of the Book of Revelation* (Grand Rapids, MI: Baker, 1940,1967), 194.

against the Church."[327]

Gary Demar makes a convincing case that the prophesied battle of Gog/Magog was fulfilled in the events of Esther which took place during the reign of Darius after the initial rebuilding of the temple. Demar argues that Ezekiel 34-37 describes the return of the exiles under Zerubbabel.[328] Haman is "Gog". He is the leader that gathers from the 127 provinces with the initial permission of king Ahasuerus to destroy the Jews.[329] These provinces are all within the bounds of the Persian empire in Esther's day.[330]

Whether the battle as depicted in Ezekiel is future or not, the imagery of John suggests that the allied nations aligned against Israel in Revelation 20 will be primarily Muslim.

Is the Islamic Mahdi the Antichrist? Are the forces of Islam gathering against the church and Israel as described by McKenzie?

We do well to remember that the Turkish empire has been identified with Gog/Magog going all the way back to the 1300s. The world did not end in the 1300s.

---

[327] Ibid., 194.
[328] Gary DeMar, *The Gog and Magog End-Time Alliance: Israel, Russia, and Syria in Bible Prophecy* (Powder Springs, GA: American Vision Press, 2016), 44.
[329] Ibid., 59.
[330] Ibid., 55.

Chapter 26
THE AMILLENNIAL SOLUTION

If the Ezekiel Gog/Magog invasion is past, then it only foreshadows the Gog and Magog invasion of the book of Revelation, which is the only battle still to be fulfilled.

If the Ezekiel Gog/Magog invasion is future, dispensationalists have a problem, as McKenzie suggests. Since they believe that the millennium is still to come, they are forced to argue that there are *two* Gog and Magog invasions. The invasion prophesied in Ezekiel would be the first (occurring before or at the beginning of the millennium), and the second invasion would be the Gog and Magog invasion prophesied in Revelation at the end of the millennium.

In McKenzie's eyes, dispensationalists correctly see the Gog and Magog invasion as one of the next events on the prophetic timeline; however, as mentioned above, *the book of Revelation shows only one Gog and Magog invasion, which happens at the end of the millennium.*

A second problem for dispensationalists is in accounting for the enemies who will oppose the saints during the invasion. "Their number is like the sand of the sea." Where did this huge coalition (that will oppose Jerusalem and the saints) come from?

According to dispensationalists, the people who populate the world in the millennium will only consist of three groups of believers: 1) those with resurrected bodies, 2) those who turn to Christ during the tribulation, and 3) the children of those who turn to Christ during the tribulation.

Given that Christ himself will be ruling on the earth (with the nations not learning war anymore), and given the huge multitude of saints with resurrected bodies to give educational guidance to those who turned to Christ during the tribulation (along with their children)—dispensationalists have trouble accounting for this massive rebellion against Christ.

From the partial preterist perspective, all the battles of Revelation have already been fulfilled with the exception of the Gog and Magog invasion. The Gog/Magog battle falls outside of the apocalyptic timeframe of the book of Revelation, namely, that "the time is near."

Amillennialists who are not preterists also believe that only the battle of Gog/Magog remains as shown in Revelation 20, although they see the battle as a recapitulation of the battle of Armageddon.

The above mentioned problems, however, in accounting for multiple Gog and Magog invasions, disappear if one accepts that we have been in the millennium since the time of Christ.

There is no problem with the Gog and Magog invasion occurring after the millennium, since the *millennium is now*. There is no problem seeing how the coalition numbering the sands of the sea is formed. The Muslim coalition that is in existence now *could* be the one prophesied in Revelation. If McKenzie is correct, Satan is now unbound to again deceive the nations. He expects the invasion to "happen in the not too distant future."

Chapter 27
FINAL CONCLUSIONS

The land of Israel became a nation again in 1948. McKenzie argues that Satan may have been released at this time to deceive the nations of the world. Since then, Satan has been concentrating on the land of Magog (Russia).

Scholars agree that the imagery of John for the Gog and Magog battle comes from Ezekiel 37 and Ezekiel 38. McKenzie devotes a number of pages in his commentary to making the case that the imagery of John from Ezekiel applies to the current conditions in the Middle East. He attempts to show that the conditions that we now see correlate with the imagery of Ezekiel to a degree never before seen.

In the words of McKenzie:

> Today – for the first time in history – the Gog and Magog invasion is a very real possibility. This has led some to accuse those who are looking for the invasion of "newspaper exegesis" (reading current events into prophecy). I find it most ironic that this invasion that has been historically dismissed because it was too unlikely is now dismissed because it is too likely![331]

Prior to the birth of Christ, the only people who had access to the Word of God as revealed in the Scriptures were the people of Israel. McKenzie believes that Satan has been released in 1948 to again deceive the nations. In other words, we are now in the beginning of Satan's Little Season. Is it possible that today we are witnessing the

---

[331] Duncan McKenzie, *The Antichrist and the Second Coming: A Preterist Examination*, Vol. 2 (Maitland, FL: Xulon Press, 2012), 503.

beginning of a process where the nations of the world are again being deceived as they were prior to the birth of Christ?

Riddlebarger believes, as does McKenzie, that once the fullness of the Gentiles comes in, God may bring the vast majority of ethnic Jews to faith in Christ. This, says Riddlebarger, is the harbinger of the end of the present age.

What we do see in recent history is an unprecedented attack on the authority of the Word of God. We see an unprecedented attack on the family. Instability in the family has led to further decline. Persecution against the church seems to be increasing worldwide. How long will it be before there is persecution in America?

Some biblical scholars, including McKenzie, believe that what we see today are the conditions necessary for the final Gog/Magog battle. Others, like Gentry, see the final battle as a long way off in the future.

The great tribulation and battle of Armageddon are past events that culminated in the end of the Jewish age and inaugurated the "coming of the kingdom." The final battle, however, will be worldwide in scope and will involve the nations from the four corners of the earth. The enemies of Christ will "surround the camp of the saints *and* the beloved city." The modern nation of Israel may be a part of this conflict.

We do know from Matthew 24:36-39:

> "But concerning that day and hour no one knows, not even the angels of heaven, nor the Son, but the Father only. For as were the days of Noah, so will be the coming of the Son of Man. For as in those days before the flood they were eating and drinking, marrying and giving in marriage, until the day when Noah entered the ark, and they were unaware until the flood came and swept them all away, so will be the coming of the Son of Man.

We do know that the number of those opposing the church at the end of history will be "like the sands of the sea."

The kingdom of God presently is between the "already" and "not yet" with Satan currently bound. This does not mean that all Satanic activity is being prevented in this current age. Satan has been cast down and Christ has already crushed his head. Although wounded, Satan still is the adversary who "prowls around like a roaring lion looking for someone to devour" (I Peter 5:8). At the end of history, however, just before the return of Christ, Revelation 20 makes it clear that Satan will be released and things will intensify. There will be one final conflict in a world that has forgotten Christ.

The Gog/Magog conflict may not take place for another two thousand years. It may come tomorrow. We just do not know. We must, however, also look for the coming of Christ.

In either case, the coming battle of Gog/Magog will end with the final destruction of the forces of evil with Satan being thrown into the fiery pit. The war will be a worldwide conflict that will bring us to the end of history and the final judgment. After the final judgment death will be cast into the lake of fire (Rev. 20:14), the curse of sin will be removed, and a renewed heavens and earth established. With the return of Christ, we will receive our resurrected bodies like unto his glorious body (Philippians 3:20,21). We will live joyfully on a renewed earth that is completely free from the curse of sin. Unencumbered by sin, we will continue to explore all of creation to the glory of God.

Today, while we are watching and waiting for his coming, we must be actively spreading the Good News throughout the world and work to redeem the various aspects of life to the glory of God.[332]

In the words of Ian Boxall:

> Revelation, through its use of apocalyptic imagery to shed light on the social situation, offers a challenge to many Christians to reconsider their own position as regards Graeco-Roman society and its perception of their own position as regards 'the way the world is…The real danger for

---

[332] An example is seen in the work of Vern Poythress. See page 224. Also visit americanvision.org.

many of John's first hearers is not so much persecution as complacency and accommodation.[333]

Life seems to be now what it was like in the days of Noah. We must:

> Put on the whole armor of God, that you may be able to stand against the schemes of the devil. For we do not wrestle against flesh and blood, but against the rulers, against the authorities, against the cosmic powers over this present darkness, against the spiritual forces of evil in the heavenly places (Ephesians 6:11-12).

In order to take on the whole armor of God, we need to study the Scriptures. We need to study and discuss all of Scripture, including the book of Revelation.

The promise in the metaphor of the Olivet Discourse and in the book of Revelation is this: just as surely as Jerusalem fell in the near-term judgment, there will be a final judgment. Just as surely as the new covenant was established, there will be a literal new heaven and a new earth. Christ is coming!

---

[333] Ian Boxall, *Revelation: Vision And Insight* (London: SPCK, 2002), 102.

APPENDIX A: PETER STEEN

One of my fondest memories of Dr. Steen is of a "daily period of physical activity" which he supervised during my sophomore year at Trinity Christian College. Trinity was a very small institution when I was a student there in the mid 60's. One of Dr. Steen's duties was to oversee this activity. I had completed a two-mile run and went down with a muscle cramp in my right hamstring. He, of course, had to give a quick demonstration to the class of both the "correct" and "incorrect" way to help someone with a muscle cramp. Fortunately, the "correct method" alleviated the pain quickly after he demonstrated both methods. He was always quick to make an educational point that led to growth, even if it induced some intellectual discomfort.

Some of his best lectures that initially gave me some discomfort were on the "new heavens" and "new earth" and the influence of Greek philosophy on the Christian view of the body and the soul. When I recently read the wonderful book *Heaven* by Randy Alcorn, I thought of Peter Steen and how similar the views of Alcorn are to those in the lectures given by Steen in the mid-sixties. In 1970, he submitted "The Idea of Religious Transcendence in the Philosophy of Herman Dooyeweerd, with Reference to its Significance for Reformed Theology" as his Doctoral dissertation at Westminster. His dissertation was published as a book in 1983 under the title *The Structure of Herman Dooyweerd's Thought*.[334] His early passing gave me a great sense of loss. He has been missed not only by his former students but his passing is felt by the entire Christian community.

---

[334] Peter J. Steen, *The Structure of Herman Dooyeweerd's Thought* (Toronto, Canada: Wedge Publishing Foundation, 1983).

APPENDIX B: DUTCH REFORMED THEOLOGICAL HISTORY

We can trace the roots of the Dutch Reformed school of thought back to Abraham Kuyper who founded the Free University of Amsterdam in 1880 where he introduced the concept of "sphere sovereignty" in his inaugural address. "Sphere sovereignty" became one of the foundations of a Christian philosophy known as "presuppositionalism" which was later developed by Dooyeweerd and Vollenhoven after Kuyper's death. Kuyper was also a newspaper man, formed the Anti-Revolutionary Party, and forged a political coalition between the Protestants and the Catholics for the public funding of all schools, including religious schools. This is today a central provision of the Dutch Constitution. Two-thirds of government-funded schools are independent.

In America, Kuyper presented his famous series of six lectures, *Lectures on Calvinism*,[335] at Princeton University in 1898. Geerhardus Vos graduated from what is now Calvin College in 1883 and earned his doctorate at the University of Strasburg in 1888. Abraham Kuyper and Herman Bavinck tried to convince Vos to become Professor of Old Testament Theology. However, Vos took a position at Calvin Theological Seminary instead, and in 1892 became Professor of Biblical Theology at Princeton. At that time both Calvin and Princeton were orthodox Calvinistic schools. Calvin College and Seminary is in the Dutch Reformed tradition and Princeton in the Presbyterian tradition. Both J. Gresham Machen and Cornelius Van Til were students of Vos.

---

[335] Abraham Kuyper, *Lectures on Calvinism*, L. P. Stone Foundation, Princeton University, 1898 (Grand Rapids, MI: Wm. B. Eerdmans Publishing Company. Copyright, 1931. Reprinted 1999).

Cornelius Van Til was born in Grootegast, Holland,[336] and at a young age his family immigrated to Highland, Indiana, in the U.S.A. Van Til graduated from Calvin College and then attended Calvin Theological Seminary for a year where he studied under Louis Berkhoff.[337] He enrolled at Princeton Theological Seminary in 1922, a year after Warfield had died. After the death of Warfield there was a shift at Princeton from Reformed conservatism to a theological liberal point of view. Machen published his famous *Christianity and Liberalism* in 1923. Van Til, a student and friend of Geerhardus Vos, received his Th.D. from Princeton in 1925 and his Ph. D. in1927. In the following year, Van Til taught apologetics at Princeton. It was during that year that the battle between the theological modernist and conservatives came to a head. Van Til left Princeton after Machen, when Princeton was reorganized along modernist lines.[338] Machen started Westminster Seminary and eventually recruited Van Til to come to Westminster, where Van Til stayed until he retired in 1972.

Van Til used "presuppositionalism" as the basis for his apologetics, although he preferred to refer to his apologetics as "Reformed apologetics." In his earlier years he was considered to be an adherent of the presuppositional approach developed by Abraham Kuyper, Herman Dooyeweerd, and Dirk H.T. Vollenhoven, although some differences developed over time.[339] Two students of Van Til were John Frame and Greg Bahnsen. According to Bahnsen:

> presuppositions are the most fundamental and coordinated convictions that a person has regarding reality, knowing, and conduct . . .[and are] considered to be . . . [the] reference point for interpreting any experience and guiding all reasoning.[340]

---

[336] Greg Bahnsen, *Van Til's Apologetic* (Phillipsburg, New Jersey: P & R Pub. Co., 1998), 7.

[337] Ibid., 8.

[338] Ibid., 10.

[339] Herman Dooyeweerd, "Cornelius Van Til and the Transcendental Critique of Theoretical Thought," *Jerusalem and Athens: Critical Discussions on the Philosophy of Cornelius Van Til*, ed. E. R. Geehan (Presbyterian and Reformed Publishing Co. Phillipsburg, New Jersey, 1971), 74-127.

[340] Bahnsen, op. cit., 446-447.

Van Til used a method of argument by examining any fact to determine what the presupposition of such a fact must be, in order to identify what it is.[341]

In 1999, Greg Bahnsen wrote *Van Til's Apologetic*, a seven hundred plus page book which goes into Van Til's Apologetic in detail. Greg Bahnsen is also a strong advocate for the early date for the authorship of the book of Revelation. Bahnsen was the adviser for Kenneth Gentry. Gentry dedicated his book *Before Jerusalem Fell* to Bahnsen.[342]

The "Already – Not Yet" approach in Dutch Reformed Theology was initially introduced by Geerhardus Voss. In the Netherlands, Herman Ridderbos completed his doctorate in 1936 at the Free University of Amsterdam and became New Testament professor at the Theological School of the Reformed Churches of the Netherlands in Kampen. One of his works, *The Coming of the Kingdom*, which greatly influenced Reformed eschatology was published in 1962. In his *Coming of the Kingdom*, Ridderbos was the first to go into detail in the "Already – Not Yet" tension of Reformed eschatology.

The coming of the kingdom of God is most certainly to be looked upon as the realization of the great drama of the history of salvation in the sense of the Old Testament and of the Jewish apocalypses. This realization is not merely a matter of the future, however. It has started. The great change of the eons has taken place. The center of history is in Christ's coming, in his victory over the demons, in his death and resurrection.[343]

Another Calvin graduate was Anthony Hoekema. Hoekema received his Bachelor of Arts degree from Calvin and Masters of Arts from the University of Michigan. He then earned his Th.B. at Calvin Theological Seminary and his Th.D. at Princeton Theological Seminary in 1953. He was an Associate Professor of Bible at Calvin College from 1956-1958 and then became Professor of Systematic Theology at Calvin Theological Seminary for over twenty years. He

---

[341] Ibid., 466.

[342] Kenneth L. Gentry, Jr., *Before Jerusalem Fell: Dating the Book of Revelation*, 3rd ed. (Fountain Inn, SC.: Victorious Hope Publishing, 1998, 2010), v.

[343] Herman Ridderbos, *The Coming of the Kingdom*, trans. by H. de Jongste (Philadelphia: P & R Pub. Co., 1962), xxviii.

was the Professor of Systematic Theology when I was at Calvin in 1969. Already at that time Hoekema was considered to be an ardent defender of Reformed amillennialism. His book on eschatology, *The Bible and the Future*,[344] was published in 1979, the year he retired. Herman Ridderbos, whom Hoekema references forty times, is the most quoted author in his book. He also defended the amillennial point of view in the millennial debate in his book *The Meaning of the Millennium: Four Views*.[345] He was considered to be one the leading spokespersons for the amillennial point of view until his death.

Another famous American theologian, R. C. Sproul, also attended the Free University of Amsterdam where he received his Doctorate in 1969. His approach to apologetics is not presuppositional, but classical. He co-authored *Classical Apologetics*[346] in 1984. He received his PhD from Whitefield Theological Seminary in 2001.

Another student of Cornelius Van Til is John M. Frame. Vern Poythress was a student and is a friend of John Frame. Poythress wrote *The Returning King: A Guide to the Book of Revelation*.[347] His book is an amillennial interpretation of Revelation similar to that of Greg K. Beale, although at a more introductory level. His work in some respects reminds me of the work of Anthony Hoekema. Hoekema contends that many passages in the Old Testament that dispensationalists interpret as belonging to the millennium actually refer to the new heaven and earth.

Let us consider Hoekema and Poythress side by side for a moment. Hoekema refers to Isaiah 11: 6-10 where the *New Scofield Bible* heading for verses 1 through 10 reads, "Davidic kingdom to be restored by Christ: its character and extent." In other words, says Hoekema, the interpretation is a description of the millennium. In verses 6-10 we see "the wolf shall dwell with the lamb, and the leopard

---

[344] Anthony A. Hoekema, *The Bible and the Future* (Grand Rapids, MI: Wm. B. Eerdmans Pub. Co., [1979], 1994).

[345] Anthony A. Hoekema, "Amillennialism," *The Meaning of the Millennium: Four Views*, ed. Robert G. Clouse (InterVarsity Press, Downers Grove, Illinois, 1977).

[346] R. C. Sproul, John H Gerstner, and Arthur Lindsley, *Classical Apologetics* (Grand Rapids, MI: Zondervan, 1984).

[347] Vern Poythress, *The Returning King* (Phillipsburg, NJ: P & R Pub., 2000).

shall lie down with the kid." In verse 9 we read, "They shall not hurt or destroy in all my holy mountain; for the earth shall be full of the knowledge of the Lord as the water covers the sea."

Says Hoekema,

> But why should it be thought of as giving a picture of the millennial state? Does it not make even better sense to understand these words as a description of the final new earth? As a matter of fact the words "the earth shall be full of the knowledge of the Lord as the waters cover the sea" are not an accurate description of the millennium, for during the millennium there will be those who do not know or love the Lord, some of whom will be gathered together at the end of the thousand years for a final onslaught against the camp of the saints.[348]

Poythress says,
> Hope for a new earth thus gives us a picture that is startlingly similar to premillennialism. I believe that Jesus will return bodily to the world, that all people will be judged, and that the earth itself will be renewed. Jesus will reign over the nations and usher in an era of great peace and prosperity. Faithful Jews will possess the land of Palestine, as well as the entirety of the renewed earth.[349]

It should be noted that Vern Poythress also has a PhD in mathematics as well as a PhD in theology. Poythress is a wonderful example of someone in the tradition of Kuyper and Van Til whose works emphasize the renewal and redemption of creation through Jesus Christ. He is a highly prolific writer. Some of his works include **Re***deeming Science*, **Re***deeming Philosophy*, **Re***deeming Mathematics*, **Re***deeming Sociology*, and *Logic: A God-Centered Approach to the Foundation of Western Thought*. (The emphasis added to the "Re" prefix is mine).

---

[348] Anthony A. Hoekema, Th*e Bible and the Future* (Grand Rapids, MI: Wm. B. Eerdmans Pub. Co., [1979], 1994), 203.

[349] Vern Sheridan Poythress, "Currents within Amillennialism," Presbyterian 26/1 (2000): 21-25.

APPENDIX C: BERTRAND RUSSELL

Bertrand Russell has had a profound influence on the entire world. His book *The Problems of Philosophy* [350] is a wonderful brief introduction to his critique of Immanuel Kant and *a priori* knowledge, knowledge that is independent of experience. Is mathematics itself, as opposed to knowledge created by mathematics, true without reference to reality? Is the knowledge, for example, that the shortest distance between two points is a straight line, knowledge that is *a priori*? Does one really need to measure a number of curved lines between two points to convince oneself that a straight line between the two points gives the shortest measurement?

> We have now seen that there are propositions known *a priori*, and that among them are the propositions of logic and pure mathematics ... How is it possible that there should be such knowledge?[351]

In his book, Russell covers what we can know about reality and matter, the world of universals, and truth, and falsehood. He developed logical analysis to focus on and solve the problems of philosophy and mathematics. He, along with Alfred North Whitehead, wrote *Principia Mathematica*[352] to set mathematics on a *purely* logical foundation. His works profoundly influenced logic, set theory, and computer science. He was truly one of the most brilliant minds of our age. However, he was wrong in that he believed that he

---

[350] Bertrand Russell, *The Problems of Philosophy* (Home University Library. 1912. Reprinted by NewYork: Oxford University Press paperback, 1959, 1962).
[351] Ibid., 81.
[352] Bertrand Russell. and Alfred North Whitehead, Principia Mathematica, Vol. 1, 2, 3. Cambridge, England: University Press, 1910, 1927.

could set mathematics on a purely logical foundation and resolve the problem of *a priori* knowledge through logical analysis.

Russell, along with his student Ludwig Wittgenstein, ran into problems in attempting to prove that logic and mathematics were just logical rules. The German mathematician, Gödel, in 1931, proved two incompleteness theorems. 1) any system of axioms is necessarily incomplete. In other words, mathematics cannot be reduced to formal proof. 2) that any consistent system of axioms could not prove its consistency.

APPENDIX D: OBJECTION TO A LITERAL INTERPRETATION OF THE NUMBER OF KINGS

An objection given to viewing ten as a literal number of kings is that there were not ten Roman provinces at the time John wrote the book of Revelation. There were more than twenty. The number of provinces kept expanding as the Romans conquered new territories. Although there were ten senatorial provinces at the time of Caesar Augustus, the empire of Rome expanded beyond Italy as provinces were added to the empire. As pointed out earlier, however, Caesar Augustus reorganized the empire into ten senatorial provinces when John was very young. Imperial provinces from conquered territories were added as Rome expanded. There is also the nature of John's audience to consider. John was writing to the churches in Asia Minor which were undergoing persecution. Asia is one of the original senatorial provinces. Judea was originally part of the imperial province of Syria.

There were economic and religious reasons for the persecution of Christians locally in Judea, which was initially part of the Roman province of Syria. In Judea the persecution began with the Jews. However, as persecution in Judea intensified, Christianity spread into Asia and eventually across the entire Roman world.

A downturn in a local economy due to Christians discriminating against local guilds, which felt they had a right to make a profit, could certainly make Christians a target for persecution. It was also the local provincial ruler who was responsible for the economic well-being of his provinces and would be politically be aligned with the local guilds.

A lucrative silver trade, for example, had been built up in Ephesus by silversmiths in silver replicas of the goddess Diana. The entire city became enraged at the apostle Paul.

> About that time there arose no little disturbance concerning the Way. For a man named Demetrius, a silversmith, who made silver shrines of Artemis, brought no little business to the craftsmen. These he gathered together, with the workmen in similar trades, and said, "Men, you know that from this business we have our wealth. And you see and hear that not only in Ephesus but in almost all of Asia this Paul has persuaded and turned away a great many people, saying that gods made with hands are not gods. And there is danger not only that this trade of ours may come into disrepute...."(Acts 19:23-27).

Not only was the livelihood of silversmiths threatened, but also those of similar trades: builders, painters, and sculptors who worked on pagan temples. Christians refused to participate in the sacrifices and celebrations to pagan gods which were part of the regular social routine of the local guilds. There was also a direct connection between the guilds and the local Roman governor.

A provincial governor gave orders to the army, was ultimately responsible for justice, and was as mentioned above, responsible for the economic interests of the province. One of the duties of the governor was to levy and collect taxes. If economic interests declined, taxes in turn would decline. Economic interests were intertwined with local religious customs, which were an integral part of the economy. Provincial governors had a direct economic interest in the local religious customs including emperor worship.

It would be natural for John, who knew since childhood the power of the ten provincial governors, to associate them with persecution from the guilds. For the Roman, their gods and religions were interwoven with their economic and social life. This was reflected on the local provincial coins that were minted. In addition, the minting

Appendix D: Objection to a Literal Interpretation of the Number of Kings

of provincial coinage was a profitable privilege given to a local governor by the emperor. In return there would be the political favoritism and expected loyalty that came along with these privileges. We also have evidence that the minting of provincial coins occurred *primarily* within the original ten senatorial provinces. Records were kept on the minting of these coins, which also found their way into the pockets of local Roman garrisons. All we have to do is follow the money. The minting of these coins in the ten senatorial provinces lends support to the point that behind the symbol of the ten kings were the provincial governors.

To follow the money, we will first examine the origin of silver and bronze that was in the possession of Roman troops across the empire. According to Reinhard Wolters, Roman legions were paid in silver and during the later empire in gold. However, it has been argued that Roman troops in the time of Augustus and after were paid in bronze.

According to Wolters,

> Such a view is supported by the spectrum of coin finds in Roman military camps, especially in those on the Rhine. Here, indeed, bronze coins, mostly asses, dominate and likewise are the more recent coins whereas silver coins only play a subordinate role in terms of numbers. Generally, the silver coins also show the earlier date of minting.[353]

In addition, Wolters tells us, even up to and through the time of Tiberius, the imperial bronze that was supplied to Italy rarely came from anywhere except Rome, and the minting of this imperial bronze was on an irregular basis. Minting of bronze was sparse under

---

[353] Reinhard Wolters, "Bronze, Silver or Gold? Coin Finds and the Pay of the Roman Army," *Zephyrus: Journal of Prehistory and Archeology*, ISSN 0514-7336, no. 54, (2001): 579-88, http://revistas.usal.es/index.php/0514-7336/article/viewFile/5010/5046 (accessed (April 9, 2016).

Claudius as it was not until the middle of Nero's rule in AD 61 that bronze coinage was again minted in Rome. Wolters contends:

> The gap in the supply of small change that had arisen due to the lacking minting of bronze in the city of Rome was bridged — at least in the provinces — by local bronze coins.[354]

We do have information on the production of provincial bronze coins. What we notice below is that all significant minting of bronze coins takes place within the ten senatorial provinces. These were centers of economic activity within the empire.

The British Museum book, *Roman Provincial Coinage*, Vol I, provides us with data showing us the provinces, number of cities, and frequency of the minting of bronze coins of each province where there was a significant production and statistics were kept. We will examine some of these statistics.[355]

In the province of Spain under Augustus, Tiberius, and Caligula there was minting of bronze coins in 62 to 63 cities with a frequency total of 3470. Under Claudius, however, there was only one issue of coins in one city and under Nero there were no provincial bronze coins issued in Spain.

In Italy itself bronze coins were minted in only one city and only under Tiberius.

In Africa, Mauretania (North Africa), and Cyrenaica there was minting of bronze coins only under Augustus and Tiberius.

However, in Crete, Achaea (including Corinth), Macedonia, Bithynia, and Asia, there was significant production under all five emperors. In Asia alone, 71 cities minted coins under Augustus, 49 under Tiberius, 21 under Caligula, 35 under Claudius, and 64 under

---

[354] Ibid., 584.
[355] Andrew Burnett, Michel Amandry, and Pau Pere Ripollès, *Roman Provincial Coinage*, Vol. 1 (The British Museum Press, 1992), 17.

Nero. In the 64 cities in Asia under which coins were minted under Nero, there was a frequency total of 1390, second only to Augustus.

Two things stand out when we examine the above statistics. The first is the amount of production in Asia Minor where John addressed his letters to the seven churches. The second largest production was when Nero was in power, although Nero was in power only a fraction of the time that Augustus was emperor. Secondly, we notice that coin production nearly died in the East under Tiberius and did die in the West. After considering a number of possibilities the following explanation is given in RPC, Vol I:

> If we take seriously the mentions of the asking for and granting of permission for coinage, we should also take seriously the possibility that such permissions might be refused (as it might be for a provincial temple), or perhaps rather that the very requesting of permission was discouraged . . . . Why it should have happened when it did or why it should have taken so long to take effect, however, remain elusive, though it took place in an atmosphere of political interference with the coinage...[356]

In other words, a governor had to be on the correct side of issues politically. He needed to show that he was strong and had his province under control. Local religious customs and related business enterprises should not be endangered. In addition, he needed to be in the good graces of the emperor or he could possibly lose the right to mint coins in his province.

Italy was not considered to be a province. If we consider Mauretania to be part of Africa, we see that all the provincial coin production was within the senatorial provinces. Two senatorial provinces are not listed, Cyprus and Gall. The island of Cyprus is believed to have had production. However, there is none cataloged in the project. The only senatorial province not listed in the above

---

[356] Ibid., 19.

statistics is that of Gaul. Gaul, however, may have been the mint of Augustus's "Spanish" coinages although there is no proof. There was production in Gaul of bronze provincial coinage under Tiberius which remained in circulation until the Flavian period.[357] Also, Lugdunum, which was the principal gold and silver mint for the empire, was located in Gallia Lugdunensis.

In conclusion, we see that the provincial bronze coin production was primarily in the senatorial provinces. There was production in Egypt. However, Egypt was considered to be the personal province of the emperor. There was also production of civic coinage in Judea, most of which was produced near the end of Nero's reign.[358] Judea was part of the huge province of Syria although Judea had its own government responsible to a Roman governor. During the reign of Nero, just before the First Jewish War, Agrippa II urged the Jews not to rebel against Roman governor Florus. The principal coinage of Syria was that of Antioch.[359] Governors of the provinces made sure local religious customs and related guilds were not endangered.

The author of Revelation was young when Caesar Augustus reorganized the government in AD 14. The apostles grew up in the midst of this political reorganization along with the sweeping power given to the governors. The records of the minting of coins and the frequency of their production show that a very high level of economic activity was maintained in the original ten provinces. In the locations where this economic activity was the highest, Christians were in danger of persecution from the guilds. It is quite possible that John literally had these provincial governors in mind when he wrote about the ten kings.

---

[357] Ibid., 19.
[358] Ibid., 24.
[359] Ibid., 24.

APPENDIX E:
FIRST CENTURY HISTORY, HALLEY'S COMET, AND MIRACLES

There are at least two written records of miracles occurring in the first century. The first are the miracles attributed to Jesus and the apostles that are recorded in Scriptures. Christians believe these miracles occurred based on eyewitness testimony. To accept this testimony as true is a matter of faith.

These are miracles in which the laws of nature were suspended. Jesus walked on water (John 6:19), he raised Lazarus from the dead (John 11:43-47), and the apostle Peter healed a lame man.

> In the name of Jesus Christ of Nazareth, rise up and walk!" And he took him by the right hand and raised him up, and immediately his feet and ankles were made strong (Acts 3:6-7).

The laws of nature were frequently suspended in the first century through miracles which were a "sign" to people at that time that Jesus Christ is Lord. Through the work of the Holy Spirit, the disciples of Christ were also able to give "signs" and do "wonders." The "signs" they gave identified them as true apostles of Christ. After Jesus raised Lazarus from the dead, "many of the Jews therefore, who had come with Mary and had seen what he did, believed in him."(John 11:45-46).

Miracles of the type that identified the apostles and identified Jesus as the Messiah ended in the "latter days" of the Jewish Age. We do not see miracles like this today. We do not see anyone walking on water like Jesus did. We do not see an "apostle" pray and then raise someone from the dead like Peter did (Acts 9:40). However, just because we do not see "signs" and "wonders" today does not mean that they did not occur in the first century.

Is it possible that some of the events recorded by Josephus were miracles? Josephus believed they were. Let us together take a look at some of the events and associated miracles recorded by the historian Josephus. The first involves the AD 66 apparition of Halley's comet and the possible miracles associated with that event recorded by Josephus.

Josephus considered this particular apparition of Halley's comet to be a sign from God of the coming destruction of Jerusalem. Just before the Jewish rebellion and only months before Vespasian began his march into Judea, the comet appeared.

In AD 66, the astronomers of the Roman world were aware that everything in the sky rotated around the North Star and the South Star except for the sun, moon, and the five "stars" we today know as Mercury, Venus, Mars, Jupiter, and Saturn. These are the five planets that can be seen with the naked eye. Educated people in ancient times knew this ever since the days of Aristotle, who was the tutor of Alexander the Great over 400 years earlier.

Alexander's legacy was the Hellenization of the areas he conquered. *Gymnasia* were set up to introduce the youth to Greek sports, arts, music, and religion. Greek became the preferred language of educated people. In 333 BC Alexander conquered Judea, and over time the Greek became the language of business and was used for communication throughout the Greek world. In time Rome became the world power. Pompey conquered Israel in 63 BC and continued the Hellenization begun by Alexander.

Aristotle's planetary system involved calculations utilizing the circular orbits of the sun, moon, and planets. They all revolved around a stationary earth. The Romans believed that the planets were gods. Each planet moved in its own "perfect orbit" with a "mind of its own" and together the planets determined the fate of men. The Jews, however, knew that the planets were not gods, they were created by the one true God.

Aristotle's model of the solar system left much to be desired in terms of predictability. In AD 66 we still have another seventy years before Ptolemy arrived on the astronomical scene and revised the mathematics involved in calculating the positions of planets with the use of epicycles. Although principles of this model were known earlier by mathematicians, it was not until AD 140 that Ptolemy wrote the *Almagest*, his book on the stars. His predictive model was not replaced for centuries. It was even more accurate than that of either Copernicus or Galileo. It was not until Kepler created his Laws of Planetary Motion in the early 1600s that the correct model was developed based on ellipses. In AD 66, however, astronomers did not have a predictive model that would even account for retrograde motion, nor did they have any idea about what comets are or where they come from. Comets, in AD 66, were referred to as broom stars and sometimes guest stars. The unpredictable and dramatic appearance of a comet indicated coming doom. In the early 1700's, Edmond Halley used the newly formed laws of gravity formulated by Isaac Newton to calculate the effects of gravity on the orbits of comets. We know today that Halley's comet reappears about every 75.3 years. The next return of Halley's comet will be in the year 2061. The calculation of a predictive model approximates its closest approach to the sun will be at 0.5 AU, and its closest approach to earth will be one of the closest approaches at 0.09 AU.[360] An AU is defined to be the distance from the earth to the sun.

Halley's comet, the apparition known as 1P/66 B1, appeared in the time of Josephus and Vespasian early in the year AD 66. Its closest distance to the sun was on January 25 of that year. It's closest approach to earth was on was on March 20 with a distance of 0.26 AU, which is only about one-quarter of the distance from the earth to the sun.[361]

The Chinese astronomers classified this comet as a "guest star," which they first observed on January 26 of AD 66. No further reference to the comet was recorded until February 20, when a "guest star" was again recorded but described as clearly cometary, with a tail of about 12 degrees in length. It remained visible until April 11.[362]

---

[360] Planetsedu.com, "Comet Halley," Planets.org.uk, http://www.planetsedu.com/comet/halley/ (accessed April 8, 2016).

[361] David Seargent, *The Greatest Comets in History: Broom Stars and Celestial Scimitars* (New York: Springer Science & Business Media, 2009), 39.

[362] Ibid., 39.

By contrast, the 1986 apparition was 0.417 AU or about 39 million miles from earth.[363]

The 1835 apparition of the comet was at its closest point of 0.19 AU from earth on October 12. The 1759 comet's closest approach to earth was on April 26 at only 0.12 AU from earth. The apparition was first observed on December 25, 1758. The apparition was still visible to the naked eye on May 26 by the Chinese. The final telescopic observation was on June 22 in Lisbon, Portugal, and was at 2.06 AU from earth. The comet was visible for six months.[364]

If a comet is close enough to the earth, it can look like it is emerging from one horizon and descending into the other. Unlike any other object in the sky, a comet has tails.

A historian who was a first-century witness to this comet was Josephus. In his book *War of the Jews*, Josephus writes:

> Thus were the miserable people persuaded by these deceivers, and such as belied God himself; while they did not attend nor give credit to the signs that were so evident, and did so plainly foretell their future desolation . . . .Thus there was a star resembling a sword, which stood over the city, and a comet, that continued a whole year...[365]

So was there one comet or two? Seargent remarks,

> As Halley's Comet approached earth following perihelion, it was moving relatively slowly and may have appeared to "hang" over the city with a dust tail resembling a sword. Maybe, as this tail faded, its appearance changed to a more familiar cometary one, but it certainly did not remain visible for a year![366]

It was probably an exaggeration of the part of Josephus that the comet resembling a sword remained visible for a year. A time of six months would be more reasonable. However, from what we know

---

[363] Ibid., 39.
[364] Ibid., 53-54.
[365] Flavius Josephus, *The Complete Works of Flavius Josephus*, trans. William Whiston (London: T. Nelson and Sons,1860), Book VI, Chapter 5, Section 3, p. 753.
[366] David Seargent, op. cit., 39.

about the comet today, with a distance to earth of 0.26 AU at its closest point, the comet must have been dramatic. Certainly, for the people of the time, the comet was a forecast of impending doom.

We know that the events recorded by Josephus occurred early in AD 66, just several months before Roman Procurator Florus seized funds from the temple treasury and triggered the Jewish rebellion in May. As mentioned above, Halley's comet made its closest approach in March of that year. Josephus continues:

> ...people were coming in great crowds to the feast of unleavened bread, on the eighth day of the month Xanthicus, [Nisan,] and at the ninth hour of the night, so great a light shone round the altar and the holy house, that it appeared to be bright day time; which lasted for half an hour. This light seemed to be a good sign to the unskillful, but was so interpreted by the sacred scribes, as to portend those events that followed immediately upon it.
>
> Moreover, the eastern gate of the inner [court of the] temple, which was of brass, and vastly heavy, and had been with difficulty shut by twenty men, and rested upon a basis armed with iron, and had bolts fastened very deep into the firm floor, which was there made of one entire stone, was seen to be opened of its own accord about the sixth hour of the night. Now those that kept watch in the temple came hereupon running to the captain of the temple, and told him of it; who then came up thither, and not without great difficulty was able to shut the gate again. This also appeared to the vulgar to be a very happy prodigy, as if God did thereby open to them the gate of happiness. But the men of learning understood it, that the security of their holy house was dissolved of its own accord.[367]

Even more dramatic is the following recounting of events given by Josephus. Josephus himself thought the event was so incredible that he cautioned that it seemed like a fable.

> a few days after that feast a certain prodigious and incredible phenomenon appeared: I suppose the account of it would seem a fable,

---

[367] Josephus, op. cit., *Jewish Wars* VI, Chapter 5, Section 3.

were it not related by those that saw it, and were not the events that followed it of so considerable a nature as to deserve such signals; for, before sun-setting, chariots and troops of soldiers in their armor were seen running about among the clouds, and surrounding of cities. Moreover, at that feast which we call Pentecost, as the priests were going by night into the inner [court of the temple,] as their custom was, to perform their sacred ministrations, they said that, in the first place, they felt a quaking, and heard a great noise, and after that they heard a sound as of a great multitude, saying, "Let us remove hence."[368]

So what are we to make of these events as portrayed by Josephus? It is accounts such as a huge door swinging open on its own accord and armies of angels running around in the clouds that have led some to doubt Josephus's reliability. However, as pointed out by R.C. Sproul,[369] the Roman historian Tacitus reports the same events.

Prodigies had occurred, which this nation, prone to superstition, but hating all religious rites, did not deem it lawful to expiate by offering and sacrifice. There had been seen hosts joining battle in the skies, the fiery gleam of arms, the temple illuminated by a sudden radiance from the clouds. The doors of the inner shrine were suddenly thrown open, and a voice of more than mortal tone was heard to cry that the Gods were departing. At the same instant there was a mighty stir as of departure. Some few put a fearful meaning on these events, but in most there was a firm persuasion, that in the ancient records of their priests was contained a predic- tion of how at this very time the East was to grow powerful, and rulers, coming from Judaea, were to acquire universal empire. These mysterious prophecies had pointed to Vespasian and Titus, but the common people, with the usual blindness of ambition, had interpreted these mighty destinies of themselves, and could not be brought even by disasters to believe the truth. I have heard that the total number of the besieged, of every age and both sexes, amounted to six hundred thousand. All who were able bore arms, and a number, more than proportionate to the population, had the courage to do so. Men and women showed equal resolution, and life seemed

---

[368] Ibid., *Jewish Wars* VI, Chapter 5, Section 3.
[369] R. C. Sproul, *The Last Days According to Jesus*, 8th ed.(Grand Rapids, MI: Baker Books, 2009), 122.

more terrible than death, if they were to be forced to leave their country.[370]

Some commentators attribute the last of the above quotes of Josephus to events which may have occurred just before the fall of Jerusalem in AD 70 as Dio Cassius makes reference to a comet that appeared in AD 69. However, this could not be Halley's comet, which reoccurs every 75 to 76 years. In addition, there is no record by any astronomers, such as the ancient Chinese astronomers, observing the appearance of another comet in AD 69. There are no other known short-term comets that could have possibly been visible at that time that would meet the description given by Dio Cassius. He tells us in his Roman History that just before Vespasian's rebellion against Vitellius that a comet was seen. Dio Cassius also claims that two suns were seen, one in the East that was brilliant and powerful (Vespasian?) and one in the West which was pale (Vitellius?).[371] It seems doubtful that there was a comet in AD 69. It could be that this was just a way that Dio Cassius was telling the world that Vespasian was born to rule.

So what was it that was recorded by Josephus? Was what he wrote just an exaggerated description of Halley's comet along with an embellishment of detail for the sake of interest? Given the eyewitness accounts, it appears to be *more* than the appearance of Halley's comet.

According to R. C. Sproul, what is remarkable is that in the Old Testament when Ezekiel was a captive in Babylon, Ezekiel had a vision of the chariot-throne with its resplendent glory departing from the temple during the fall of Jerusalem in 586 B.C. Sproul quotes from the book of Ezekiel at length. He compares the account of Josephus to the sight witnessed by Elisha's servant when his eyes were opened.[372]

> Then Elisha prayed and said, "O Lord, please open his eyes that he may see." So then Lord opened the eyes of the young man, and he saw, and

---

[370] Cornelius Tacitus, *The History of Tacitus*, trans. Alfred J. Church and William J. Brodribb (London: Macmillan and Co., 1873), 199-200.
[371] Dio Cassius, *Roman History*, Book XLV., ch. 7.
[372] R.C. Sproul, op. cit., 124.

behold, the mountain was full of horses and chariots of fire all around Elisha. (2 Kings 6:17).

Despite the fact that the length of time that the comet of AD 66 was visible was more likely closer to six months rather than the year that Josephus records, a portion of what Josephus recorded from the eyewitnesses, the priests, may have occurred. The chariots of fire were recorded by two different historians, Josephus and Tacitus. I believe that even the most skeptical must admit that something happened that was unusual. Josephus believed that the March apparition of Halley's comet was a sign of the impending fall of Jerusalem.

The Jewish revolt which began six months later, after a victory against the troops under the local provincial governor, Cestius Gallus, led to the involvement of imperial Rome. Nero ordered Vespasian in December to put down the rebellion. Vespasian began his Galilean campaign in the Spring of AD 67, and Jerusalem fell in September of AD 70, forty-two months later.

In addition to the miracles recorded by Josephus, Josephus recorded the fall of Jerusalem.

Forty years earlier Jesus, in the Olivet Discourse, prophesied the destruction of the temple and the fall of Jerusalem within a generation:

> For there will be great distress upon the earth and wrath against this people. They will fall by the edge of the sword and be led captive among all nations, and Jerusalem will be trampled underfoot by the Gentiles, until the times of the Gentiles are fulfilled (Luke 21: 23-24) Truly, I say to you, this generation will not pass away until all these things take place (Matthew 24:34).

The Jews were led captive among all nations in September of AD 70. Just as Jesus prophesied, Jerusalem was trampled underfoot.

Josephus was a Jewish historian who is considered a reliable historian given the standards of the time in which he wrote. It was common for historians in the first century to either exaggerate or minimize some of the details in their accounts for the sake of what we today would call "political correctness." An historian in ancient times was often in the service of a king or a military leader, in which case the historian certainly did not wish to write something which was "politically incorrect." Consequences could follows. We know that Domitian, the youngest son of Vespasian,

> put to death a scholar of Paris, the pantomimic, though a minor, and then sick, only because, both in person and the practice of his art, he resembled his master; as he did likewise Hermogenes of Tarsus for some oblique reflections in his History; crucifying, besides, the scribes who had copied the work.[373]

Josephus was a captive of Vespasian, who not only was a general in the Roman army, he was also to become emperor. Josephus, a Pharisee, was well educated. He also believed himself to be a prophet and worked his way into Vespasian's good graces by prophesying that Vespasian would become emperor.

Josephus was an eyewitness to the destruction of Jerusalem and was in the unique position to be able to write history from both the Jewish and Roman point of view. Josephus has been criticized by some to have exaggerated the body count of certain battles because he was a captive of Vespasian. It is assumed by some that Josephus would naturally tend to exaggerate his accounts of the efforts of Vespasian and Titus in order to show them in the best possible light.

Josephus gives 1.1 million as the number of Jews who perished in the fall of Jerusalem, while another source, Tacitus, places the number at 600,000. Of course, Tacitus had his own motivations to minimize the achievements of both Vespasian and his son, Titus. It can be argued that the numbers given by Tacitus were too low.

Josephus would eventually have access to the emperor's libraries, the records of Herod and other rulers in the Empire such as Pilate and Felix. He gives a passionate account of the preliminary events and battles fought as Vespasian moved relentlessly across Palestine, circling in and isolating Jerusalem. Later, Vespasian used Josephus to

---

[373] Suetonius, C. *Lives of the 12 Caesars*, Titus Flavius Domitianus, X.

plead with the Jews to give up Jerusalem. Josephus believed the Jewish people were duped by the zealots into rebelling against Rome. Eusebius referred to Josephus with these words:

> If any one compares the words of our Saviour with the other accounts of the historian concerning the whole war, how can one fail to wonder, and to admit that the foreknowledge and the prophecy of our Saviour were truly divine and marvelously strange.[374]

---

[374] Philip Schaff and Henry Wace, *A Select library of Nicene and post-Nicene fathers of the Christian Church*, Second Series, Vol. 1, Eusebius: *Church History, Life of Constantine the Great, and Oration in Praise of Constantine* (New York: The Christian Literature company, New York. 1890), 142.

APPENDIX F:
AGRIPPA II AND THE EXPANSION OF HIS TERRITORIES

Agrippa died in AD 44. However, Claudius refused to let Herod Agrippa's son, Agrippa II, have control over Judea because of his youth and instead gave him control of his uncle's small kingdom of Chalcis in AD 49. Claudius also gave him supervision of the Temple and its treasury along with the right to appoint the high priest. Both Agrippa II and his sister were devout Jews. Agrippa II's sister Bernice was married to Agrippa's uncle Herod, the brother of Agrippa I.

As reported by Josephus,

> But as for Bernice, she lived a widow a long while after the death of Herod [king of Chalcis], who was both her husband and her uncle; but when the report went that she had criminal conversation [sexual relations] with her brother, [Agrippa, junior,] she persuaded Poleme, who was king of Cilicia, to be circumcised, and to marry her, as supposing that by this means she should prove those calumnies upon her to be false; and Poleme was prevailed upon, and that chiefly on account of her riches. Yet did not this matrimony endure long; but Bernice left Poleme, and, as was said, with impure intentions. So he forsook at once this matrimony, and the Jewish religion.[375]

This passage from Josephus is considered to be a parallel to Acts 26:27-28.[376] In Acts 26, we read about Agrippa II's exchange with Festus on the legal case of the apostle Paul in AD 59. Paul perceived

---

[375] Flavius Josephus, *Antiquities of the Jews*, Book XX, Chapter 7, Sections 3, p. 541.
[376] Josephus.org, "Agrippa II and Berenice ," Joesephus.org, http://josephus.org/ntparallels2.htm#AgrippaII (accessed April 8, 20116).

that he may be given by Festus into the hands of the Jews for trial by a change in venue and possible sentence by them. That sentence could then be carried out with Roman approval. Paul appealed to Nero. Judging by way he astutely evaluated the case against him, we must believe that Paul was acutely aware of the politics of his time. This indicates that Nero, at this point, had no interest in persecuting the Christians at that time in AD 59/60.

It took Agrippa II from AD 49 to AD 71, over twenty years of loyalty to Roman emperors, to expand his territories.

In AD 53 Claudius transferred Agrippa II to the old tetrarchy of Philip, and in AD 56 Nero added the toparchies of Tiberias, Tarichaeae, Abila, and Livias-Julias. In AD 61 he received parts of Galilee, including Tiberias, from Nero. Unlike his predecessors, Agrippa II had provincial coins minted in the image of Caesar. Agrippa changed the administrative capitol's name to Neronias, where the coin depicted above may have been minted. The profitable right to mint coins was not given without political favor and loyalty was expected.[377]

Festus was replaced as procurator by Albinus in AD 62, who was replaced by Gessius Florus in AD 64. Florus plundered the temple due to low tax revenue, and riots broke out. Agrippa II urged restraint upon the part of the Jews as recorded by Josephus (War of the Jews ii 16 §§ 4, 5). His "restraint" was not to the liking of the Jews who burned the palace in further rioting. Agrippa and Bernice fled to Galilee where Bernice fell in love with Titus. Agrippa and Bernice sent over 2000 soldiers to support Vespasian.

James Stuart Russell observes:

> Tacitus speaks of the bitter animosity with the Arab auxiliaries of Titus were filled [with] against the Jews, and we have a fearful proof of the

---

[377] JewishEncyclopedia.com, s.v. "Agrippa II, http://jewishencyclopedia.com/articles/913-agrippa-ii (accessed April 8, 2016).

intense hatred felt toward the Jews by the neighbouring nations in the wholesale massacres of that unhappy people perpetrated in many great cities just before the outbreak of the war. The whole Jewish population of Caesarea were massacred in one day.[378]

These were not the worst atrocities. However, even more are brought to our attention as Russell continues, quoting Josephus:

> In Syria every city was divided into two camps, Jews and Syrians. In Scythopolis upwards of thirteen thousand Jews were butchered; in Ascalon, Ptolemais, and Tyre, similar atrocities took place. But in Alexandria the carnage of the Jewish inhabitants exceeded all the other massacres. The whole Jewish quarter was deluged with blood, and fifty thousand corpses lay in ghastly heaps in the streets.[379]

As John prophesied in Revelation 17:16:

> They will make her desolate and naked, and devour her flesh and burn her up with fire.

The temple was burned with fire when the city of Jerusalem was destroyed. For his loyalty Agrippa was rewarded with more territory by Vespasian and was made praetor in AD 71.

---

[378] James S Russell, *The Parousia: A Critical Inquiry into the New Testament Doctrine of Our Lord's Second Coming* (London: Daldy, Isbister & Co., 1878), 503.
[379] Ibid., 503.

BIBLIOGRAPHY I

Modern Writings

Adams, Jay Edward. *The Time is at Hand*. Woodruff, SC: Timeless Texts, (1966), 2004.

Bahnsen, Greg L. *Van Til's Apologetic*. Phillipsburg: NJ: P & R Pub., 1998.

Baird, William. *History of New Testament Research*, Vol. 2, *From Jonathan Edwards to Rudolf Bultmann*. Minneapolis, MN: Fortress Press, (2003).

Barnes, Timothy D. *Constantine and Eusebius*. Cambridge: Harvard University Press, 1981.

Bauckham, Richard. *Jesus and the Eyewitnesses: The Gospels as Eyewitness Testimony*. Grand Rapids, MI: William B. Eerdmans Pub. Co., 2006.

Bauckham, Richard. *The Climax of Prophecy: Studies on the Book of Revelation*. Edinburgh: T. & T. Clark, 1993.

Beale, G.K. *The Book of Revelation (The New International Greek Testament Commentary)*. Grand Rapids, MI: Wm. B. Eerdmans Pub. Co., (1999), 2013.

Boxall, Ian. *Patmos in the Reception History of the Apocalypse*. Oxford: Oxford University Press, 2013.

Boxall, Ian. *Revelation: Vision And Insight*. London: SPCK, 2002.

Boxall, Ian. *The Revelation of Saint John (Black's New Testament Commentary)*. Grand Rapids, MI: Baker Academic, 2009.

Bruce, F.F. *The New Testament Documents: Are They Reliable?* 6th ed. Grand Rapids, MI: Wm. B. Eerdmans Publishing Co.: IL, Downers Grove: InterVarsity Press, 1943, 1946, 1953, 1960, 1981.

Burnett, Andrew. Amandry, Michel. Ripollès, Pere Pau. *Roman Provincial Coinage*. Vol. 1, London: The British Museum Press, 1992.

Caird, G. B. *The Language and Imagery of the Bible*. London: Gerald Duckworth & Co., 1980.

Collins, John J. *Sibylline Oracles of Egyptian Judaism*. Missoula, MO: Society of Biblical Literature and Scholars' Press for the Pseudepigrapha Group. Dissertation Series, Number 13, 1972, 1974.

Coxe, Arthur Cleveland. *Ante-Nicene Fathers. Vol. 5, Hippolytus, Cyprian, Caius, Novatian, Appendix*, ed. Alexander Roberts and James Donaldson. Revised by A. Cleveland Coxe. New York: Christian Literature Publishing Co., 1886. http://oll.libertyfund.org/titles/1972.

DeMar, Gary. *The Gog and Magog End-Time Alliance: Israel, Russia, and Syria in Bible Prophecy*. Powder Springs, GA: American Vision Press, 2016.

Dooyeweerd, Herman. "Cornelius Van Van Til and the Transcendental Critique of Theoretical Thought." *Jerusalem and Athens: Critical Discussions on the Philosophy of Cornelius Van Til*, ed. E. R. Geehan, Phillipsburg: P & R. Pub. Co., 1971.

Edmundson, George. *The Church in Rome in the First Century: An Examination of Various Controverted Questions Relating to Its History, Chronology, Literature and Traditions. Eight Lectures Preached Before the University of Oxford in the Year 1913*. London, and New York, and Bombay and Calcutta: Longman, Green and Co., 1913. http://www.archive.org/details/churchinromeinfi00edmuuoft.

Ellis, Edward Earle. *The Making of the New Testament Documents*. Leiden: Brill, (1999), 2002.

France, R.T. *The Gospel of Matthew*. Grand Rapids, MI: Eerdmans Publishing Co., 2007.

Friesen, Steven J. *Imperial Cults and the Apocalypse of John*. Oxford: Oxford University Press, (2001), 2006.

Friesen, Steven J. *Twice Neokoros: Ephesus, Asia, and the Cult of the Flavian Imperial Family*. Leiden: Brill Academic, 1993.

Ferguson, Everett. *Church History*, Vol. 1, *From Christ to Pre-Reformation*. Grand Rapids, MI: Zondervan, 2005.

Gentry, Kenneth L., Jr. *Before Jerusalem Fell: Dating the Book of Revelation*, 3rd. ed. Fountain Inn, SC: Victorious Hope Publishing, 1998, 2010.

Gentry, Kenneth L., Jr. *He Shall Have Dominion*. Tyler, TX: Institute for Christian Economics, 1992.

Gentry, Kenneth L., Jr. *Perilous Times*. Texarkana, AZ: Covenant Media Press, 1999.

Gentry Jr., Kenneth L. Postmillennialism.com, "The Temple Problem for Revelation's Dating." Postmillennialism.com. postmillennialism.com/the-temple-problem-for-revelations- dating/ (accessed April 11, 2016).

Gentry Jr., Kenneth L. *The Olivet Discourse Made Easy*. Draper, VA: Apologetics Group, 2010.

Gregg, Steve. "Is Dispensationalism Indispensable?" *Christian Research Journal* 35, no. 04 (2012),
http://www.equip.org/article/dispensationalismindispensable/.

Gumerlock, Francis X. "Nero Antichrist: Patristic Evidence for the use of Nero's Naming in Calculating the Number of the Beast (Rev 13:18)." *Westminster Theological Journal* 68, (2006).

Gumerlock, Francis X. *Revelation and the First Century (Preterist Interpretations of the Apocalypse in Early Christianity)*. Powder Springs, GA: American Vision Press, 2012.

Gundry, Robert H. *A Survey of the New Testament*, Grand Rapids, MI.: Zondervan, Fifth Edition 2012.

Gundry, Robert H. "The Apostolically Johannine Pre-Papian Tradition concerning the Gospels of Mark and Matthew." In *The Old is Better*. Tübingen: Mohr Siebeck, 2005. Reprinted Eugene, OH: Wipf and Stock Pub., 2010.

Hendriksen, William. *More Than Conquerors*, Grand Rapids, MI: Baker Books, (1940), 1967.

Hill, C. E. "The Debate Over the Muratorian Fragment and the Development of the Canon." *Westminster Theological Journal* 57, no. 2 (Fall 1995).

Hoekema, Anthony A. "Amillennialism." In *The Meaning of the Millennium: Four Views*, ed. Robert G. Clouse. Downers Grove, IL: InterVarsity Press, 1977.

Hoekema, Anthony A. *The Bible and the Future*. Grand Rapids, MI: Eerdmans, (1979), 1994.

Ice, Thomas, and Kenneth Gentry Jr. *The Great Tribulation--Past or Future?: Two Evangelicals Debate the Question*, Grand Rapids, MI: Kregel Academic & Professional, 1999.

Kovacs, Joe. World Net Daily, "666 Wrong Number of Prophetic Beast?" World Net Daily. http://www.wnd.com/2005/05/30211/ (accessed April 11, 2016).

Kruger, Michael J. Jkruger.com, 'Ten Basic Facts about the NT Canon that Every Christian Should Memorize: #6: "At the End of the Second Century, the Muratorian Fragment lists 22 of our 27 NT books."' michaeljkruger.com/ten-basic-facts-about-the-nt-canon-that-every-christian-should-memorize-6-at-the-end-of-the-second-century-the-muratorian-fragment-lists-22-of-our-27-nt-books-2/ (accessed April 11, 2016).

Kuyper, Abraham. *Lectures on Calvinism*. L. P. Stone Foundation, Princeton University, 1898. Grand Rapids, MI: Wm. B. Eerdmans Pub. Co., (1931), 1999.

Lawlor, Hugh. "Hegesippus and the Apocalypse." *The Journal of Theological Studies* 8 (April 1907).

Lawlor, Hugh. *Eusebiana: Essays on the Ecclesiastical History of Eusebius Bishop of Caesarea*. Oxford: Clarendon Press, 1912. https://archive.org/details/eusebianaessays00lawluoft.

Levick, Barbara. *Vespasian*. London: Routledge, 2002. https://books.google.com/books?id=IHiFAgAAQBAJ.

MacArthur, John. "Why Every Calvinist Should be a Premillennialist." Grace to You. http://www.gty.org/Downloads/PDF/macarthur_on_future_israel.pdf.

Mathison, Keith. *Dispensationalism: Rightly Dividing the People of God?* Phillipsburg, NJ: P&R Pub., 1967, 1995.

Mathison, Keith. *From Age to Age, The Unfolding of Biblical Eschatology*. Phillipsburg, NJ: P & R Pub., 2009.

Mathison, Keith. "The Eschatological Times Text of the New Testament." In *When Shall These Things Be? A Reformed Response to Hyper-Preterism*, edited by Keith A. Mathison (Phillipsburg, NJ: P & R Pub., 2004).

McDonald, Lee Martin. *The Biblical Canon*. Grand Rapids, MI.: Baker Academic, (2002), 2007.

McKenzie, Duncan. *The Antichrist and the Second Coming: A Preterist Examination. Vol. 1*, Maitland, FL: Xulon Press, 2009.

McKenzie, Duncan. *The Antichrist and the Second Coming: A Preterist Examination. Vol. 2*, Maitland, FL: Xulon Press, 2012.

Minear, Paul S. "The Wounded Beast." *The Journal of Biblical Literature*, 72, no. 2 (June, 1953): 93-101. doi:10.2307/3261346.

Pappano, Albert Earl. "The False Neros." The Classical Journal 32, no. 7 (1937): 385-92. http://www.jstor.org/stable/3291534.

Poythress, Vern Sheridan. "Currents within Amillennialism" *Presbyterian* 26, no. 1 (2000).

Poythress, Vern. *The Returning King*. Phillipsburg, NJ: P & R Pub., 2000.

Ridderbos, Herman. *Paul: An Outline of His Theology*, Translated by John Richard DeWitt. Grand Rapids, MI: William B. Eerdmans Publish. Co., 1975, 1997.

Ridderbos, Herman. *The Coming of the Kingdom*. Translated by H. de Jongste. Philadelphia: P & R Pub. Co., 1962.

Riddlebarger, Kim. *A Case for Amillennialism: Understanding the End Times*. Grand Rapids, MI: Baker Books, 2003.

Riddlebarger, Kim. *The Man of Sin: Uncovering the Truth about the Antichrist*. Grand Rapids, MI: Baker Books, 2006.

Robinson, John A.T. *Redating the New Testament*. Philadelphia: Westminster Press, 1976.

Rosenberg, Joel, host. *Epicenter*. DVD. Studio: Tyndale House Publishers, 2008.

Rosenberg, Joel. *Epicenter 2.0: Why the Current Rumbling in the Middle East Will Change Your Future.* Carol Stream, IL: Tyndale House Publishers, 2008.

Rosenberg, Joel. *The Third Target.* Carol Stream, IL: Tyndale House Publishers, 2015.

Ruffin, Bernard C. *The Twelve. The Lives of the Apostles After Calvary.* Huntington, IN.: Our Sunday Visitor Pub., 1977, 1984.

Russell, Bertrand., and Whitehead, Alfred North. *Principia Mathematica.* Vol. 1-3, Cambridge, England: University Press, 1910, 1927.
https://archive.org/details/PrincipiaMathematicaVolumeI.
https://archive.org/details/PrincipiaMathematicaVol2.
https://archive.org/details/PrincipiaMathematicaVol3.

Russell, Bertrand. *The Problems of Philosophy.* New York: Home University Library, 1912. Reprint, New York: Oxford University Press paperback, 1959, 1962.

Russell, Bertrand. *Why I am not a Christian*, 1927. New York: Touchstone, 1967.

Russell, James S. Foreword by R. C. Sproul. *The Parousia: The New Testament Doctrine of Our Lord's Second Coming*, new ed. Grand Rapids, MI, Baker Books, [1887],1983, 1999.

Russell, James S. *The Parousia: A Critical Inquiry into the New Testament Doctrine of Our Lord's Second Coming.* Daldy, Isbister & Co, 1878.
https://books.google.com/books?id=0PgUAAAAYAAJ.

Seargent, David. *The Greatest Comets in History: Broom Stars and Celestial Scimitars.* New York: Springer Science & Business Media, 2009.

Slater, Thomas B. "On the Social Setting of the Revelation to John." *New Testament Studies* 44 (1998). doi:10.1017/S0028688500016490.

Smith, Kym. *Redating the Revelation and …a Reconstruction of the Sixties of the First Century, Giving the Context and Completion of the New Testament.* Blackwood, South Australia: Sherwood Publications, 2001.

Sproul, R.C, John H.Gerstner, and Arthur Lindsley. *Classical Apologetics.* Grand Rapids, MI: Zondervan, 1984.

Sproul, R.C. Foreword to James Stuart Russell's book, *The Parousia*, new ed. Grand Rapids, Michigan: Baker, 1999.

Sproul, R.C. *The Last Days According to Jesus*, 8th ed. Grand Rapids, MI: Baker Books, 1998, 2009.

Steen, Peter J. *The Structure of Herman Dooyeweerd's Thought*. Toronto, Canada: Wedge Publishing Foundation, 1983.

Stevens, Mark B. *Annihilation Or Renewal? The Meaning and Function of New Creation in the book of Revelation*. Tübingen, Germany: Mohr Siebeck, 2011.

Storms, Sam. *Kingdom Come*. Fearn, Scotland: Mentor Imprint of Christian Focus Pub., 2013.

Thompson, Leonard L. *The Book of Revelation: Apocalypse and Empire*. New York: Oxford University Press, (1990), 1996.

Vos, Geerhardus. *The Pauline Eschatology*. Princeton University Press, 1939. Reprinted Phillipsburg, New Jersey: P & R Pub., 1979.

Wallace, Daniel B. Religion News Blog, "Daniel B. Wallace responds to article on 'the number of the Beast,'" Religion News Blog. http://www.religionnewsblog.com /11139/daniel-b-wallace-responds-to-article-on-the-number-of-the-beast (accessed April 10, 2016).

Wilkinson, J. H. "Bousset's Die Offenbarung Johannis." In *The Critical Review of Theological and Philosophical Literature*. Vol. 8, edition by Stewart Dingwall Fordyce Salmond. T. & T. Clark, 1898. https://books.google.com/books?id=8N4ZAAAAYAAJ.

Wolters, Reinhard. "Bronze, Silver or Gold? Coin Finds and the Pay of the Roman Army." *Zephyrus: Journal of Prehistory and Archeology*. ISSN 0514-7336, No. 54 2001.

Wright, N.T. *Jesus and the Victory of God: Christian Origins and the Question of God. Vol. 2*, Lanham: Fortress Press, 1997.

BIBLIOGRAPHY II

Ancient Writings

Dio, Cassius. *Complete Work of Cassius Dio (Illustrated)*. Delphi Classics, 2014. books.google.com/books?id=cm6PBAAAQBAJ.

Eusebius. *The Ecclesiastical History and the Martyrs of Palestine. Vol. 1*, Translated by H. J Lawlor and J.E.I Oulton. London: SPCK, (1927), 1954.

Irenaeus. *Against Heresies*. Literature Publishing Company, 1885. Republication by Veritatis Splendor Publications. Copyright 2012. Kindle Edition.

Schaff, Philip. and Wace Henry. *Nicene and Post-Nicene Fathers: Second Series Volume 6, Jerome: The Principal Works of St. Jerome*. Translated by W. H. Freemantle. New York: Christian Literature Publishing Co., 1892. Reprint, Grand Rapids, MI: Christian Classics Ethereal Library. http://www.ccel.org/ccel/schaff/npnf206.html.

Josephus, Flavius. Translated by William Whiston. *The Complete Works and Historical Background (Annotated and Illustrated)* (Annotated Classics), Annotated Classics (January 21, 2013), Kindle Edition.

Josephus, Flavius (Author). Translated by William Whiston. *The Complete Works of Flavius Josephus*. London: T. Nelson and Sons, 1860. https://books.google.com/books?id=wQ1MAAAAYAAJ.

Martyr, Justin, and St. Irenaeus. *ANF01. The Apostolic Fathers with Justin Martyr and Irenaeus*. Ed. Philip Schaff, 1885. Reprint, Grand Rapids, MI: Christian Classics Ethereal Library. http://www.ccel.org/ccel/schaff/anf01.html.

Pliny the Younger. *The Letters of the Younger Pliny* (Penguin Classics). Translated by Betty Radice. London: Penguin Books Ltd., 1963, 1969.

Schaff, Philip. *ANF07. Fathers of the Third and Fourth Centuries: Lactantius, Venantius, Asterius, Victorinus, Dionysius, Apostolic Teaching and Constitutions, Homily, and Liturgies*. 1885. Reprint, Grand Rapids, MI: Christian Classics Ethereal Library. http://www.ccel.org/ccel/schaff/anf07.html.

Schaff, Philip. *NPNF 1-02. St. Augustin's City of God and Christian Doctrine.* The Christian Literature Publishing Co., 1890. Classics Ethereal Library. http://www.ccel.org/ccel/schaff/npnf102.html.

Schaff, Philip. *NPNF 2-03. Theodoret, Jerome, Gennadius, & Rufinus: Historical Writings.* New York: Christian Literature Publishing Co., 1892. Reprint, Grand Rapids, MI: Christian Classics Ethereal Library. http://www.ccel.org/ccel/schaff/npnf203.html.

Schaff, Philip and David Schaff. *History of the Christian Church.* Vol. 1, Charles Scribner's Sons, 1910. https://books.google.com/books?id=vonYAAAAMAAJ.

Schaff, Philip., and Henry Wace. *A Select library of Nicene and post-Nicene fathers of the Christian Church.* Second Series. *Vol. 1, Eusebius: Church History, Life of Constantine the Great, and Oration in Praise of Constantine.* New York: The Christian Literature company, 1890. https://books.google.com/books?id=boIXAAAAIAAJ.

Schaff, Philip., and Wace, Henry. *Nicene and Post-Nicene Fathers: Second Series Vol. 6, Jerome: The Principal Works of St. Jerome.* Ed. Philip Schaff, Henry Wace. Translated by Freemantle M.A., The Hon. W.H. New York: Christian Literature Publishing Co., 1892. Reprint, Grand Rapids, MI: Christian Classics Ethereal Library. http://www.ccel.org/ccel/schaff/npnf206.html

Tacitus, Cornelius. *The History of Tacitus.* Translated by Alfred John Church and William Jackson Brodribb. London: Macmillan and Co., 1873. https://books.google.com/books?id=cCwYAAAAYAAJ.

Tranquillius, C. Suetonius. *The Lives of the Twelve Caesars.* Translated by Alexander Thompson, London: George Bell & Sons. 1896. https://books.google.com/books?id=Ad2Gom01ERQC.

Weinrich, William C., and Victorinus. *Latin Commentaries on Revelation.* Downers Grove, IL: IVP Academic, 2011.

Notes

"1. I do not know how it is that some have erred[i,ii] following the ordinary mode of speech, and have vitiated the middle number in the name,[i,ii] deducing the amount of fifty from it, so that instead of six decads they will it that there is but one. Others then received this reading without examination; some in their simplicity, and upon their own responsibility, making use of this number expressing one decad; while some, in their inexperience, have ventured to seek out a name which should contain the erroneous and spurious number.[iv] Now, as regards those who have done this in simplicity, and without evil intent, we are at liberty to assume that pardon will be granted them by God. But as for those who, for the sake of vain glory,[v,vi] lay it down for certain that names containing the spurious number are to be accepted,[iii] and affirm that this name, hit upon by themselves, is that of him who is to come; such person shall not come forth without loss, because they have led into error both themselves and those who confided in them.[vi]

3. It is therefore more certain, and less hazardous, to await the fulfilment of prophecy, than to be making surmises,[vii] and casting about for any name that present themselves. For if there are many names found possessing this number, it will be asked which among them shall the coming man bear.[viii] It is not through a want of name containing the number of that name that I say this, but on account of the fear of God, and zeal for the truth: for the Evanthas contains the number, but I make no allegation regarding it[ix].... Then also Latenios has the number six hundred and sixty-six; and it is a very probable [solution], this being the name of the last kingdom [of the four seen by Daniel].[x] For the Latins are they who at present bear rule:(5) ... Teitan too, Teitan too ... is rather worthy of credit ... Among many persons, too, this name is accounted divine. So that even the sun is termed "Titan" by those who do now possess [the rule] this name "Titan" has so much to recommend [xi] ... We will not, however, incur the risk of pronouncing positively[xii] as to the name of Antichrist;[xiii] for if it were necessary that his name should be distinctly revealed in this present time, it would have been announced by him who beheld the apocalyptic vision. For that was seen no very long time since, but almost in our day, towards the end of Domitian's reign

www.ingramcontent.com/pod-product-compliance
Lightning Source LLC
Chambersburg PA
CBHW050549160426
43199CB00015B/2593